To Craig —
Good hunting!
Chuck Adams
1/05

LIFE AT FULL DRAW
THE CHUCK ADAMS STORY

by Gregg Gutschow

Book Number One in the
SUPER SLAM® SERIES

P.O. Box 1148, Chanhassen, MN 55317-1148

Cover photo by Phil Aarrestad

ISBN 0-9721321-0-4

10 9 8 7 6 5 4 3

ISBN 0-9721321-0-4

8 24274 02495 7

To Dad, for buying me
a bow when I was 11.
To Mom, for writing a
letter to the high school
principal the day that
I had to track a buck. ...
To Barb, for loving a guy
in love with the outdoors.

CONTENTS

ACKNOWLEDGMENTS

W riting a book or editing a magazine, something that I did for a number of years, is, I suppose, comparable to architecture. You start with a vision of what the completed, multifaceted structure might look like. You construct a plan, assemble the parts, adjust the plan to accommodate any oversights, and, most importantly, gather together a great team—a construction crew. Every good book has one, and I was especially fortunate in this regard from the outset.

At home there is a foundation upon which I believe that I can attempt to do anything to which I might set my mind. That foundation exists because of my wife, Barb. Oh, the countless late evenings that she had to listen to me complain about this onerous task that lay before me—that I couldn't make headway because the kids were raising a ruckus, or that I didn't know how to handle the technical problems that I encountered with the computer or the printer or the software. I'm a writer, not a scientist! Always, she'd offer reassurance, shush the kids and solve the haywire technical stuff. And then, with calm restored, she'd listen to me read a page that I had written and she'd tell me how wonderful it sounded. And with that, I could go on to write another, with a smile.

And as the pages turned to chapters, I handed them off to Tom Carpenter and Cory Pedersen, two journalists whom I respect. Tom, a book author and editor in his own right, went to work with his red pen, sometimes wounding my pride, but always improving upon what I had built. He gave my manuscript a fresh coat of paint. Cory ensured that my facts were indeed factual. He did the dirty work, the heavy lifting, making the telephone calls and doing the research to ensure that everything hit the bull's eye. Each of these men asked only for a signed book in return. I've promised that I'll pay in real money some day.

At the same time, my friend, Jim Shockey, paged through chunks of the manuscript, sometimes in distant hunting camps, and would listen over the telephone from thousands of miles away as I'd read a passage of which I was particularly proud.

6

Jim's work is some of the finest outdoor writing of our day in the popular outdoor press. So when he'd tell me that he liked something, I knew that my writing and re-writing had paid off.

Designer Mark Simpson took the finished manuscript and more than 100 of Chuck's photos, out of the 400 or so that he sent in, and breathed life into this book. Mark's son, Gary, also an avid bowhunter, volunteered the many hours of photo scanning. If a picture's worth 1,000 words, Mark's expertise in layout and design are equally important to this volume as the manuscript itself. Like Tom and Cory, Mark's putting it on my tab and banking on future considerations, whatever that means.

I also owe my sincere gratitude to Chuck for granting me the opportunity to pen his biography. He made himself accessible and went far out of his way to help at many times during this nearly two-year project. And he agreed to share experiences and a side of himself during those marathon interviews that confirmed to me, even more, that the Chuck Adams story had been long overdue.

Thanks, all of you, for helping to construct a book that's everything that I had envisioned and more.

FOREWORD

So, do not follow where the path may lead,
Go, instead, where there is no path
And leave a trail.
—*author unknown*

Like many, I purchased my first "Chuck" book way back in the 1980s; that book, "The Complete Guide To Bowhunting Deer," I still have. It's a cornerstone in my library of mostly less-er-read tomes. Dog-eared now, yellowed and filled with notes to myself, Chuck's work is as valid today as it was when he wrote it nearly 20 years ago. At the time, I was inspired to make Chuck's accomplishments my goal. But, alas, after two marginally successful seasons as a bowhunter, I discovered that what Chuck Adams "did" was not so easy to "do."

So I switched to a muzzleloader and took up Chuck's trail, following him to the edges of this continent, hunting for every species of North American big game. And as any hunter will come to know the animal that he is tracking, I feel that I have come to know Chuck Adams ... the hunter. Chuck's is a trail wrought with challenge, a trail that leads where few, if any, have gone before and where few will ever go. Chuck's is a trail that leads to the top and then down the far side of many a Rocky Mountain; cold and ancient, these heights defy all but the most determined hunters.

Following Chuck's trail has meant enduring the frightening wrath of the untamed arctic, surviving more like, but it had to be done, for that is the way that Chuck went for polar bear and muskox. It has meant living in tents and less on sheepy peaks, it has meant fording glacial rivers for goats, it has meant toil and discomfort so many times, and yet the path presses onward to new adventure and greater achievement, always the high road.

Many, many times I've stood on some remote, inhospitable mountain, surrounded by others of the same ilk, and wondered at the limit, or lack of limit, to Chuck's desire. How driv-

8

Jim Shockey

en was this man? He'd done first what I was attempting to do, but he'd done so in such an infinitely more difficult way, with bow and arrow. Even more importantly, he was the trailblazer, the one who found the way. How did he keep his focus when it would have been so easy to give up or compromise by picking up a rifle? What made this man, this great hunter, tick?

Chuck Adams is more than an enigma, though, far more. He is truly a living legend in this hunting industry of ours. He is a man who has accomplished much, a man who has earned his way. He, by virtue of his profile, (and undeniable smile) has been the subject of many a conversation in the wild lands, taxidermy shops, sporting goods stores and taverns, but most who do the talking don't know Chuck from Adam. The ones who do, the guides who've been in the trenches with Chuck, every single one whom I've encountered, says the same six words, "Chuck Adams is the real thing." These are words of high praise from men and women who walk the walk.

Chuck Adams is the real thing.

—*Jim Shockey, well-known outdoor writer, outfitter and guide*

INTRODUCTION

An editor of a hunting magazine got lost for a second, staring at a cover mock-up. The dead elk in the photo would break the bowhunting world record, and the happy hunter clutching the titanic antlers happened to be the editor's "Bowhunting" columnist. He'd struck gold again. The editor wondered, "Could Adams possibly be this good?" And if he really was this good, why hadn't anybody written a book about him? Why not?

Legends like Fred Bear and Jack O'Connor are gone. Today, only one man survives in the hunting world with what can truly be considered a household name. You've seen bowhunter Chuck Adams in magazine advertisements and on posters in archery pro shops, grinning widely beside some big game trophy. You've read his magazine articles or studied his bowhunting how-to books. You've heard about his "Super Slam" conquest of 27 North American big game species with a bow. And from these glimpses, you've likely formed a strong opinion of the "world's most successful bowhunter." You despise him. You idolize him. You think that he's a walking billboard with a Montana-sized ego. You rave at his hunting equipment innovations and insights. You think that he's a fraud. You consider him the Michael Jordan of bowhunting.

There's little consensus and even less middle ground in judging Chuck Adams. Many of us have made up our minds, though we've never had the chance to see the man behind the magazine pictures ... until now. This is the true story of Chuck Adams—a behind-the-scenes, unabridged account of the least-understood, best-known hunter ever.

Many interviewed within render their own judgments. This book sets out to neither make Chuck Adams a sinner nor saint. There is no agenda here other than to write the true story of Chuck Adams' life and to finally place you alongside him in the mountains, at a hunting camp and in his everyday life at full draw.

— *Gregg Gutschow*

CHAPTER ONE: **BORN TO HUNT**

"You have become a different person in the course of these years. For this is what the art of archery means: a profound and far-reaching contest of the archer with himself. You will see with other eyes and measure with other measures. It happens to all who are touched by the spirit of this art."
— *Eugen Herrigel, "Zen in the Art of Archery"*

Beneath the soil and rock of Deer Creek Canyon, somewhere, are the tools and footprints of bowhunting. Geographically, Deer Creek Canyon is a speck on a California map. To a 13-year-old boy with a Ben Pearson recurve bow, however, the headwaters of that creek, near Mount Lassen, marked the most important place in the world ... almost heaven.

Black-tailed deer skulked in the manzanita. Rainbow trout

Pop and Chuck's grandfather, Dick Brockman, with Pop's 1958 California black-tailed deer.

swirled in Deer Creek's currents. And there were Indian arrowheads to find in the dirt. Though he didn't know it at the time, Charles Adams Jr. was treading on hallowed ground and on a collision course with history.

Grandpa Brockman, with Pop and young Chuck in 1958.

In 1911, Ishi, the last survivor of the Yahi Tribe of American Indians wandered south from his home country between Deer and Mill creeks and appeared, disheveled and hungry, at a slaughterhouse outside of Oroville, California.

White settlers hell-bent for gold and land had decimated the Yahi over the course of five decades. Ishi expected to meet the same fate. But two anthropology professors arranged living quarters for Ishi at an anthropology museum and requested that Dr. Saxton Pope, a professor at the University of California in San Francisco, conduct a physical examination of Ishi. Pope befriended Ishi and slowly learned from him the Yahi language and how to craft Yahi bows, arrows and arrowheads. Pope's friend, Art Young, who lived on Clear Lake a couple hundred miles north of San Francisco, joined in Pope's fascination with Ishi's teachings. And in the years before Ishi's death in 1916, the trio walked the Deer Creek country where the Yahi had lived and bowhunted for more than 3,000 years.

Pope and Young learned enough about bowhunting from Ishi, and were so captivated by it, that they became known as the fathers of modern archery. Today, the Pope and Young Club keeps records of trophy big game animals taken by bowhunters. The highest honor that the Club bestows, the Ishi Award, is given only when the Club convenes and determines that an exceptional animal has been taken in an honorable manner.

If you mark on a California map the Yahi home territory, and the homes of Pope and Young, the resulting triangle contains a small town called Chico, the place where Charles "Chuck"

In the late 1960s, after three years of bowhunting trial and tribulation, Chuck took his first big game animal with a bow—a forked horn blacktail. Chuck's parents, Charles and Neva, right, always supported Chuck's bowhunting passion.

Adams Jr. was born in 1951. As this is written, Chuck Adams, who shot his first deer with a bow in Ishi Country, owns the coveted Ishi Award and 111 Pope and Young-qualifying animals, more than double that of any other bowhunter in history.

"I shot my first deer in Deer Creek Canyon when I was 12 years old with a rifle," Chuck says. "And then I shot quite a few deer with a bow at the headwaters of Deer Creek Canyon up high around Mount Lassen, which was Ishi's summer range. I always thought that was an interesting coincidence. It's eerie. I have a pretty big collection of arrowheads that I picked up from Ishi's territory over the years."

Today, Chuck Adams is a bowhunting icon. Yesterday, he was just a kid who fell in love with the California hills. Today, most every bowhunter in America knows the name Chuck Adams. Yesterday, he was just a teenage boy reading about Fred Bear and wondering if he'd ever bag an animal with a bow.

FOLLOWING FOOTSTEPS

Though all humans are born with the hunt in their blood, many are born into families where they are not allowed to act on those instincts. Chuck was a fortunate son. His father, Charles Sr., came from generations of hunters like Grandpa Paul Adams, and

13

thrilled to the pursuit of both big and small California game. Even Chuck's mother, Neva, hunted and killed deer. Her father and Chuck's grandfather, Dick Brockman, was also a serious deer hunter, using his old .30-30 Winchester with open sights to deadly effect. Family lore indicates that Grandpa Brockman rarely missed.

In the 1960s, Chico was a tiny, rural, everyone-knows-everyone sort of town. Two steps from the back door put you in game-rich hunting country. Even today, the hills of northern California stand in stark contrast to L.A.'s smog and Hollywood's glitz—

Like most kids, Chuck cut his hunting teeth on small game.

images that spark faulty stereotypes of the entire state. California was a fine place for Chuck Adams, or any young hunter, to grow up. In fact, it might have been the very best setting in the world for Chuck to become the world's most successful, best-known bowhunter today.

The oldest of four children (he has three younger sisters), Chuck's hunting initiation began early. Even as a toddler, he followed his dad in the pheasant fields. Chuck toted a stick, pretending that it had 12-gauge powers.

A BB gun and Chuck's first confirmed kill, a sparrow, came at age 5. To practice his marksmanship, Chuck would hang the 1-inch-diameter cardboard BB tube canisters from tree branches with a piece of string. Out to 15 yards or so, the tube danced at most every trigger squeeze. When that became too easy, he'd increase the distance or figure out some other way to make the target more difficult. Grandpa Paul bragged about the youngster, Charles Sr. bought hundreds more BB's, and Chuck honed the God-given hand-eye coordination that he'd been blessed with.

Already he craved challenge. Even in games played with his younger sisters.

"Usually Chuck was on one team, and the three girls were on the other team," middle sister Becky True remembers. "And he usually won. Whether it was baseball or soccer or whatever, if he couldn't get something he would just work harder at it. Like sometimes he would do it left-handed so he had a handicap, you know. Three against one, but he'd do it a little harder and try to do it just to see if he could."

Chuck learned early on, though, the difference between childhood games and the BB gun. It came with stern rules, the foundation of hunter safety: no pointing the gun—ever—at anything that you didn't intend to shoot. No toy gun pointing at other people, even during cops and robbers games with the cousins and other kids. Charles told Chuck in no uncertain terms that if the muzzle of his BB gun ever pointed at another person for even a split second, it would be gone until he was 12.

For a kid whose little life was already consumed with a love for the outdoors, that was all the warning required. He might not wash his hands before supper or clean up his room, but he'd not dare to break the gun safety rules and have hunting taken from him. Hunting tools were gold.

At age 5, Chuck cobbled together a "bow."

"I made my first bow and arrow out of a piece of lath and a string when, I think, I was 5 years old," Chuck says. "I remember the first shot I took because I picked up another stick out of the board pile, and I shot and I looked out in front of me, and I couldn't see the arrow anywhere. That stick had a little nail in it, and I looked down and it was sticking in my hand, and I have a scar 'til this day that I could show you right on top of my thumb. My arrow was sticking in my hand with the nail driven in. I pulled it out, and the blood was squirting like crazy, and I ran into the house.

"That was my first experience with a bow. I had my first blood trail, and it was mine. So I marked myself for life."

But Charles was a gun hunter, and as a grade-schooler Chuck couldn't have cared less what kind of tool he hunted with, as long as he was hunting. So, most Saturdays starting at around age 7, Chuck and Charles "Pop" would trek afield after northern California's most abundant and detested rodent, the ground squirrel.

In the almond orchard country around Chico, ground squirrels were, and still are, Public Enemy No. 1. Farmers often resorted to large-scale squirrel poisoning in a futile attempt to control their numbers. As a result, the father-son Adams squirrel hunting team was welcomed on a number of nearby orchards.

15

"That was the bonding experience for Pop and me virtually every weekend in the spring and summer," Chuck says. "I was quite fortunate. I looked forward to Saturdays because we'd leave mid-morning and go out for most of the day. We'd stop by the same little grocery store coming back and get a candy bar.

"Today, I think about that. The anti-gun people who are saying we should take 'em all away, they just don't get it. On those ground squirrel weekends I got exactly what, in my opinion, is what these school-shooter kids have never gotten—a good, strong family tie and a mentor in their parent. I think I was extremely well-adjusted and I had a gun in my hand."

At 7, Chuck tumbled his first rooster pheasant using his Grandpa Paul's Mossberg bolt-action .410. He bought his own .22 at age 9, a Winchester Model 69A bolt-action, earned with lawn-mowing money. Eventually he added a 16 gauge Winchester Model 12 to his collection of hunting tools. Birds were a big deal back then in California. Doves, pheasants and quail thrived. Grandpa Paul, in fact, used to line up 10 shotshells on the kitchen table each September 1st, the opening day of dove season. Known among his family and friends as an accomplished wing-shooter, he'd often fill his 10-dove bag with those 10 shells.

"Grandpa Paul was the more avid of the two grandfathers when it came to hunting and guns. He was a gun nut like my dad," Chuck says. "He collected firearms.

"We were out jackrabbit hunting one time. Dad had one of his high-powered rifles, and I had my little Winchester 69A with a Weaver scope on it and I shot a jackrabbit at 220 yards. We paced it off later, way out in this field. It was luck. I held about 10 feet over its back and just nailed it. My grandad talked about that the rest of his life. It's not something you can brag about, but I think I was blessed with the same hand-eye coordination that my dad and my grandfathers had, because they were all great shots. And I've always had good eyesight—which helped. I've had 20-15 eyesight most of my life, and it just all came together."

Of course, there were missteps along the way. When Chuck was about 10 he and his father were preparing to hunt pheasants one day. Chuck had loaded his shotgun, switched the safety off for some reason and accidentally bumped the trigger. Fortunately, he'd been properly trained, and the gun was pointing at the ground at the time. It still cost him a full week without the gun during California's two-week pheasant season. "Dad got quite upset about that," Chuck says.

"I also have fond hunting memories of Mom and Grandpa Dick from those early years," Chuck continues. "At age 70, Grandpa Dick joined Pop and me for an all-day hike deep into the rugged Devil's Parade Ground area near Deer Creek. I managed to shoot a little forked horn blacktail with my .270 midday, and all three of us took turns carrying deer halves for six hours. Grandpa Dick was wiry and tough as nails. At age 80, he climbed over 2,000 feet from the nearest road to the top of Mount Lassen in the heart of Ishi Country.

"I wouldn't call Mom an avid hunter, but she's always been a hard walker and a crack shot. One time when I was in my early teens, Mom and Pop went deer hunting near home. Mom shot a buck with her little .25-35 lever-action carbine as it ran by at 75 yards. Only after the deer went down did she discover that she had forgotten to snap up the folding rear peep sight. I still laugh about that one. I need a peep on my bowstring for best accuracy, but Mom did fine without hers."

Besides his parents and Grandpa Paul and Grandpa Dick, most of Chuck's relatives were, as he describes, "casual hunters." Chuck took his hunting anything but casually, even at a very young age. None of his three younger sisters—Beth, Becky and Sylvia—hunted. So Chuck hunted with his father and, in his teenage years, occasionally with his cousin, Bob Adams. But as bowhunting gripped his life more firmly, he hunted less with family and more with friends who were serious bowhunters.

BOWHUNTING BEGINNINGS

Like a lot of young boys whose greatest heroes were famous hunters, Chuck devoured hunting magazines, especially *Outdoor Life* and the articles by Fred Bear, famed bowhunter and bowhunting pioneer. Archery gained steam in the '60s, and Chuck found himself fascinated by Fred's tales of adventure and hunting challenge. It was too much for a 13-year-old to take. He had to try it, even though Dad wasn't a bowhunter. Fred Bear would serve as a surrogate bowhunting mentor.

One day Chuck happened to be visiting relatives in the San

Francisco Bay area with the rest of his family. A pocket full of lawn-mowing money was burning a hole in his pocket. It was springtime. Bowhunting season would open soon. Chuck had his sights set on a new bow. At a discount store, a Ben Pearson recurve with a fancy wood handle caught his eye. Sold. A six-pack of broadheads and handful of Ben Pearson fiberglass arrows later, Chuck was ready and raring to go.

"I couldn't hit the broad side of a barn with that setup," Chuck says. "But I wanted to bowhunt because I think my dad taught me too well. In California you had one deer tag; you had to shoot a forked-horn buck or better. They were black-tailed/mule deer crosses where I grew up on the west side of California's Sierra Nevada Mountains, close to home. I always had my deer within a week during the rifle season. The season was six weeks long. I thought about deer season all year long, and then it was over so fast. I figured the bow would give me a chance to hunt more and kill less because I only had one tag to work with and I'd have more fun per year if I did this. I was hooked, even though I didn't shoot a deer for three years."

For those three seasons, Chuck withstood the frazzled frustration of trying to piece together a workable bowhunting setup. With little literature or general bowhunting information available, Chuck scoured G. Howard Gillelan's bowhunting columns in *Outdoor Life* for any morsels of bowhunting know-how that might smooth out the bumps in his teenage bowhunting road. By the second season, he'd pitched the fiberglass arrow shafts in favor of some aluminum arrows from Herter's, and his groups tightened. By the fourth season, a 53-pound Wing recurve replaced the old Ben Pearson, and Chuck put his faith in Easton aluminum arrows and Fred Bear broadheads. Bit by bit, his bow-shooting shaped up, and the fun factor skyrocketed. He hadn't shot a deer, but he swore that he wouldn't quit until he did.

FIRST DEER

Chuck's California deer license and the bow in his hand suggested that he was a bowhunter. But he wouldn't call himself one until the day came that he killed a buck with a bow. He'd already had some chances. He would earn more.

Early in his fourth season, he crossed paths with a black-tailed

Though Chuck turned primarily to bowhunting later in his teenage years, the bird hunts of his youth continue to occasionally call him back to the fields with a shotgun.

buck at 15 yards. So overcome by the fortuitous opportunity dangling there for the taking, Chuck couldn't quell his buck fever and muster enough energy to draw his bow. All he could do was watch the deer walk off. Days later, another chance. This time Chuck forgot to place the arrow shaft on the rest and instead released with the arrow still on the shelf. It caromed harmlessly six feet below the deer. His hunting skills, like those of a wolf pup, were a work in progress.

Then came late August. Charles had been taking Chuck to a place called Butte Meadows, north of Chico, to let the boy stalk deer in their high summer range. Pine tree plantations lined the hills where the manzanita had been dozed off. After three or four years, the new manzanita brush started sprouting again. The deer loved the lush habitat and flocked into the area. But despite the high deer density, the ghostly little hunter-shy deer kept giving young Chuck the slip.

19

"I had hunted on and off for two or three weeks and was frustrated to tears," Chuck says. "Finally, late one afternoon I spotted this little fork-horn out in the middle of a plantation a couple hundred yards away. I sneaked up on him using rows of dozed up brush for cover. I tip-toed along an edge and got within 40 yards of him. He was slightly downhill, just feeding away. He quartered, I shot, he jumped the string, and I hit him right in the middle of the ham. He just ran down out of sight. I had read enough of Howard Gillelan and Fred Bear to know that I should wait. And then it was dark."

Chuck headed back to the truck, flooded with emotions that spiraled from elation to dread and back again by the second. He couldn't wait to find Pop. Charles was at the vehicle when Chuck charged up and recounted what had happened, barely able to keep his breath. After talking it over, they decided to head back for camp. Cool evening air settled into the hills, and they figured that the meat from the deer would be all right, even if left until morning. Camped about 20 miles away on a small U.S. Forest Service campground, father and son started a campfire and talked more about what had transpired in the moments leading up to the fateful shot.

"I was on pins and needles," Chuck says. "I couldn't sleep. Up to that point part of my mindset was that it wasn't possible that I could see an arrow go from my bow into an animal. I just didn't believe that it could happen. And when it did happen, I hit that deer in the butt, and I hadn't had any experience with arrow-hit animals before. So I was understandably worried.

"But I had read Fred Bear, and he had said that butt shots were deadly on animals. I actually felt pretty confident based on that, but I didn't know for sure what was going to happen the next day. So I didn't sleep that night.

"Pop and I talked about scenarios for several hours. We just sat around that campfire and wondered what was going to happen, or what was likely to happen—how far the deer was likely to go and all that. We pretty well decided the deer would go 250 yards or less because he wasn't spooked; he didn't really know what had hit him."

At daylight, like two bloodhounds, Charles and Chuck set out on the thin bloodtrail. It was slow going. Chuck, having read enough to know to stay with the blood, sorted it out spot by painstaking spot. Charles flanked him and began crossing ahead side to side in a sight search for the buck. After 200 yards or so, Chuck snapped to attention when he heard Pop call out. He'd found him!

"I was the most excited kid you can imagine," Chuck says.

Finally. Finally, Chuck Adams considered himself a real bowhunter. He had heeded the sage advice of Papa Bear, had endured the agony of shabby equipment, failed stalks and missed shots and had finally savored a taste of sweet success known only to those who have bow-killed big game. Through all the heartache of failure he leaned on the broad shoulder of Fred Bear's encouraging words and banked on persistence to some-day pay off. He swears that he never considered quitting.

"Never," Chuck says. "I tend to be like a bulldog about stuff and I was just determined to get it right. And part of it was that there were people—well, Fred Bear primarily—who were doing it right, so I knew it could be done. And so I just fumbled around. I finally went to the pro shop and that's what got me on the right course. Pioneer Archery Shop in Chico, California was my salvation. I went in there and Harold and Frances Durff set me up. And I've been a life-long fan of pro shops, too, for that reason."

A DIFFERENT PATH

Chuck continued to gun hunt even with that first bow-killed forked-horn blacktail under his belt. The more time that Chuck could be out there hunting game of any type, the happier he felt. But even back to his pre-teen years in pursuit of ground squirrels, he sensed that some other aspect of the hunt called him. Shots from some far-away rifle didn't trip his trigger. He could get a marksmanship test at a target range. Getting ultra-close to animals, however, could challenge him in so many spell-binding ways: stealth, patience, cunning, persistence and self-control. Though at age 12 or 13 his thought process might not have considered all of these reasons individually, he felt it. He felt the close-range, cat-and-mouse thrill and thirsted for it.

So while Pop practiced the skills of precision rifle work as he plucked distant squirrels, Chuck turned down the barnburner rifles and stuck with his .22-caliber Winchester 69A.

"When we stopped at that country store afterward for a

candy bar, I liked Almond Joy and Pop liked Mounds," Chuck says. "And we never crossed over on that one either."

The closest Chuck came to turning Pop into a bowhunter came the season after Chuck bow-killed his first deer. Charles had a second-hand Bear recurve bow that he reluctantly toted into Ishi Country after Chuck's constant prodding finally got the best of him.

"One morning I was across the canyon glassing that same plantation where I got my first deer, and this forked horn buck came down past Pop, obviously within bow range," Chuck says. "It looked to be about 15 yards away. Dad was behind one of those rows of dozed-up brush. The deer walked right past him, and Dad didn't draw his bow to shoot. We met after the hunt was over at the truck, and I said, 'Why didn't you shoot that deer?'

"He kind of kicked a rock with his toe and looked embarrassed and said, 'Well, I was afraid that I'd kill it and that I wouldn't have my tag for gun season.' And that was the last time that Dad bowhunted in California. He didn't want to spoil his season by shooting something with a bow."

Though polar opposites in their approaches to the hunt, Chuck and Charles became and have remained life-long hunting partners: a father and son team sharing one of the finest gifts given to man—a love of the hunt. Charles didn't begrudge Chuck his growing bowhunting passion. Chuck's respect for his hunting mentor would never diminish. Instead, they shared the outdoors, encouraged and congratulated one another. And they'd recall with one another and the rest of the family, in a tradition as old as man, the thrills of the hunt.

"Hunting was just endemic," Chuck's sister, Becky, says. "It was just a way of life. They'd tell us in detail about their hunts together. It was like oratory, detail by detail. They can tell stories, both of them, in a wonderful way. To me, that's an awesome talent—the memory for detail they have of their hunts and the way the wind was blowing and which way they stalked up the ridge and how far it was.

"In our garage they had the antlers of every animal that they had ever killed hanging over the rafters. And they could tell you what year, where they were, what the stalk was like. It was real typical for us at home on a Saturday night to sit around the fire and we'd hear everything about what happened on the hunt that day."

CHAPTER TWO:
COLLEGE & CAREER

"I think everybody's an individual. Some people focus like a magnifying glass—focus all the light in one spot. Others diffuse that energy in different directions. That's just a matter of individual choice. It's been my observation that people who focus all or most of their energy in one spot, like a magnifying glass, burn up the spot."

R espect and discipline. Many teenage kids today would need a dictionary to get at the meaning of these fundamental character traits. In Chuck's family, they went without saying. Hard work, respect and discipline put food on the table whether one had a shovel or a shotgun in his hand.

Grandpa Paul pulled up stakes and left Oklahoma in the 1930s when Charles was 8, and headed for California. The family picked

Chuck expanded his bowhunting horizons in 1971 with a do-it-yourself Colorado elk hunt to the Flattops Wilderness Area.

23

cotton and did whatever they had to do to survive during the Depression. The memories of those hardships, and the knowledge of what it took to get through the hard times, passed from father to son early on.

"Everybody in my family is proud of doing any kind of work. That was a tradition in our family," Chuck says. "There was no free ride, and my parents did pretty well financially, but they said that us kids had to pay our way. I was never afraid of work, and I was always proud of working with my hands."

As a teenager, Chuck helped his grandfather, who was a plumber, dig septic tank holes and ditches. With uncles and aunts in farming, he also spent a lot of steamy summer days hauling hay and stacking bales with his cousins.

Chuck with the "Golden Hammer" award earned in junior high shop class.

So when it came time for Chuck to make important decisions about college and what he'd do with the rest of his life, Charles and Neva didn't meddle. They'd brought him up right. He'd learned self-reliance, and at 18 it was time for Chuck to start making his own decisions.

Sure, his parents offered support when needed, just the way Charles had supported Chuck's foray into bowhunting. But when you're a college professor and chairman of the university's English department, as Charles was, staying out of your children's academic affairs is not easy. Yet Charles and Neva couldn't complain about the way in which their kids conducted themselves in the classroom.

Maybe it was the work ethic that had been instilled in him from a young age. Maybe it was the respect and discipline that he had been taught in the hunting fields. Maybe it was a combination of the two with a good dose of genetics thrown in. Chuck graduated from high school in Chico as class valedictorian. In fact, throughout his high school career, he turned in straight A's.

Now that's a high school graduation present! The father-son hunt to Wyoming produced trophy mulies, but Chuck confesses that he would rather have been bowhunting.

Amazingly, so did his three younger sisters. All three of them were class valedictorians as well. Granted, Chico Senior High School wasn't huge with a total enrollment of 1,200, but a perfect 4.0 grade point every year is uncanny.

"I was just well-disciplined," Chuck says. "But it was not like pulling teeth at all; it wasn't like I was book-bound or anything. I think I was best at writing, and my teachers said that. Again, I think it's pure luck that the two things that I've always done best are write and hunt and I've combined that really weird combination into what I do now."

Not only did he ace English and math tests, but Chuck earned the "Golden Hammer" award in junior high shop, too. After the presentation, Chuck's physical education teacher approached him, offered congratulations and said that he'd never seen a kid earn top honors in academics *and* shop. Of course, Chuck's shop projects were mahogany gun racks, steel ammo boxes and other items that would serve a useful purpose.

Whatever Chuck chose to put his mind to had to be done right. Whether it was a composition for his English class, the

25

solution to a math formula, the finish on a piece of woodwork or target practice with his bow ... satisfactory just didn't cut it. For Chuck, there was a right way, a wrong way and nothing in between.

As a reward for his academic achievement, Chuck could have enrolled at Harvard, Stanford or any number of distinguished universities. Despite all of the professional opportunities and doors that would have opened to him with a degree from some Ivy League school in his hand, leaving home would mean unfamiliar ground. And unfamiliar ground would mean the likelihood that for four years, bowhunting would have to stop. That's as far as the collegiate decision-making process ever made it. There was a university right down the street. It was called Chico State. It was cheaper, but most of all, it was in the blacktails' backyard and not far from the archery club.

Bowhunting already ruled his life. It had, probably, even before he arrowed his first deer in Ishi Country at age 16, maybe even before he bought the Ben Pearson bow at 13, maybe even back to those early issues of *Outdoor Life*, or maybe all the way to that day when he tied some string to a lath and shot the stick into his hand at age 5.

Bowhunting kept Chuck mostly out of sports in high school because sports were played after school when he could be hunting. Even when he noticed girls, there was no more tempting young love than bowhunting. Sure, Chuck dated. But a date might be a shad fishing trip to the Sacramento River or a hike into Ishi Country to look for arrowheads. The outdoors had seduced his heart and soul.

"You might say that my priorities were screwed up from an early age," Chuck says. "I discussed going to Chico State with my parents and I just decided to stay close to home because I loved the outdoors. My dad was such an outdoorsman, I think he understood.

"I would say that my childhood was really normal in some ways and not so normal in others. Hunting was what I loved to do the most, and I was abnormal in that way, I think, because I preferred to hunt rather than play sports in school. I viewed sports as something that robbed me of hunting time.

"My hunting activities decreased a little bit the last couple

26

years of high school because I discovered girls. But some things were very telling. We had a day when everybody went and did what they wanted to do after high school graduation, and three friends of mine and I took our girlfriends shad fishing. It was late May or early June and that's what we wanted to do. Fortunately, many of the girls in my area were outdoors-women and they liked doing stuff like that. I remember I took my girlfriend bowhunting quite a few times in high school. It was enough of a passion with me that I didn't just let it drop."

As a high school graduation present for a job well done, Charles bought Chuck—what else?—a four-day horseback mule deer hunt near Wyoming's Star Valley. The outfitter charged only $25 per day and led father and son to a pair of beautiful, 30-inch bucks. But it wasn't easy. Chuck, though only 18, had been reading enough magazine articles and sizing up enough pictures of mulie bucks to determine that he wasn't going to squeeze that rifle trigger until his crosshairs focused on a real trophy. The outfitter urged Chuck to shoot smaller bucks earlier in the hunt, but he refused and eventually killed a big 5x6.

Driving home to California with a buck three times bigger than anything that he'd ever shot, and having experienced his first "out West" adventure like those he'd read about in *Outdoor Life*, Chuck nonetheless felt unfulfilled. He loved being out there, but he couldn't help but imagine what each moment of the four days would have been like if he'd have had his Wing recurve bow in his hand instead of that rifle. Someday, he promised himself, he'd find out.

"Shooting that buck with a rifle didn't thrill me as much as shooting a little forked-horn blacktail with a bow," Chuck says. "And I remember feeling conflicted at the time. I was grateful that I had this fantastic high school present, but I was wishing I had a bow in my hand instead."

MAKING A WAY

While Chuck's vision of his hunting future gained clarity, he had no such clairvoyance as it pertained to his life's work. Sure, he dreamed. He fantasized about being like Fred Bear, Grancel Fitz or Jack O'Connor traipsing about the continent, one hunting adventure greater than the next. What a life. What a dream.

27

The reality that he saw was a future much more comparable to that of another hero—his father.

As a college English teacher, Charles had made a fine life for his wife and children. Chuck seemed to possess the same gift for the language and composition. He excelled at academics, so it was logical to devote his life's work to the field. He could get a bachelor's degree at Chico State, maybe even a master's, buy a nice home, and use any leftover money to take bowhunting trips for elk and other big game that he dreamed of hunting. He loved Ishi Country and being around home to hunt with Pop. Maybe someday he'd even start a family.

So he enrolled at Chico State and focused his energy and attention on making a good life for himself. From the first semester to the last day of his bachelor's degree in English, he was perfect. Straight A's. Valedictorian of his collegiate class. The faculty at Chico State pored over the university's records and found only one other student among 650,000 to have achieved a perfect 4.0 throughout the bachelor's program. And despite the fact that his major was English, Chuck also became Chico State's first student to graduate with honors in philosophy.

While Chuck recognized why some might consider the achievements extraordinary, to him they seemed perfectly ordinary and something that he fully expected of himself. Par for the course. Standard operating procedure. Perfection, or why bother?

Closer to beginning an occupation in front of a classroom teaching others, Chuck enrolled in the master's program at Chico State. Taking classes and student teaching at the same time, he could feel the day approaching where he'd enter the working world.

But childhood dreams wouldn't let go. Every time that he found himself immersed in books instead of bows and arrows, his mind wandered. Suddenly, the concentration that he'd been able to channel so effortlessly throughout grade school, high school and four years of college began to wane. He worried. Could he be truly happy as an English professor? It was certainly an honorable profession and one that he deeply respected. But how could he reconcile the fact that he'd never even tried to attain his dream? Why couldn't he do it?

"Dad used to chastise me for spending too much time reading

28

Chuck with his first black bear taken in the early 1970s while hunting with friend Dennis Johns and his trusty hounds.

Outdoor Life on the weekends when I was in grade school," Chuck says. "I would read the articles over and over and over, and I used to wait for that magazine to come every month. The three people who I remember being in awe of were Fred Bear, Jack O'Connor (the shooting editor of *Outdoor Life*) and Grancel Fitz. Fitz was one of the early members of the Boone and Crockett Club and, I think, might have been the first person ever to take a North American Super Slam with a gun.

"I remember reading those guys in particular and thinking, 'Wow, what a way to go!' And from the time I was old enough to read, I was thinking that I wanted to be an outdoor writer. That was my boyhood dream—to be an outdoor writer."

Bowhunting became increasingly impossible to put aside, too. Archery deer season opened August 20th, and every summer from high school until college Chuck would work for his grandfather's plumbing business until the 19th. Then he'd bowhunt all day every day until he had his deer or until college started in early September. If he still had his tag when school was in session, he'd bowhunt every weekend.

Since his deer tag was usually gone, Chuck started looking for more big game bowhunts to satisfy his thirst. Though Chuck preferred to do most of his bowhunting alone, a friend, Dennis Johns, whom he'd met at the local archery club, became a bowhunting partner. Dennis ran Walker hounds, and he and Chuck chased black bears together in California.

Later on in college, Chuck and Dennis, who was about 10 years Chuck's senior, loaded up Chuck's 1971 Ford pickup and headed for Colorado's Flattops Wilderness Area in pursuit of elk. Chuck toted his same 53-pound recurve bow, but never killed an elk during his college days. Yet, just the way that bowhunting had stirred him starting out as a 13-year-old, the new adventures and challenges of elk hunting kindled another fire inside of him.

In the off-season Chuck honed his archery skills at the local club and as a member of his collegiate team.

"I shot winter leagues religiously with both my hunting bow and target bow during those late high school and college years," Chuck says. "But those were finger shooting days, and releases weren't even legal when I started shooting a target bow. Then

30

they went to ledge releases and then they legalized mechanical releases for target, and everything changed. I rebelled against releases at that point. I was beating everyone in my club until releases came along. I stayed with fingers because, again, I thought it was more of a challenge than shooting releases.

"I was captain of the college team, but it was pretty small, minor-league stuff. My coach tried to get me to try out for the Olympics. Years before, she had coached at another college and one of her guys made the Olympic team. She said that she thought I had a chance. But I didn't do it because I couldn't shoot both a target bow and a hunting bow well, and I didn't want to sacrifice four years of hunting to shoot a target bow on a hope and a prayer that I'd get to the Olympics.

"I knew if I was good with my Wing recurve, I was too strong to shoot my old HC300 target bow because the average tournament shooter then was shooting about 32 or 33 pounds at full draw. When I was strong with my hunting bow, I was too strong for my target bow and I was doing things with the string that hurt accuracy. When I was really good with my HC300 was in the winter and spring when I hadn't been shooting a hunting bow in a while. So I made the decision that I didn't even want to try out for the Olympics. And who knows? I'm not saying that I would have gotten to first base, but she thought I had a chance. But hunting was more important to me so I just passed on that."

If he were going to set his mind to do something, he'd have to do it all the way. Training to become an Olympic archer; completing a master's program to become an English teacher ... neither could capture his complete, undivided attention. Only two things could captivate his thoughts when he dared to look down the road into his future—bowhunting and writing for a hunting magazine.

Finally, he acknowledged the hunger pangs that had been increasingly bothering him during his post-graduate work. He didn't want to be an English professor. He could be one. He would be if that's what it came down to. And if that's what it came down to, he'd make sure that he did a great job at it and make the best of that life.

But he wanted to be an outdoor writer. He knew it from the first years that he could read *Outdoor Life* without having a grownup read it for him. And he wouldn't be happy unless he tried. Six units away from his master's degree, Chuck retrained his focus on a new target—the most tantalizing and challenging target that he'd ever taken aim at in his young life.

"Much to the chagrin of my college advisor, I said, 'You know, I want to go and try to be an outdoor writer,'" Chuck says. "I didn't like the fact that college starts about the same time that bow season does, particularly out of state. I had gone elk hunting in Colorado a couple of times, and that was again a late-August season, and it went into September. But school started, and I had to be teaching and doing coursework when the elk bugle was going on, and I didn't like that. So I said, 'You know, I'm tired of school. I'm going to try to get a job with a magazine and learn the ropes.' I bailed on the master's program six units before I completed my master's. And I actually never regretted it."

"I figured if anybody could do it, Chuck could," his sister, Becky, says. "He was not happy. He knew he would be bored teaching. He never took typing in high school, so he taught himself to type in just a few weeks' time. He had a plan. There was nothing but support from the family, and, I mean, his determination just comes through. You say, 'If anyone can do it, Chuck can.' And what was he going to lose?"

DREAM JOB

With an English degree in hand and a lifetime of hunting in his head and heart, Chuck began his quest to gain an editorial staff position at a national hunting publication. He aimed application letters and resumes at every hunting magazine publisher that he could locate. But back in the early 1970s, few potential employers existed.

Of course, everyone knew the "Big Three" of *Field & Stream, Sports Afield* and Chuck's boyhood bible, *Outdoor Life*. At that time all of them, though, were headquartered on the East Coast. Chuck applied, but didn't know what he'd do if *Outdoor Life* actually called. He had, after all, chosen Chico State over more heralded universities because he couldn't see himself moving far from home. Even if he received a response from *Outdoor Life*'s New York offices, he couldn't be sure when the time came that he'd be able to leave California in the rearview mirror.

Six months passed. Chuck hadn't heard a peep in response to any of the many letters that he had mailed hoping for work in the outdoor publishing business.

Then, in 1974, a new magazine based in Los Angeles hit the newsstand—*Petersen's Hunting.* Chuck bought it off the newsstand and scoured the content. He scrolled down the masthead, spotted Ken Elliott's name listed as editor and went about making his sales pitch.

"I wrote Ken Elliott a very aggressive letter," Chuck says. "I said, 'I think you have some problems with your editing of the magazine and I can help.' And I'll be darned if he didn't call me back. He looked at my resume and he said, 'I really like what I see. I'd like you to fly to L.A. I think we can probably use you.'

"First airplane I'd ever been on; I'd never been on a commercial flight in my life. I flew into L.A. and could smell the smog before I landed and I said, 'What the heck am I getting myself into?' Talk about falling off the turnip truck."

Twenty-two years old, a California resident, and Chuck had never been to Los Angeles. Chico's population was 10,000; plenty big enough as far as Chuck was concerned. Now he faced his first job interview—at a hunting magazine!—following his first commercial airline flight and after stepping foot into the first skyscraper that he'd ever seen. "It was total culture shock," Chuck says.

It was also the best opportunity, the only opportunity, that looked like it might pan out up until that point. Charles went along to offer moral support before and after the interview. Though Chuck found himself entirely out of his element in the city, all the years of magazine reading and immersing himself in hunting paid off. Elliott queried Chuck mostly with hunting questions. Once again, just as he had through high school and college, Chuck aced the exam.

"I remember distinctly that Ken Elliott asked me about what a Grand Slam on sheep was," Chuck says. "He told me later that he had interviewed a number of local guys who were writers, but not hunters, and nobody could tell him what a Grand Slam of wild sheep was. And he asked me what the 27 varieties of North American big game were, and I told him. He later told me that he was impressed with that. I was preparing my whole life

33

for that one interview. I knew the stuff."

Elliott offered the associate editor's job, and Chuck accepted. The reality of what he'd "gotten himself into" would sink in soon enough—a 75-hour-per-week job that included a lot of weekend work and late nights at the office editing copy sent in by free-lance outdoor writers ... all for an annual salary of $9,800.

But Chuck knew that Petersen's could eventually be his ticket to bigger and better things if he played his cards right. Not so fast, though. It was May. Chuck knew that once he moved to L.A., it wouldn't be easy to get home. He told Elliott that he'd be ready to report to work July 1; that he had some unfinished business to attend to back home. The master's thesis? Not exactly.

"I wanted to go pig hunting," Chuck says. "I decided that if I was going to go to this foreign, smog-ridden city, I had to get a hunting fix that would last me a while. And wild pigs are rampant in northern California. I shot 29 wild pigs in 40 days from May to late June on ranches around there just because I knew that I was going to have very little hunting while I was down there; that thought distressed me. Hunting those pigs was more important to me than finishing those six units of master's work. I don't know if my priorities were screwed up, but that's the way it was.

"I hated L.A. And to this day I hate L.A. intensely because it's a big, smoggy city. I told Ken up front that I probably wouldn't be working there for more than two years."

Chuck had just landed the job that would launch him toward his dream, and already he had an exit plan. The master plan, after all, wasn't to be a relatively unknown editorial staffer whose name only appeared in small type buried in a busy masthead.

No, he made the sacrifice of leaving Ishi Country—the black-tails, the black bears and his family and friends—500 miles away because he had set a course attempting to follow the footsteps of his boyhood idols: O'Connor, Bear and the others whom he'd read in *Outdoor Life*. To get there, he knew that he needed the start that Petersen's could give him. And he recognized that Petersen's could only take him so far. Before long he'd have to strike out on his own.

As July 1 approached, Chuck packed his bags for the big city.

Chuck chose Chico State over more acclaimed universities so that he could stay home and continue to bowhunt his beloved blacktails.

He rented a tiny apartment in the Wilshire District about five miles from the Petersen Publishing headquarters, determined to work hard, pinch pennies and return to Ishi Country to hunt as often as possible. Most single guys in their early 20s might have decided to spend most of their free time and spare cash seeing L.A.'s sights. Chuck decided instead to live life like a hermit.

"I spent most of the money I made flying back to northern California to hunt," Chuck says. "I got out of L.A. as much as I could. It was very tough on me, being there in that city environment. I was a duck out of water. I've always budgeted myself very carefully and I decided that student loan payoff was a priority. I got $3,000 in student loans all paid off during those two years."

At the same time, a revolution was taking place in the hunting industry. Bowhunting stood at the brink of innovation that would create a watershed for the world of archery. The compound bow was preparing to take center stage. And what had been a tiny faction of hunters and a tiny fraction of the hunting industry's total economic output was about to become an entire industry unto itself.

COMPOUND INTEREST

Chuck went to L.A. with his recurve bow. But when he finally left Petersen's two years later, he was a compound bow shooter. Much of it can be traced to a meeting between Chuck and Tom Jennings, whom many regard as the father of compound bow technology, at the Jennings Archery headquarters just north of L.A.

"I made an appointment to see Tom Jennings," Chuck says. "I'll never forget the first time I walked into his office. He didn't have a secretary. He was a great guy—a hands-on guy. Well, I walked in, and he had this big desk. It was piled so high with stuff that you had to kind of peek between the piles to see him.

"He took me under his wing and showed me around the factory. They were just coming out with metal-handled bows then, and I got an old S-handled Jennings and went to Montana and shot nice mule deer and white-tailed bucks with that S-handled bow. I was hooked on compounds.

"I started shooting compounds because that was the way of the future," Chuck continues. "I liked compounds, and most of

36

the magazine editors after I left Petersen's were asking for stories related to compound bows because that's where the market was, that's where the advertising was.

"At that point, I didn't even know that there were people who looked at compounds with a jaundiced eye. After I became a full-time outdoor writer, I started getting letters from people with serious objections to compounds, but I just naturally went with the flow and I figured archery was archery and all bows are difficult to shoot. I didn't shoot a compound any better than I did a recurve. But compounds did impart more energy to the arrow, and I just liked them. I figured they were more efficient killing machines."

As Chuck considered the evolution underway in the bowhunting business, he contemplated the chance for a perfect marriage—a match made in heaven. As an associate editor at *Petersen's Hunting*, he had the responsibility of editing all manner of hunting columns and feature stories. The vast majority, big game and small, centered on some type of firearm as the hunting tool. In Chuck's personal hunting life, however, the bow ruled. He rifle hunted on a couple of business trips while employed by Petersen's. But that was it. He knew that his future was as a bowhunter or an English teacher.

With compounds catching hold, Chuck lobbied Elliott to launch a bowhunting column in *Petersen's Hunting*. He agreed, and Chuck authored the column during his second year of employment at the company and for 19 years after he left. In fact, having the regular column in his back pocket helped Chuck to leave after the two-year warning that he'd given Elliott before he took the job.

The time at Petersen's had also bought Chuck a ticket to the industry's annual trade show, the National Sporting Goods Association (NSGA) Show in Chicago. There Chuck rubbed elbows with well-known outdoor writers and fellow editors from other hunting publications around the country. He talked with representatives from the top archery manufacturers like Easton and Hoyt. He'd constructed enough of a network and safety net that two years and one month after hiring on with Petersen's he plunged into self-employment as a full-time freelance writer.

"It took me another year and a half to get out of L.A. because I was so busy writing," Chuck says. "Thank goodness Ken Elliott agreed to buy a lot of my stuff after I left. I was writing for bowhunting magazines and everybody else I could."

With that, he was on his own in the hunting world at age 25, and on schedule for the rest of his professional life to unfold. Grandpa Paul, still alive at the time, reminded everybody of a day deer hunting with Chuck in California when Chuck was a teenager. Paul lost his hearing aid out in the woods and offered Chuck $5 if he found it. Chuck asked his grandfather what kind of percentage $5 was of the purchase price. Smiling at the question, Paul turned to Chuck's father and said, "That guy's going to be an entrepreneur."

GOING IT ALONE

At the center of the network that Chuck had woven during his two years at Petersen's was a California company called Easton.

Chuck had met the Easton folks at an NSGA show in Chicago. He saw a company poised to flourish as the archery industry gained momentum and noted that Easton was producing its catalogs and product releases in-house. Chuck figured that it couldn't hurt to ask if the company could use some help with its publications and someone to help test new equipment.

So one day while still employed at Petersen's, Chuck picked up the telephone and placed a call.

"It amazes me that I had the courage to call Easton," Chuck says. "I had met these folks, but never Jim Easton, the owner. I called and got an appointment with Jim Easton, saying that I would like to talk to him about doing some consulting work for him because I was trying to leave L.A. I'll be darned if he didn't allow me to come down there.

"I had about an hour meeting with him and Joe Johnston, who was the president of Easton at the time, and they were the nicest guys in the world. They treated me with respect—this young, punk kid—and Jim hired me as a consultant on a monthly retainer. That retainer was enough to give me the courage to go ahead and leave Petersen's."

"I guess it was his strong passion for doing what he was trying to do," Jim Easton says, looking back on his decision to hire Chuck back in 1976. "It was his dedication to that goal in his life that made me feel that this young man is going to be successful. Sometimes you make good decisions, and in this case it was a good one."

Still, Chuck wasn't sure that it would all work out. Easton could turn its publications over to some agency and leave Chuck out in the cold at any time. The freelance writing gigs with hunting magazines could dry up. Like any small business, there were no guarantees. So Chuck sought assurance in the fact that if it all crumbled down around him he could go back to Chico State, complete the six units remaining in his master's, and get a job as a teacher. It helped him sleep at night. That is, when he managed to find time to sleep.

In addition to *Petersen's Hunting*, Chuck helped with the launch of *Petersen's Bowhunting*, and wrote for *Archery World* (later called *Bowhunting World*), *Bowhunter*, AquaField Publications, *Guns & Ammo* (as knife editor), and a couple of other publications. All the different assignments and deadlines required organization and discipline in order to get the job done. Freelancers who make a habit of missing deadlines find themselves out of work quickly. So Chuck burned the midnight oil, not exactly sure where the journey would lead him.

"Making money was not my motivation," Chuck says. "Somehow, I wanted to make a living doing what I loved to do most. Certainly, being a journalist is not a route that's going to make you rich. I was working seven days a week and basically, except for occasional hunting trips, 52 weeks a year. I was trying to stay afloat and I was hustling like crazy."

Eighteen months after quitting Petersen's, Chuck finally found enough time to gather his things, escape L.A., and return to Chico. He rented a small apartment in town. Two years later, with business picking up, he had scraped together enough cash for a down payment on a home. "My machine was starting to move," he says.

But as Chuck's writing career crystallized, his bowhunting took a back seat. There simply wasn't spare time. Sure, Chuck slipped away for a few hours here and there to hunt around Chico, but extended hunting trips of more than a few days were rare. Chuck knew that a big part of what allowed him to write and endeared him to editors was his field experience and

39

bowhunting expertise. Even the best writer has to have something to write about.

To continue to deliver fresh-from-the-field bowhunting insights, he knew that he had to bowhunt, even though it didn't directly pay the bills. That meant planning a trip and then working like a maniac to get far enough ahead on his freelance work that he wouldn't have to worry about any deadlines or panicked calls from editors while he was gone. From there, he just had to be able to break away mentally and leave the office at the office.

"My main problem was that I was always dead tired when I went hunting because I was always up day and night trying to get everything done so I could leave," Chuck says. "There was a July blacktail season, I think the earliest deer season in the Lower 48, in the California Coast Range. I always made opening day. But I was always up all night the night before, either driving to a hunting spot or getting the last article in the mail before I left. It was difficult.

"Then it would take me a few days to decompress after I got there. I made more bowhunting mistakes during the first few days after I'd leave the office than I would the rest of the season because I was still in high gear. I found myself walking too fast, sneaking too fast, poking my head too high over the ridges because I was still in that churn-out-the-articles mode. I'm happy to say that as the years have gone by I've learned to shift gears more rapidly and have gotten into other businesses besides writing that have allowed me to not work so frantically all the time."

Ultimately, Chuck Adams the hunter made Chuck Adams the writer. As had been the case with Bear, O'Connor and the other *Outdoor Life* heroes that Chuck had admired as a kid, the hunting stories and experiences eventually immortalized them. They gained respect in the hunting world for having "been there" and "done that."

Chuck knew what he wanted from those heroes as he impatiently waited for each new issue of *Outdoor Life* to arrive in his mailbox. He wanted to escape on a hunting adventure alongside one of them. He wanted to learn from them along the way about equipment, destinations and species that he'd never hunted. Chuck the reader, too, had helped to make Chuck the writer.

40

As Chuck eyed a teaching career, he wondered how he'd live with less bowhunting.

41

In O'Connor and Bear, Chuck had found more than boyhood idols. He had discovered a blueprint of the finished product that he wanted to be. It didn't include step-by-step instructions on how to get there, but it helped to define success in this business that he'd gotten himself into. With the blueprint in his mind, the audience provided by a number of hunting publications, the industry support from Easton and a bow in his own well-trained hands, Chuck set out to earn his place.

He'd hunt as much as possible, as hard as possible, across as much of North America as possible. And he'd retrace those footsteps across the continent in the words that he'd scrawl and clack to paper between adventures. There wouldn't be time for much else in his life, but he had in this career everything that he wanted.

"Hunting was always very strong in my life," Chuck says. "I was focused. I just loved it. I think everybody's an individual. Some people focus like a magnifying glass—focus all the light in one spot. Others diffuse that energy in different directions. That's just a matter of individual choice. It's been my observation that people who focus all or most of their energy in one spot, like a magnifying glass, burn up the spot. They tend to do a real good job in that one area.

"When you diffuse your energy you don't tend to stand out as much in a particular area. It doesn't mean you're a better or worse person, but I've always been one to tend to focus on particular spots. And hunting's been my big focus. I don't know if it's healthy or unhealthy. Knowing how happy I've been my whole life, I can't imagine that it was unhealthy for me."

CHAPTER THREE:
FAMILY & MARRIAGE

"I'm too intense about hunting. It's not a hobby. It's a lifestyle. It's a passion. So, I think almost without exception, both the men and the women I've known over the years who I've gotten along with best were outdoors people."

Focus. It had brought Chuck Adams a long way quickly. Valedictorian, straight A's through high school and college, an editorship at *Petersen's Hunting*, consultant for Easton and out on his own—his own boss—as a freelance writer while still in his 20s. But while the focus undoubtedly "burned up the spot"— Chuck's vision to make bowhunting his life's work—it blurred most everything on the periphery.

When he wasn't hammering the keys of his typewriter at

Chuck and Joanne with Quebec caribou, 1990.

hyper-speed to hit another deadline or road-tripping to be on a mountain at the crack of dawn, he found a few spare moments to reflect. And, on rare occasion, he'd manage enough introspection to deliberate his drive, his direction, his choices and where all of it might lead.

His life (which for a time appeared as though it might mirror his father's life) now stood in stark contrast to it and to tradition. Any thoughts of a wife or kids only clouded the focus that he enjoyed when consumed by all things bowhunting. And Chuck knew himself well enough to know that it would be difficult if not impossible for anyone else to know and understand him. He acknowledged and accepted the vanity inherent in such a view, and was ready to move on.

Then, in late winter 1981, before the Super Slam was even a twinkle in Chuck's eye, he noticed someone else.

"I was 29 years old," Chuck says. "I don't necessarily believe in love at first sight, but it was darn near that. I met Joanne at an indoor archery shoot in Chico, and we shot next to each other on the archery range. I'll be darned if a year and a half later I wasn't married and the happiest guy in the world. Here was a gal from a hunting family herself who was out there shooting a bow before I met her. We just absolutely hit it off. For the first time, I thought marriage. I met someone who could enhance my life.

"I had girlfriends prior to that, but never had the desire to get married. They were either city girls who didn't understand what I did, or it just wasn't the right mix that would lead all the way to marriage. I had two girlfriends in my 20s who both dabbled in hunting. They understood what I did, but not everyone you meet is your soulmate and your marriage partner. If you find one or two people like that in your whole life, I think you're fortunate."

Proof that Chuck had found the right partner was evident on the first date—a picnic in, where else, Ishi Country. In May 1982, Chuck and Joanne were married.

But Chuck couldn't and wouldn't allow marriage to change his life, something that he had made abundantly clear before saying "I do." He couldn't afford to slack. To make ends meet, he had reached "12-12" status in the outdoor publishing realm; that's 12 articles each and every month for 12 months of the year—144 in all, just to pay the mortgage and keep the lights on.

44

In between it all, he had to find enough time to bowhunt in a business where a writer like Chuck is judged as much by his kills as by his words. His editors demanded it, his readers demanded it, Easton and the other companies he was consulting for demanded it. Chuck knew that he had to perform equally well in both areas if he was going to summit the mountain that he had set out to climb when he called Ken Elliott back in 1974. And because Joanne supported his goals and dreams, the train stayed on track.

The stocking cap works on birds, too! Chuck with Montana partridge, 1987.

"I was going on three or four major out-of-state hunts a year at that point," Chuck says. "Joanne was and is a very independent person. And she didn't have a problem with that. She said, 'I would love to have some time to myself during hunting season.'

"I had been a happy bachelor and I thought that I would make a difficult husband because I was gone so much and because I was so passionate about what I did. I think most of the women in the world wouldn't put up with someone like me, and I think that's very legitimate. Most marriages are fairly traditional. The spouse, whether it's the man or the woman, is around most of the time, around on weekends and whatnot. I found a gal, though, who was happy with my lifestyle."

Chuck had found room for a wife, but that made a full house in his mind. He and Joanne agreed: there would be no kids, at least not right away. It would be hard enough to be away from home and Joanne for 100 or so days each fall. He knew that it would be impossible if a baby entered the equation. And if he couldn't maintain the freedom and the flexibility to schedule a two- or three-week hunt when necessary, then everything that he had done to get this far would be wasted.

He'd never settle for being an average outdoor writer with average success as a hunter and average celebrity in the industry. In school only A's were acceptable; at Petersen's he had told Ken Elliott that he'd stay only a short time so that he could move on to bigger and better things flying solo. If he were going to be a dad now, he might as well go back to Chico State, finish his master's and become a college professor, just like Pop. He loved Joanne, but children would not make him any happier at the time.

"We discussed it all in detail—what I did and the issue of children," Chuck says. "I didn't want children right away. Joanne said she could go either way. She wasn't one of those ladies who had such a strong maternal instinct that she thought she had to have children. We discussed it and we went into our marriage agreeing that those two things were not issues. And they never were issues in our marriage, either.

"I had the philosophy that the biggest problem we have in the world is overpopulation. One of my biology professors in college spent a whole week talking about the population explosion. I've never felt any desire to duplicate myself. In some ways I think I'm almost doing the world a favor by not having another person helping to wipe out wildlife habitat. Everybody makes life choices. There are consequences and downsides to your choices. You can't have everything, and I decided to do what I'm doing and to have kids right away would be incompatible.

"If I had children, my first priority would have been to be a good dad. I would have hunted less. I made the conscious choice and paid the penalty of not having kids. You can't have everything in life, and Joanne agreed with me. She said, 'Fine, if that's what you want to do, I love you and that's what we'll do.'

"I'm wistful now because Joanne and I never did have children. One of my best hunting buddies, Doyle Shipp, lives in Montana. He manages a cattle ranch and he's a serious bowhunter. He has two little boys, 6 and 7 years old. I visit them, and those little boys are all over me. I take them out with their little toy guns and take them fishing and play baseball and do what a surrogate dad does, and it makes me wistful.

46

The Shipp family of Montana has been like family to Chuck, who calls Doyle one of his best hunting buddies. Colleen, Reo and Ryley enjoy Chuck's elk hunting visits, too.

"But you can't have everything. I have a nephew and two nieces. I spend a lot of time with them and I spend time with literally hundreds of little, up-and-coming bowhunters at sport shows and kids that friends of mine have and love every minute of that."

Chuck and Joanne stayed in Chico for two years after they were married and then decided that it was time for a change in scenery. Chuck was in his early 30s and traveled to Montana most every September in search of elk. He'd grown to love it, so he took Joanne to see the Bitterroot Valley with him. She fell in love with the vast, empty spaces, too, and a year later they packed their belongings and left Ishi Country behind.

In Montana Chuck also found a hunting partner—someone who over the years probably bowhunted by his side more than anyone else before or since.

"Joanne loved to hunt and as she hunted more and more with

47

me with a bow, she discovered that she got excited and loved big antlers," Chuck says. "Pretty quick it was Joanne saying, 'You know, we gotta go get a big elk this fall,' before I could say it. She didn't want to be on a mountain hunting bighorn sheep, and we couldn't have afforded two tags anyway. So we went on the hunts where she'd have fun. She absolutely loved it. Like many women I know, once she got into it, she was a great hunter and had a great time.

"We hunted the Missouri River Breaks every year for elk. We'd spend 10 days to two weeks and just hunt elk. She finally got a nice 7-point elk in New Mexico in 1991 and she was doing cartwheels, she was so excited."

Being married to a man like Chuck, it's no surprise that bowhunting began to take over Joanne's life, too. She was hunting more and gaining a clearer vision of where Chuck was steering his career. It quickly became a team effort with Joanne quitting her job as a dental assistant to guide another endeavor aimed at capitalizing on Chuck's notoriety.

With outdoor magazines buying so many of Chuck's articles and photos, and Easton starting to make him the focal point of its arrow ads, bowhunters across the country increasingly dissected the details of how Chuck Adams did what he did. They scrutinized his techniques and his equipment. And they started noticing that unlike most bowhunters of the day, Chuck's compound bow didn't have a bow-attached quiver. He carried his arrows at his hip and he wrote about the reasons why he liked a hip quiver better than one that attached to the bow. The hip quiver became a signature, and bowhunters figured that if it was good enough for Chuck Adams, it was good enough for them. They wanted one. Thus, Chuck entered the mail-order and retail market for the first time with a product solely designed and marketed by Chuck Adams.

"We started a little hip quiver business," Chuck says. "I started using a hip quiver instead of a bow-attached quiver back in the early '80s because after experimenting quite a bit I decided it was a more accurate way to go, it took weight off my bow, and it made my bow bounce around a little less in crosswinds. People started seeing my hip quiver in photographs—my one and only hip quiver that I had designed—so they started asking, 'Where can we buy that?'

The Adams Arrow Holster, circa 1988. This product marked Chuck's first foray into merchandising, and proved extremely successful, as have his more recent archery product innovations.

"So shortly after we married and moved to Montana, Joanne and I started selling the Adams Arrow Holster by mail-order. That business grew so rapidly that Joanne quit her day job to run the business. It worked out very well. It gave her the chance to work like me—frantically part of the year and then have the time to take off and go like we did one year to Hawaii. We combined a mouflon sheep hunt with relaxing on the beach. If she'd had a day job, it would have been hard for us to do that when we wanted to."

Of course, Chuck wasn't sitting there in his garage building your Chuck Adams Arrow Holster for you. He and Joanne hired a handful of craftsmen, trained them and kept them busy filling orders. Chuck had more important things to attend to.

As 1985 approached, he directed his bowhunting focus on far-away adventures, tirelessly researching outfitters and studying hunting areas as he planned to embark on his most exotic, expensive and important hunts to date—those that would take him in pursuit of the Grand Slam of wild sheep.

As he plotted and dreamed about arrowing a Stone, a Dall, a bighorn and a desert sheep—something that nobody, not even the great Fred Bear, had ever done—he brazenly dared to look even further. Out there loomed a goal so seemingly unattainable for a bowhunter, that no one had even put a name to it yet. The summit, though still perilously distant, slowly gained focus.

"I just got to thinking one day, 'You know, I've got about half of the species of the North American 27,'" Chuck says. "This is the thing that Grancel Fitz had done with his rifle. And I thought, 'Well, here I am a bowhunter and writer and I like variety. Why don't I try to go and get all the species, the rest of the ones that I don't have? It'll make me more credible as a writer because I'll have more diversified experience. It'll be a real adventure and a lot of fun.' So that's when I deliberately started to try to harvest the rest of the species."

The quest for "Super Slam" began.

CHAPTER FOUR: **SUPER SLAM**

PART I: MAN ON A MISSION

"I kept it under my hat until I had it because I already knew in my heart that if I made it known that I was going for the Super Slam somebody else with a lot more money than I had would try to beat me to it."

Hanging up the telephone, his exhaustive interview of another Stone sheep outfitter in British Columbia complete, Chuck leaned back in his chair and counted again.

Columbia black-tailed deer, black bear, mule deer, Canada moose, white-tailed deer, pronghorn, Alaska-Yukon moose, mountain goat, Rocky Mountain elk, barren ground caribou, Sitka black-tailed deer. Eleven. Sixteen to go: the four wild sheep, three caribou, the three dangerous bears, a Coues' deer, a Shiras

Outfitter Duane Nelson helped Chuck tag a Dall ram in 1985—the first in his Grand Slam. Here, they share sheep tenders.

moose, a bison, a muskox, a Roosevelt elk and a mountain lion. If the sheep hunts played out as he imagined, a Dall, Stone and bighorn would be his before 1985 ended. That would make at least 14—more than halfway. If. *If* circumstances beyond his control didn't conspire against him. *If* the bank would give him the money. Because *if* it didn't go right the first time, there might not be money for a second time.

Still, in Chuck's mind, only something unforeseeable could stand in the way of his goals for 1985. He would find outfitters who sounded right to him when he inquired about how they'd handle a bowhunter. He'd arrange with them to have extra days available on the back end of the hunt, even if it would cost him more money at that point, to stay longer and get what he had come for. With the right people, in the right places, at the right times and for a long enough time, only two elements remained— his own ability, in which he had no doubt; and chance, over which he had no control.

"The first 13 years of my career I was basically enjoying myself and working my butt off and not making a heck of a lot of extra money," Chuck says. "Part of it was that I was spending virtually everything I had going after more exotic animals in the Super Slam. In 1985 I pulled the plug and really went after them. I mean, I went to my local banker. People ask who paid for the Super Slam. I did. I took out several bank loans to go on these hunts because I just didn't have the money in the bank. And I owned a house and I had some collateral and took out loans and paid them back. Those were expensive hunts even then.

"I paid for all my hunts—always have and I like it that way. There are fewer strings attached. Certainly, I cut deals with outfitters to stay longer and I think anybody who had the ability to cut deals because he was a magazine writer would do the same thing. I make no apologies for that. It was in Jerry Knap's best interest to say I could hunt a few extra days (for polar bears) because he got good publicity out of it. Same thing for Brent Jones. He got his full money for those Alaska brown bear hunts. Bighorn sheep, I paid full boat for that with Charlie Stricker and I arranged to come in and scout before season and arranged for extra days on that one as well. A lot of people assume that because I work with industry people that I'm 'sponsored.' I don't

Outfitter and guide Keith Holmes on the edge of a British Columbia abyss with Chuck's 1985 Stone ram.

even like the word 'sponsored.' Some of the people I work with use that term occasionally, but the word 'sponsor' implies that they're paying for my hunts, and that's never happened. I wish they would. But nobody's ever offered to pay for a hunt."

Chuck's claim that the Super Slam wasn't a sponsor-funded publicity effort is supported by Hoyt President Randy Walk and Easton Outdoors CEO Erik Watts. Both corroborated Chuck's story and say that they sensed that Chuck was extending himself financially in an effort to complete his quest. "We never put a penny into that," Watts said. "Chuck funded every bit of that on his own. We supported Chuck over the years on our staff, but that had nothing to do with any endeavors to go after Super Slam. Until he got really close, I never even heard of it."

As a result, Chuck says that the only person counting on him to come through was himself. "Any time I go hunting there's always a certain amount of pressure to perform," Chuck says. "And I suppose you could make the argument that the pressure would have to be a little higher when the cost of the hunt is on the line. But the pressure wasn't coming so much in that case from, 'Geez, what's going to happen if I don't get this animal career-wise?' The pressure came from the thought that, 'Well, if I don't get one, I'm going to have to try to find a way to go back and spend more money a second time.'"

THE GRAND SLAM

It was the early summer of 1985—beautiful days to kick back and soak in the splendor of Montana's Bitterroot Valley. But Chuck allowed himself no such luxury. Dozens of articles needed to be written to satisfy a couple months' worth of deadlines before he'd escape the real world. In July, Chuck's focus could concentrate all of its substantial energy toward its most natural, enjoyable dimension—as human predator.

He'd travel to the Northwest Territories first, aiming for a Dall ram with Duane Nelson. In August he'd stalk the mountains of British Columbia for a Stone with Keith Holmes; then in November to Alberta with Charlie Stricker and guide Rod Collin in search of a bighorn.

Most hunters, even savvy bowhunters with miles in the mountains, knowing that they would be in the hands of some of the finest sheep hunting outfitters and that they'd be in the right places at the right times, would have been pleased to celebrate Christmas, 1985, two sheep richer. Two-for-three would be good. To most bowhunters, that is. To Chuck, it would have been cause for disappointment. He expected three legal rams.

After two days of backpacking into the MacKenzie Mountains with Duane Nelson in July, Chuck set out on day three for his first real day of hunting. Later that morning, he spun his dial-operated rangefinder on a bedded ram in the first band of sheep that they found. Fifty-four yards and no way to get closer, pinned down by sheep eyes and lacking cover. So he drew smoothly and confidently, settled his sight pin firmly and released ... and took his first of four giant steps toward the Grand Slam of North American wild sheep—an expensive and esteemed component of the Super Slam.

Less than a month later and on his first day out with Keith Holmes, the duo found a legal ram, again in the first band of sheep spotted. A stalk put Chuck within 40 yards but sharply downhill from the ram. His first shot from an awkward, kneeling position missed clean, but the next nailed the ram center-chest facing straight on. The Stone scrambled 100 yards over the dangerous terrain, faltered, then fell, just inches from tumbling over the edge of a cliff. Two sheep hunts, two days of sheep hunting, two legal rams, one-half of a Grand Slam.

"I found the sheep to be relatively easy," Chuck says. "A lot of people put sheep up on a very high pedestal. And I love sheep— they're gorgeous, and the country is gorgeous. And they live in fairly challenging terrain. But once I got into the country and once I found the animal I wanted, I didn't find them to be the most challenging animals I ever hunted. I found them to be very bowhuntable, which surprises a lot of people. And my impression was that if I had wanted to shoot all four varieties of sheep at 20 or 25 yards, if I had allotted more time to hunt, I probably could have gotten closer shots."

While in the MacKenzie Mountains back in July, Chuck added a mountain caribou bull to his list of species and now sat on 14 of the 27. Oozing optimism, he readied for Alberta bighorns in November.

Then the uncontrollable Mr. Murphy paid a reality check. No

55

one around the town of Canmore, Alberta to this day can remember November cold quite like that of November 1985.

"I've never hunted sheep in that kind of cold weather or in as much snow," says Rod Collin, a Canadian hunting guide with 24 years of experience. "There was a fair bit of snow there, and it was terribly cold. It wasn't a whole lot of fun."

Chuck and guide Rod Collin had toughed it out for nine days in a tent on the mountainside nearly within view of a warm, cozy motel in Canmore, just two hours' hike down the mountain.

"My bighorn was tough—nine days of grueling hunting in severely sub-zero weather," Chuck says. "It was 31 degrees below zero the day I took my ram. And the warmest I saw it during that whole trip was 25 below zero during the day. That was the roughest sheep hunt by far."

The pain paid off on the ninth day when Chuck made a steep 25-yard downhill shot on a big ram and then coolly plucked, nocked and delivered another arrow to the ram's chest as it hurried past at six feet. Looking back, Chuck cherishes what he and Rod went through during those nine days enough to regard his bighorn hunt as one of his five greatest hunts ever. (The details of the numbing adventure come in Chapter Five.)

As Chuck celebrated the holidays in 1985, he had a lot to be thankful for. Three-fourths of his Grand Slam stood completed, proof once again that the front-end investment of time and effort researching far-away outfitted hunts is of equal importance to the effort invested once you arrive. The controllable had been masterfully controlled. And when Mother Nature struck with fury, Chuck countered with persistence and optimism—the attitude that each passing day earned him odds that would eventually pay out in his favor.

"I was confident in my ability to shoot and hunt. I had researched areas and was always going to an area with a track record for fairly numerous animals and good trophy animals," Chuck says. "And I always went with an outfitter with a good track record in the cases where an outfitter was legally required. I prefer not to hunt with an outfitter unless legally required. Some of my best friends are outfitters, but even those guys don't hunt with other outfitters. They feel confident in their ability to

Chuck summited the Grand Slam of sheep in 1986 on the Hualapai Indian Reservation in northern Arizona. That's outfitter, Larry Heathington, supervising from above.

go do it themselves. I enjoy doing it all myself whenever possible because the challenge is higher and the mental rewards are higher for me. If I've done all the scouting and even set up my tent myself, when I take an animal the reward's a bit higher because I did it independently. But 13 of the 27 species that I hunted legally required a guide. I did as much research as I could and in every case I did arrange to stay extra time if I needed it if the hunt was going poorly."

In October 1986, Chuck swept the Grand Slam. He traveled to the Hualapai Indian Reservation in northern Arizona, the cheapest place that he could find to hunt desert sheep and one of the few places where he could deliberately go without having to put in for years in hopes of drawing a lottery tag. Three days into the hunt, he arrowed the first and only legal desert ram that he stalked on the trip. A good shot from 30 yards did the job on the bedded sheep.

Four hunts, a North American Grand Slam of sheep, with a total of six arrows. Only one of those six missed. Sounds easy. But the Grand Slam hadn't come without its share of pressure-packed moments. The hunt on the Hualapai proved to be a perfect example.

"The Hualapai Indians told me if I drew blood on a sheep, my hunt was over either way," Chuck says. "If you wanted it to be a pressure cooker, it was. I had one chance. I can tell you that those Hualapai Indian guides, after I shot, they ran over there to see if I hit that sheep. I'd have gone away minus my money without a sheep had I drawn blood, even if I'd have nicked the hock of a sheep. So I was very careful and I really did turn into a machine during that decade. I was lucky. There could have been a problem on any of those hunts. But it just didn't happen, and I think partly because I was sure of the distance. During the '80s I had enough experience behind me that I was extremely careful.

"My Grand Slam made a fairly good splash in the archery industry," Chuck says. "I was the fourth bowhunter to take the Grand Slam on sheep. Jack Frost was first, Tom Hoffman was second, Paul Schafer was third and I was fourth. That helped my career."

Though Chuck completed his Grand Slam a full year after Jack Frost had, he knew that being the first to Grand Slam was not the Grail so far as his career was concerned. He knew before he started his pursuit of the sheep, in fact, that the Grand Slam quest was likely begun too late in the game to give him a realistic chance at being first anyway.

He was, of course, thrilled to have taken each of the four majestic sheep. But as much as anything, Chuck could now count four more of the North American 27, his Super Slam, to his credit: Columbia black-tailed deer, black bear, mule deer, Canada moose, white-tailed deer, pronghorn, Alaska-Yukon moose, mountain goat, Rocky Mountain elk, barren ground caribou, Sitka black-tailed deer, Dall sheep, mountain caribou, Stone sheep, bighorn sheep, bison, desert sheep. Seventeen. He was well over the hump to 27. And by now he'd spent enough time mulling the idea to know what being the first archer to 27 might mean. The challenge now would be maintaining the perspective and the focus that had spurred his journey in the first place.

"I would like to say that I planned to shoot up my career with the Super Slam, but that's really not true," Chuck says. "It was for other reasons. It's like the reason that I went to Los Angeles at less than $10,000 a year and worked for Petersen's. I was just trying to figure out a way to do what I love most and make a living. The Super Slam made sense because I was having fun and I thought it would help me write more magazine articles on more subjects. And I really didn't fully anticipate the spike in my career that resulted. It was not a publicity stunt or anything like that.

"I knew that the Super Slam had implications, but I can honestly say that the financial gain wasn't my prime motivation. My prime motivation was the challenge of getting it done. My prime motivation for bowhunting is challenge. People talk about enjoying the woods and enjoying wildlife, and that's certainly part of bowhunting and I love every aspect. But challenge is my prime motivator and always has been. I knew that Super Slam would have strong business implications, but that was secondary to just the challenge of doing it. I enjoy hunting. And, so, I was out there having fun, but I also wanted to succeed."

A WORLD RECORD ALONG THE WAY

To succeed, Chuck also realized that he had to keep quiet about his ultimate goal. That would be difficult. The excitement alone made it difficult to contain the idea. And with so many people reading his articles, hearing about his hunts and the different species, sooner or later someone would put it together and see that this wasn't some random trek of the continent purely for bowhunting fun. Chuck had a purpose and a method.

Still, he couldn't be everywhere at once. September lasted only 30 days. Seasons came and went. Completing the Super Slam would take time ... years more. So when he couldn't hunt for a new species, he'd hunt the ones that he enjoyed the most and the ones that presented the ultimate challenge. On Kodiak Island, Alaska, thrived an animal that Chuck especially liked for thrill and challenge.

In 1984 he traveled to Kodiak to hunt Sitka blacktails for the first time. It was August in bowhunting paradise. The lush island, cradled by the northern waters of the Pacific Ocean, was famous enough. In the 1960s it had been home to fleets of commercial fishing vessels that probed the deep, icy waters for king crab. With millions of dollars at stake, greedy captains sometimes pushed their vessels and their weary crews too far in the most hellacious weather that the North Pacific could brew up. Working on a crab boat was the most dangerous career choice a man could make anywhere in North America.

Decades earlier, the island had gained fame far and wide for its huge brown bears. And wealthy hunters came from around the globe to pursue the beasts under the guidance of outfitters like Bill Pinnell and Morris Tallifson, who became legendary. Kodiak spewed adventure of all sorts. And its abundant blacktailed deer lured Chuck there early in his career.

With a liberal limit, no guide required and a season that started in August, Kodiak had "Chuck Adams" written all over it. Hunting with his friend, Richard Long, in 1984, Chuck arrowed three nice bucks that all qualified for the Pope and Young record book. Following the trip and studying the P&Y records more closely, and then comparing the best bow-killed bucks to some of those that had been taken by rifle hunters on the island, Chuck concluded that the island harbored a bowhunting world record, so long as a bad winter kill didn't strike before his next trip there.

In 1986 he was back with his friend, Jim Clark, and the two hunters bivouacked in separate directions from base camp.

Chuck with his former P&Y world record Sitka blacktail taken on Kodiak Island in 1986. The buck marked the first of five P&Y world records that Chuck has posted.

Dall sheep: July, 1985.

Stone sheep: August, 1985.

Three days later, Chuck was heading back to camp with the meat and antlers from two Sitka bucks, both of which would be large enough to shatter the standing P&Y world record, the larger of the two measuring 108⅛.

The great buck didn't help him closer to Super Slam, but it earned his first world record recognition in Pope and Young. Again, he'd gone with a deliberate goal in mind and achieved it by researching the hunt harder, hiking farther and hunting smarter than most others could imagine. The maps that he had pored over had revealed an area where he felt assured that no other hunters would have pressured the deer. If true, that would mean more deer and bigger, older bucks. It would also mean a nine-hour hike just to get into the area.

"I researched a more remote area of Kodiak because when Richard and I went to a semi-remote area in 1984, we saw evidence of other people," Chuck says. "There were a few footprints around. So, the next time I picked the most remote part of the island I could find that I could get into. It took me nine hours one

62

Bighorn sheep: November, 1985.

Desert sheep: October, 1986.

In little more than a year's time, Chuck went on four sheep hunts and killed four legal rams, becoming only the fourth bowhunter in history to complete the Grand Slam.

way to backpack to where I killed those two big Sitka deer. It was difficult, heavy alder brush. It was thick. I climbed 3,000 feet and went in a long way toward the backbone of the island. It all worked out because I got into an area where people just don't go. And, as with other species I've hunted, the more remote, less accessible areas have the bigger animals just because they survive."

THE RACE IS ON

Again, Chuck had cast the spotlight on himself. The world record Sitka earned a lot of mention in the outdoor press. Also in 1986, after completing the Grand Slam, Chuck tagged his muskox. A year later, in 1987, he arrowed a Wyoming moose. Eighteen, nineteen. Super Slam was going to happen. One way or another, it was going to happen. He could feel it. It was his destiny. But would he be the first?

In all of his time spent talking with people throughout the archery industry and other well-known bowhunters, he hadn't heard anyone speak of another hunter aiming to conquer the North American 27. Nothing. Why? How could no one else be working toward it? What about guys like Jack Frost and Tom Hoffman? They'd accomplished the Grand Slam on sheep. They had the skill, the money and the time away from their careers if they wanted it. But it seemed as if the Super Slam secret remained safe in the imagination of Chuck Adams.

Then he slipped.

"I didn't let anybody know until the summer of 1988," Chuck says. "I was talking to someone at *Petersen's Bowhunting* and just mentioned something about it, and I'll be darned if it didn't come out in the magazine. It said something like 'Chuck Adams is likely to be the first bowhunter ever to take all 27 varieties.' I had several species left to get.

"Well, Jimmy Ryan, who got the second Super Slam, I believe, in October of 1990, started chasing me, and chasing me with a lot of money, and he was catching up fast. I promise you that if I had said anything about it five years earlier, I would not have been the first guy with the Super Slam. Somebody would have semi-retired or retired and just gone after it. It took me 23 years to get all those species.

"The article worried me. Jimmy Ryan and Tom Hoffman and Jack Frost had quite a few species already and these people were competitors. I knew that there were a number of serious competitors that if you put the idea in their mind, they were going to go for it. I hadn't heard anybody in archery talking about it and I thought, 'I'll just keep this under my hat.'"

But the secret that Chuck had kept from the world for three years was secret no more. And when the news hit in 1988, there remained a long distance to travel, with three particularly monstrous obstacles standing in the way.

CHAPTER FOUR: **SUPER SLAM**

PART II: THE DANGEROUS BEARS

"Maybe I was just too dumb to know better, but I had a talk with myself before I went on these hunts and said, 'If you're going to be scared about this, don't do it.' And I honestly wasn't. I was focused, like my brain was that magnifying glass, and I was focused on getting a shot, and that was it."

I n little more than one year, Chuck conquered the Grand Slam of wild sheep. So maybe it stood to reason that he should plan to kill a grizzly, polar and Alaska brown bear in a year's time. Or maybe he was delusional for ignoring the blatant flaws in the plan. One, finding a grizzly, Alaska brown bear or polar bear is a lot more difficult, even in a great area, than finding a wild sheep. Two, even if you find a bear, sneaking within bow range means defeating the best nose in the business. Three, do you really want to be within bow range of a grizzly, polar or Alaska brown bear

Chuck follows shotgun-wielding guide/outfitter Dick Blewett through the British Columbia jungle in search of his first dangerous bear in mid-October 1988.

in the first place?

Think about it. Imagine yourself huddled there in the alders 20 yards from a hungry, 1,000-pound Alaska brown bear as it rumbles along a stream bank probing for a salmon snack. Imagine yourself anchored at full draw, muscles quaking, sweat beading your brow, waiting for the right angle as the bear's head inexplicably snaps to attention and beady eyes focus on your form.

Imagine a polar bear hunt in minus 30 degrees, wondering if your bow can even withstand the cold when it comes time to draw the string. And imagine what a minuscule equipment failure might mean 15 yards from Nanook.

Imagine a grizzly—that cantankerous, unapproachable, unpredictable beast that will be foraging on berries one second and leaping on the back of a caribou the next. Imagine having planned your approach perfectly, arriving at your ambush to intercept a moving griz only to watch in horror as the bruin changes course and veers into the heavy cover 10 yards downwind of you, now just steps from entering your scent stream. Will he run? Away, or right at you?

These are the types of thoughts that might cross the minds of most bowhunters facing the proposition of hunting any of these three beasts, not to mention all three of them in one year. Chuck considered momentarily the things that might go awry and then chose instead, in his typical fashion, to focus on the positive.

"Maybe I was just too dumb to know better, but I had a talk with myself before I went on these hunts and said, 'If you're going to be scared about this, don't do it.' And I honestly wasn't," Chuck says. "I was focused, like my brain was that magnifying glass, and I was focused on getting a shot, and that was it. And I knew from the research that there hadn't been anyone hurt who had bowhunted dangerous bears and that the actual danger before an animal was hit was very low. I thought the danger was a little bit overrated anyway until the bear was hit. And I figured if I hit him in the right place, and he didn't know I was there before I shot, and he wasn't facing me, I'd probably be all right. There are no guarantees. But I can honestly say I wasn't scared. I always get excited.

"I did the same thing with the dangerous bears that I did with the sheep. I researched areas and outfitters all at once. I went to areas that I thought had the potential for big animals. I went with guides who had really solid track records. And in the case of the bears, the dangerous animals, I picked guys I thought were cool heads who could save me if we got into a problem with a charging bear, but who wouldn't perforate my bear with bullet holes if it wasn't charging.

"I asked all three of my guides not to shoot their gun unless the bear was actually chewing on me because I regard (and, you know, I'm sticking my neck out here) an animal with a bullet hole in it as not a legitimate archery trophy. It's a fine trophy and something that I'd be proud of, but I couldn't enter it in the books and I wouldn't consider it part of a Super Slam. So I told all of those people that, and they all agreed to that. Then I went hunting."

A GRIZZLY TALE

A fine line exists 50 yards or less from a dangerous bear. Though charging bears and attacks are incredibly rare, that knowledge is not enough to allow any bear hunter or guide ever to erase the possibility from his mind. And, so, all nonresidents hunting for dangerous bears are guided. And all guides carry guns as extra insurance in case the unthinkable happens.

But being close to a bear that might weigh 1,000 pounds or more heightens the tension to incomparable levels and can cloud one's judgment. A bear that might appear relaxed and totally unaware at one second might smell or see you and turn aggressive the next second. One might only bluff-charge, while the next might never bluff, but just come and get you. It has been said that a dangerous bear can cover 100 yards or so as fast as the finest quarter horse. Knowing when and how to act can be the difference between life and death. And for the guide watching a bowhunter's back, the stress multiplies exponentially. Two guns are better than one.

As Chuck planned his bear hunts in 1987, he hoped to find outfitters and guides who had hosted bowhunters before. That experience, he knew, would make everything easier for everyone involved. As it turned out, he only went 1-for-3 in that component of his search. He tabbed Brent Jones and AAA Alaskan Outfitters for his Alaska brown bear hunt in October 1989, and Brent himself was a bowhunter who had shot a brown bear with

67

a bow. But for his grizzly and polar bear guides, this would be their first go-round with a bowhunter.

"The biggest problem with guided hunts is, if you get with somebody who doesn't understand bowhunting, at least part of the trip is devoted to increasing their understanding of bowhunting," Chuck says. "And that takes away from your chance of killing animals. The first three days you get your act together, and then the rest of the trip you go after animals. I had that with Dick Blewett a little bit, but within a day we had our act together. He was staying back behind me a bit, so I could stalk and do my thing.

"Dick had never guided a bowhunter in his life, but I couldn't find anybody I liked the sound of who had taken bowhunters. And this guy was a 30-year veteran of grizzly bear hunting. I got his name through Jack Atcheson and Sons as a good, solid guide. He was near the Bella Coola area of British Columbia, which is famous for big grizzlies. I talked to him on the phone for several hours, and he promised me that the average shot with a gun up there was like 20 or 30 yards. He told me that he had saved several gun hunters' bacon when they had mis-hit bears that charged. And he told me that he didn't think that if I hit the bear in the right spot there'd be a problem. He promised me he wasn't going to be trigger-happy about it."

So in mid-October 1988, Chuck left for Rivers Inlet, about 100 miles south of the Bella Coola. As the floatplane circled, he peered down at the large freshwater lake and a maze of rivers and creek arms below. He knew from his research that bears from miles around would be drawn to the waterways because the salmon would be making their annual spawning trek up a river that flowed all the way to the Pacific Ocean. A simple plywood cabin on the lakeshore would serve as the base of the grizzly hunt operation, and a 14-foot boat would be the pair's primary mode of transportation to get to the various streams. From there they'd head out on foot along a particular stream where the wind was right, allowing them to move near the banks, glassing ahead for sight of a mature bear.

It didn't take long for Chuck to realize that he was in for a great deal more in terms of time and effort than he had expended in his quest to complete the Grand Slam of sheep. In his first

Grizzly bear camp, Rivers Inlet, British Columbia, October 1988. These swanky wilderness accommodations would be the finest that Chuck would enjoy during his quest for the three dangerous bears during 1988 and 1989.

four days of grizzly hunting, he and Dick spotted 14 bears—a lot on a grizzly hunt, but nothing compared to seeing one band of 20 or more sheep on the first day. Plus, sows accompanied by cubs were illegal, and Chuck didn't want to shoot a smallish single bear, even if it was a legal animal.

Glassing in the more wooded cover was a challenge, and Chuck could see that he wouldn't have the luxury of wide-open terrain where he could keep track of the animal and execute a stalk all at the same time. This was going to be more straightforward, down-and-dirty—see the bear, check the wind, wait 'til he's not looking and move in—aggression. On the third day of the hunt, opportunity number one arrived.

"We were hunting these little creeks that averaged probably 15 feet across where salmon were spawning," Chuck says. "It was morning. We were walking up these creeks and we had downdrafts morning and evening, so it was good hunting. This big bear came out of the brush at about 15 yards, and Dick hissed at me. Dick said he would square a little over 7 feet. The bear just popped out and started splashing through probably about a foot and a half of water toward us. Dick was right behind me, about two or three feet, and we had some good cover in front of us. But that bear just kept coming, and he was right on the other side of a tree branch from me. I could have reached out and touched his nose with my broadhead. Then he saw something. I think he saw Dick move behind me, and he just turned and ran. I never had an opportunity to get a clear shot, and everybody had told me don't shoot a dangerous bear straight-on in the chest. Well, not only is it a small target and I wouldn't shoot for that reason alone, but bears tend to run the way they're facing when they're hit. So I would never have taken that shot."

That would be the biggest bear that Chuck would see during his hunt. Two days later, on the morning of the fifth day, he and Dick spotted a good bear farther out and watched it cross a meadow on the opposite side of a creek, about 100 yards away. Then the bruin crossed the stream to Chuck's side and headed toward the hunters.

"It came within 10 yards of me in the brush, then turned upstream on our side," Chuck says. "It stopped in an opening. I shot it through both lungs at 18 yards and killed it. It ran 46 yards

70

Chuck's grizzly came on the fifth day of his hunt. An 18-yard shot double-lunged the bruin which piled up less than 50 yards from where he was shot.

at a dead gallop and then just collapsed. It was one of the fastest bow-kills I had ever seen. It let out a huge roar that almost blew the stocking cap off my head.

"Only after that did Dick tell me that he was very nervous about the whole deal. He had talked to his wife and his family about this and he didn't know at all how a bowhunt was going to turn out. He didn't share any of that with me until it was over. But he was very impressed with how lethal an arrow was and how well the hunt went."

Added to the woodland caribou that Chuck had taken earlier that same October, Chuck now had 21 of the 27. A polar bear and an Alaska brown bear lurked nearby.

POLAR EXPEDITION

In May 1989, approximately seven months after arrowing the Rivers Inlet grizzly, Chuck embarked on a journey to the Far North—Baffin Island in the Northwest Territories. Some say that polar bears are the most fearless and dangerous of all the North American bear species. They are almost exclusively carnivorous, feeding primarily on seals. And they can grow huge, with old boars tipping the scales at more than 1,000 pounds.

But the most daunting circumstance facing Chuck as he journeyed to the far-away island was the fact that he would be hunting with an Inuit guide who spoke no English. Polar bear tags are allocated to Inuit communities which then have the right to utilize them for their own subsistence or to sell them for commercial hunts that they host. The outfitter is more of an agent working between the Inuit communities and the nonresident hunters interested in hunting a polar bear. Thus, the Inuit can set their price on the few coveted polar bear tags that they make available to sport hunters each year. Chuck turned to his old friend and owner of Canada North Outfitting, Jerome Knap, who organized the polar bear hunt.

Chuck knew that the two bears that he had arranged to hunt in 1989 would be, next to moose and bison, the largest animals in terms of sheer body size that he'd encounter on his way to 27. Combine a mass of bone and muscle with sharp claws, teeth and crushing jaws, and these hunts were no place for any malfunction. Thus, Chuck paid particular attention to maximizing and

May 1989, on Baffin Island in the Northwest Territories. A nice spring day in the arctic.

perfecting his bow and arrow setup.

Chuck started shooting a Hoyt GameGetter bow back in 1984 on his hunt for Sitka blacktails and immediately fell in love with it. Shooting without the aid of a mechanical release, Chuck appreciated the forgiveness that the Hoyt bow offered a finger shooter. Before his grizzly hunt in 1988 he switched Hoyt models to a ProVantage set at 80 pounds and shooting a 2219 Easton aluminum arrow. Chuck acknowledges that the bow, despite the heavy draw, was slow. But he contends that it was also one of the most accurate finger bows ever designed because of the strongly deflexed riser. Earl Hoyt had focused his eye on accuracy when he conceptualized the ProVantage, and Chuck appreciated the philosophy of accuracy over speed—a perspective that he strongly maintains to this day and one that he banked everything on in 1989. In preparation for the polar bear hunt, he painted the ProVantage in removable white, cranked it to 86 pounds and went to a heavier 2317 shaft tipped with his standby four-blade, 125-grain, Zwickey Black Diamond Eskimo broadhead.

Fortunately, Chuck had the arctic bowhunting experience for muskox in his hip quiver and knew how to prepare for bow-shooting in extreme cold. Huge, elbow-length mittens would keep his hands warm on the dogsled and could be dropped quickly if he closed in on a bear. Same for the traditional caribou hair parka—the only thing that could keep him warm on arduously long, monotonous dog sled rides.

Even though Chuck felt comfortable that he had controlled every possible aspect leading up to the hunt, and even though he felt supremely confident working with Jerome, he knew that Knap wouldn't be out on the ice with him once the hunt started. It would be Chuck, an Inuit guide, and Inuit helpers. Jerome had taken bowhunters in pursuit of other species before, but it wouldn't matter. Head guide, "Akashu," never had.

"That hunt was fairly grueling," Chuck says. "It was 25 to 40 degrees below zero. We were on a dogsled and we covered about 50 miles one direction by dogsled across ocean bays and peninsulas before we found a bear. It was an adventure from start to finish. I'd never seen so much white in my whole life.

"The only legal place you could hunt polar bears then was the Northwest Territories of Canada. Back when they hunted polar bears in Alaska, it was legal to use bush planes on skis. Sometimes they'd spot bears from the air and land well ahead and try to intercept them. In the Northwest Territories it was illegal to use any motorized vehicle in the hunt. It was dogsled only. So the standard hunting method is: When you see a bear or fresh track, you turn a few sled dogs loose. They're supposedly trained to bay up the bear on the ice, and then you tip-toe up and try to get a shot.

"Akashu's two sons spoke English and they served as interpreters. They were in and out of camp during the hunt and said if the polar bear's head is down facing the ice when the dogs are around him, he's fairly safe to approach. If you run into a bear that keeps his head high and is watching outside of the ring of dogs, it can be really dangerous and he could charge."

But Chuck never experienced the classic method of getting close to a polar bear. Early in the hunt, Akashu had bragged to Chuck that his sled dogs were the best bear dogs in the world. He hadn't bothered to tell him that those good dogs had been lost the week before during a hunt with a German client. Akashu had cut the dogs loose on a bear for the German, and the bear

Head polar bear guide Akashu spoke no English, smoked a couple packs a day, and carried his trusty .243 Win. just in case.

turned tail and ran out of sight, with the dogs in pursuit. They never returned. The dogs tethered to Akashu's sled now, unbeknownst to Chuck, were second-stringers.

"The fifth morning we stepped out of the tent, Akashu was yelling, 'Nanook! Nanook!' and here was this big bear walking across the ice a couple of miles away," Chuck says. "We hitched up the dogs and mushed after the bear. That sled only went, I figure, a couple of miles an hour. It was a big, heavy cargo sled, so we got out to where the bear was about an hour later.

"The bear was just fiddling around on the ice and wasn't really going anywhere. He was looking for seals at the holes where seals come up for air. Akashu was cracking his sealskin dog whip, the dogs were yammering away, and the bear heard all that as we got close. He started to walk away.

"Akashu just reached up to the front of the sled and cut loose four of the dogs, just cut the lines, and the dogs ran after the bear with the lines still attached to them. When they got to the bear, the bear turned around and took a swipe at them, and they all ran back to the sled and hid behind the sled. At that point I was thinking, 'What am I doing on the most expensive hunt I've ever been on in my life—I definitely went to the banker and got a loan for this one—when the only way I'd ever heard of anybody in modern times taking a polar bear was after it was bayed up with dogs?'

"Well the bear ran close to a mile across the frozen ocean bay and climbed a peninsula. I was watching through my binoculars. He went right up under the cliff at the top and laid down and appeared to go to sleep. He wasn't worried about us. We mushed to the base of the peninsula. Akashu tried to put those dogs on the smoking-hot tracks going up the hillside, and they tried to crawl under the sled!"

Some things you can't control on a hunt far from home. Like the dogs. Like the additional fact that Akashu's bear gun of choice turned out to be a .243 Winchester with 100-grain bullets. Or the fact that Akashu was a 60-something chain smoker who torched a couple packs a day and coughed almost non-stop day and night. This was the first legal, single bear that Chuck had seen in five days of hunting, and as he glassed the bear high on the distant ridge, he assessed his limited options.

Even in sub-zero cold, Chuck filled down-time ensuring that his rig was perfect.

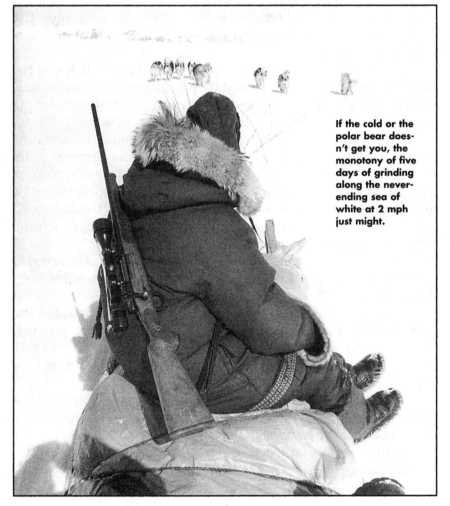

If the cold or the polar bear doesn't get you, the monotony of five days of grinding along the never-ending sea of white at 2 mph just might.

"I looked at Akashu," Chuck says, "and I thought, 'He probably can't climb this hill.' It looked like about 500 vertical feet to the top. 'If he can, he's going to go slowly and he's probably going to make a lot of noise, and he'll either scare the bear away or make the bear mad. And because of the size of the rifle, I wasn't too worried whether he was beside me or at the bottom of the hill when he backed me up. He could see everything that was going on.

"The wind was strongly crosswind. I decided I could circle up the hill well away from the bear and get on top of the cliff above the bear and be safe because it was a pretty substantial, 15- to 20-foot high sheer cliff and it went in both directions for a ways. The cliff was covered with ice, so I didn't think the bear had any chance of getting at me.

"I stepped out above the bear about 45 minutes later, and the bear jumped out of his bed and he was lunging at the cliff base and popping his teeth and growling when I shot him under the chin. He took about four wobbly steps and collapsed.

"It was faster than my grizzly bear kill. He fell in an ice chute that ran to the ocean and he gathered speed like a freight train. He hit the ice right beside my guide, and when I got down there, Akashu's eyes were as big as saucers, and I don't know what he was saying, but he was really revved up. That was the only bow-kill that he had ever seen on a polar bear. That was a lucky hunt. That could have been a disaster.

"So that was a gift from heaven as far as I'm concerned. I could have very well not gotten a polar bear the first time. But I had good luck. I'll take luck every time."

Chuck's 2317 Easton arrow, as it turned out, penetrated the bear's chest, passed through one lung and the liver, and was buried in the ham in the rear of the bear. The bruin was estimated at approximately 1,000 pounds live weight, and its hide squared nearly 9 feet.

Two bear hunts, two shots; a grizzly and a polar bear were his. Adding the Coues' whitetail that Chuck had tagged in Arizona in December the previous year, his tally now stood at 23. Four to go, including Alaska's famed beast—the brown bear—less than five months away.

Given the circumstances, Chuck calls his polar bear expedition, "a lucky hunt." Still, he made his luck by stalking the monster and then shooting him straight-on at close range.

WIDE BAY CANNIBAL

Between his polar bear kill on Baffin Island and the October 1st start of his Alaska brown bear hunt near Wide Bay, Alaska, Chuck killed a Quebec-Labrador caribou in August near Fort Chimo, Quebec and a Roosevelt elk while hunting with friends in Oregon. Twenty-five. Only the brown bear and a mountain lion remained in his Super Slam quest. And the pressure mounted.

It wasn't a self-imposed kind of pressure worrying about his ability to pull it off. On the contrary. Chuck at this point of his career exuded confidence in his bowhunting abilities, regardless of the sharp teeth and claws that he might be staring at less than 20 yards away. Instead, the pressure came in the form of a human pursuer. For the first time, Chuck worried that he could conceivably be caught.

"I've got a pretty upbeat attitude," Chuck says. "I was hopeful. I just figured what will be will be. I did everything I could. If I had not gotten that brown bear, I would not have gotten the first Super Slam. I knew Jimmy Ryan was chasing me. I found out that spring. I didn't know how close he was, but I could feel him breathing down my neck. I can honestly say, though, I was enjoying the hunt as much as I would have 10 years before or as much as I would now. I was enjoying it and I just figured what was going to happen was going to happen. I was confident in my brown bear guide, Brent. He was a great guide, and I'd been shooting my bow a lot. I was confident in my shooting ability and just thought what's going to happen is going to happen."

But as an insurance policy, Chuck worked out a plan that would avail him the maximum possible odds. During his desert sheep hunt on the Hualapai in 1986, Chuck had forged a friendship with his guide, Larry Heathington. As they searched for sheep, Chuck told Larry about his plans to set up a brown bear hunt in Alaska. Larry, a rifle hunter, expressed an interest in partnering with Chuck on that hunt. So when Chuck talked to Brent Jones at AAA Alaskan Outfitters about arranging the hunt, he asked Brent if he would be willing to modify his normal bear hunting schedule slightly. Instead of the two 10-day hunts with a one-day break in between, Chuck asked whether he and Larry could book the full 21-day season from October 1-21. Brent would

As Brent Jones and Chuck tracked a colossal brown bear in October 1989, Chuck knew that he was being tracked by another bowhunter attempting to beat him to the first Super Slam.

get the same amount of money; he'd just have to sacrifice the one day off in between. Brent agreed.

Now Chuck had 21 days instead of 10. Larry agreed to allow Chuck to try to go after every good bear that they thought he could get to with a bow. Any bear that didn't present a good bowhunting opportunity because of the terrain or cover would be Larry's to go after.

"That gave me the entire season to get a brown bear and took a lot of the pressure off," Chuck says. "And I was pretty confident with that much time that I could shoot a brown bear the first trip even with bad weather. I figured I'd have enough hunting days. And thank goodness I did that. Larry shot his bear the fourth day with his rifle and he flew out. Brent had his money, and I had the rest of the season. So it worked out."

On that fourth day, Brent, Chuck and Larry spotted a big, single legal bear high on the mountainside above the valley where the hunters tent-camped. The mountainside was choked with terrible alder thickets that blocked visibility and made climbing painstaking. The bear had moved into the center of a sweeping draw swallowed in alders, and the trio of hunters could only manage glimpses of the bruin as it rumbled slowly along foraging for whatever edibles it could locate. Brent had seen enough of the bear to call it a good one of about 9 feet. Though he desperately wished there were a way, Chuck knew that it would be impossible to stalk within bow range of the bear in those alders. For half the day, the trio watched from above, but the bear refused to leave the cover.

"He didn't seem inclined to go down to the stream to look for salmon," Chuck says, "so we sneaked to that bottom edge of the thicket, and Larry actually said, 'You get in position, and I'll try to call the bear out.' He was really working for me. That's what a good friend is all about. We were on the underside because there was a downdraft, so we got the wind right. I planted myself on the bottom edge. And Larry actually did call that bear down. I could hear it crashing in the brush. He was using a dying rabbit call. But I never saw the bear. I was within bow range, but I never saw it. Brent and Larry were on a higher point and they said the bear came within about 20 yards of me. But he wouldn't poke his nose out where I could get a shot. He fiddled around for a little

"Sit on your (rhymes with glass) and glass, and don't be afraid of the dark." That's the advice of veteran brown bear guides in Alaska. Chuck and Brent did plenty of glassing during their 15-day quest, and lots of hiking, too.

bit and then went back up and in."

At that point, Chuck decided that this bear wasn't in the cards, and Larry didn't have to think twice about whether he wanted a crack at the thick-coated boar. Because of the dense cover, the trio moved uphill of the alder thicket and purposely let the bear smell them. When he did, he thundered from the other side of the thicket and Larry made the shot.

"I didn't ever think, 'Darn it, I didn't get that bear,'" Chuck says. "I was really happy for Larry and I was really happy I had 17 days left to hunt one-on-one with Brent. We had seen quite a few bears. I think I saw 37 bears on the trip. So we were seeing more than one bear a day."

But the number of bear sightings belied the bear hunting conditions that Chuck faced. He'd gone to Wide Bay on a fall hunt anticipating, like on his grizzly hunt, that the bears would be focused on the salmon run and would be concentrated near the waterways. Instead, the runs were weak that fall, and the storms were heavy. Flooding washed what few salmon remains there were back out to sea. That's why Larry's bear had been high on a hillside foraging for other food sources instead of the high-protein salmon meat. What's more, ugly weather cut into precious hunting time as rain and wind pounded the Alaskan Peninsula.

"The salmon run was really poor, and the bears were moving around a lot," Chuck says. "Our strategy basically was to climb the hills on the edge of the valley, glass all day, then go down into the alder brush after the bears we saw. We lost track of some of the bears and couldn't get close to the rest. The bears are hunted pretty hard there and they're pretty spooky anyway.

"I went after four more single, legal bears the first 14 days. My goal was to just get a good, representative bear that would square 7 or 8 feet. I would have been tickled. But I couldn't get close to one because they were standing up on their hind legs and looking around all the time. And it's always more difficult for two people to stalk an animal, and you legally have to have a guide there. Those two factors—spooky bears and two people—made it impossible for me to get a bow-shot.

"We found two brown bears that had been killed and eaten where we were hunting. The back track of the bear that had killed them was 16 inches long, and the front track was just under 11 inches wide. We kept wondering where this big bear was and figuring that he was making the rest of the bears in the valley very spooky."

Suddenly, one night in the tent, Chuck counted the days and realized that 11 of them were gone. And he began to fathom the fact that if he could go 11 days without killing a brown bear, he could go 21 days, too. He was down to a 10-day bear hunt—the thing that he had been trying to avoid when he set the whole thing up two years prior. Then things got worse.

"A typhoon struck the area with winds, we found out later, in excess of 90 miles an hour for three days," Chuck says. "We were tent-bound for those three days—days 12, 13 and 14. It was raining so hard we couldn't see, and just simply couldn't hunt.

"I was worried because we could have been weathered in right to the end of the 21-day season. But we had been seeing enough bears every day that I was still hopeful. The weather is just a factor you can't control. I thought there was a possibility we would sit there until the end of the season and not be able to hunt. That was certainly bothering me, and when you sit there 24 hours a day in a tent, you have plenty of time to think."

To escape the harsh reality that existed outside the tent flap, Chuck pulled out one of his ever-present paperbacks. He read the first 20 pages of "The Hunt For Red October," tore those pages out and passed them to Brent. During the next few days, the duo feasted on a regular diet of rice and read the whole book in 20-page chunks to pass the time. Sometime in the middle of the 14th night, the storm subsided.

"The morning of the 15th day we got up, the storm was over, and I saw the first clear, blue sky of the whole trip," Chuck says. "We changed strategy. There were five little creeks that flowed out of this big valley that was about five miles wide and 10 miles long. We just walked up the nearest creek, up this little gravel bed with about 6 inches of water flowing on average. And about half a mile above camp we rounded a sharp bend in this little creek with alder walls on each side, and here was this bear walking away from us. First, we saw a splash that went like 20 feet into the air. We actually heard the splash, and Brent said, 'There's a bear up there.' We went around the bend, and here was this bear just swaggering up the creek looking for salmon.

Basically, he was looking for salmon for an hour-and-a-half and didn't find one.

"I was a green-horn; I'd seen sows with cubs; he looked huge to me. He was wet because it had been raining and because he'd been messing around in the creek, and Brent said, 'Oh, my God, that's a huge bear.' He had been on 80 or 90 brown bear kills, so he knew what he was looking at. And he said, 'We're going after that bear.' The bear was about 125 yards away. He was moving away from us up the valley with the wind in his face which was great for us."

As soon as Chuck and Brent saw the great bear, they wondered if they were looking at the animal that had mauled the other two bears that they had found dead earlier in the hunt. Was this the bear with the 16-inch back track and the 11-inch-wide front paw? For an hour-and-a-half the two men tailed the bear as it zig-zagged upstream searching for salmon and carrion to feed on. With Brent trailing 30 to 50 yards behind, Chuck slipped to within bow range of the bear several times in the brush, but never had a good shot opportunity because of the cover or the angle.

"That bear was walking around with his head under the water for a couple of minutes at a time. He was looking for salmon. I tried to get close to him when his head was under the water, but he wouldn't leave his head under quite long enough," Chuck says laughing. "It was the funniest thing. But there were no salmon in that hole, I guess, because he went on.

"I had told Brent at the beginning of the hunt that I planned to hunt these bears just like I would mule deer—that I was going to be aggressive and not timid at all because I wanted to get close. If I was going to be scared of bears, I shouldn't be there, and he agreed. But he was kind of nervous, he told me later, that I was so aggressive on the bear because I was doing just what I would on a deer or anything else. I was going right into the brush and trying to set up a shot, and the bear never knew I was there. At one point, I was within 20 yards of the bear in heavy brush and couldn't see him. I could just hear him. I don't think at any point I got as close as I did when I finally shot."

After an hour-and-a-half, the huge boar finally got lucky and unlucky. He caught a salmon, his first success in the 90 minutes

Chuck's brown bear might be the largest-bodied bear ever taken by a bowhunter. Though at this point in his odyssey he would have been happy with a 7-footer, Chuck took one of his finest trophies ever and the second-to-last step toward the Super Slam.

of hunting, and carried it into the brush to devour it. Chuck had watched enough bears during his previous grizzly hunt and during his Sitka hunts on Kodiak to know that the bear usually returns to the same spot on the stream bank after finishing its meal. So he tip-toed up to the trail where the bear had gone in and parked himself only five yards away. From his hideout on the stream bank, Chuck could occasionally see the top of the bear's back approximately 50 yards farther into the brush.

When the mammoth bear consumed all he wanted, he tramped out on a different trail 25 yards in front of where Chuck waited. But instead of turning and continuing upstream, the bear rolled its broad chest right at Chuck and plodded directly at him with the wind at his tail.

"I was on the front edge of some brush, and there was some brush about 15 yards in front of me," Chuck says, detailing the scene. "I was probably 10 yards from the water. It was shallow water right there, probably 6 to 10 inches deep. But I was standing in the open on a gravel bar when the bear came out. I was backed up against the cover, so I was blending in, but there was nothing in front of me. I had a clear field to shoot, except there was that little ribbon of brush that came out in front of me about 15 yards, and then beyond that it was clear again. He came out beyond that. That's why I couldn't shoot right away. It was about 25 yards when he came out, and there was a cut-bank there. He was hooking his paws under the bank trying to feel for salmon. That's when he turned and walked back toward me.

"I drew before he came into the open. I could see he was moving steadily toward me. I could see he was gonna clear the brush and so I drew when he was behind the brush. I could see his form behind the brush, but I knew he couldn't clearly see me, so that's when I drew. I was standing upright—one of the few times I've been able to shoot from a classic open target stance. I felt exposed, but it happened so fast. He had been moving steadily away from us for more than an hour and then, suddenly, he came back. It happened very quickly. Ten seconds and there he was. I didn't have time to think about much except drawing my bow and taking the shot.

"As soon as he cleared that ribbon of brush, he walked out into the open at 12 yards, and that's when I shot him. When he put his right leg forward, I put my arrow right behind it, and he let out a huge roar. The arrow went to the fletching, he lunged away from me and then came right up on his hind legs and looked down at me from about 15 yards (we paced it off later). I say, 'looked down' because this bear would stand 9 feet at least. His head looked as big as a garbage can lid, and he looked right at me, and I was frozen. I had already decided in a case like that the worst thing you can do is move. He was dead, but didn't know it yet. He looked for three or four seconds and then turned and ran away. He went 163 yards at a dead gallop and just collapsed."

And so did Chuck. His legs turned to rubber as a euphoric Brent rushed in to congratulate his hunter.

"My legs got really weak after that," Chuck says. "A lot of people ask, 'Were you excited?' I was so tired and cold and wet over the last 14 days all I was thinking about was killing that bear. I was looking at the spot I wanted to hit. I hit him, and as soon as he turned and ran, it hit me, and my legs got so shaky I could hardly stand up—not from fear so much, although I got to thinking about that later, but just from sheer excitement."

Chuck and Brent knew that the bear would be dead not far away. But, playing it conservatively, they decided to head back to camp and grab the camera gear before following the bruin into the heavy brush. When they returned to the scene, they realized that they would not have to blood-trail the beast. Huge tracks had cratered the mud and tundra like a bulldozer barreling at full-throttle. And when they came upon him, they marveled at the magnificence of the bear.

A tape stretched to 97 inches around the bear's chest. Bear charts, based on that circumference, put the animal's live weight at nearly 1,400 pounds. His front paws were almost 12 inches wide, and his hide squared 10 feet, 8½ inches in front of a dozen witnesses back at base camp. The bear's skull scored 27⅟₁₆ inches, placing it number three in the Pope and Young record book at the time.

The Easton arrow and Zwickey broadhead had done the job cleanly on one of the largest animals ever taken by a bowhunter in North America. It buried to the center of the fletching with a full-length arrow, for nearly 30 inches of penetration. Chuck theorizes that the fact that the bear was walking when he shot might have hampered penetration slightly. The arrow sliced the thick hide and an amazing 10 inches of meat before drilling a thick rib dead center. It completely penetrated the right lung and was just scratching the left lung, illustrating the bear's incredibly massive body size.

Though Chuck remained focused on his goal, with one piece of the Super Slam puzzle remaining, a look back over what he had just achieved provides enlightening perspective. He had gone on four hunts for the wild sheep over a 16-month span and completed the Grand Slam in a sweep, missing just one shot. He had gone on three hunts for his three dangerous bears in less than one year, loosed three arrows and killed all three animals (with a combined weight of more than 3,000 pounds) as quickly and humanely as any rifle ever could.

"Keep in mind that I try to take only high-percentage shots, and I carried a rangefinder and used it whenever I could," Chuck says. "That made a difference. I had marginal shots present themselves in some cases and I didn't take them. The shots that I took at the bears were pretty close. You're not talking that challenging a shot in any case. The bears presented a fairly large target, and people who know me know that I weigh my arrows meticulously. Everything is as perfect as I can make it before I go. So I had everything working to my advantage."

Getting back to camp, the sun that had shined on Brent and Chuck on day 15 vanished in a sea of clouds followed by a torrent of rain and wind that stretched for 12 more days, giving Chuck plenty of time to think about what might not have been. But he had made his luck and had a familiar bowhunting realization hammered home once again—a bowhunter's fortunes can turn on a dime.

Twenty-seven days after arriving in Wide Bay, Chuck finally climbed aboard a plane headed for civilization one step removed from history.

This famous photo graced the center of the Hoyt USA Super Slam commemorative poster and provides perspective on Chuck's imposing quarry.

CHAPTER FOUR: **SUPER SLAM**

PART III: EPILOGUE

Capped off by the Alaska brown bear, 1989 marked Chuck's most successful calendar year during the 20-year Super Slam. A world record Coues' deer on the San Carlos Indian Reservation of Arizona in January, the polar bear in May, two Quebec-Labrador caribou bulls in two shots in August, and a Roosevelt elk in September. The elk, the third-to-last animal, was another point of stress.

A denizen of the Pacific Northwest's rainforests, the Roosevelt elk was one that befuddled Chuck in his planning. An outfitted hunt for Roosevelt elk would be expensive, and Chuck couldn't see how he'd be able to afford that knowing that every spare cent was tied up in his big bear hunts. Besides, he had enough elk hunting experience from his time in Montana to feel confident that if he could just get into the right area, even if it was on public land, that he could pull it off solo.

Mike Hillis, president of Easton Archery at the time, told Chuck that he knew of an archery dealer in Oregon who was respected for his Roosevelt elk expertise. So Chuck called Del Moore, the archery shop owner, who referred him to Dave Griffith and his wife, Gail. Dave, a real estate agent in Oregon at the time, bowhunted Roosevelt elk fanatically. Each year, he and a group of friends set up their traditional elk camp in early September. In 1989, they welcomed Chuck along.

"Dave and Gail were kind enough to invite me right into their elk camp, and I was hunting on my own in early September," Chuck says. "It was difficult hunting. It was public land with very spooky elk, and some clear-cutting had been done the year before. Dave said it had hurt the elk hunting pretty significantly because there had been a lot of logging activity in there."

In the middle of the hunt, on about the fifth day, Chuck finally got a chance when he called in a satellite 5-point bull to 30 yards. Settling the sight pin, he calculated for the thin screen of grass directly in front of him, but failed to recognize a limb closer to the elk. The arrow arched on line and then deflected wildly off the limb, spooking the bull out of sight in a blur. Would an elk, one of the big game animals that he had cut his teeth on

It's a small Roosevelt elk, but no animal was bigger in the Super Slam. Chuck arrowed the bull on Oregon public land just days before the season closed in September 1989.

93

since his college days, prove to be the nemesis that would keep him from the first Super Slam? Even with more than a week left to hunt, Chuck began to wonder.

The days kept slipping by, each one without any sighting of another bull elk. Before he knew it, Chuck had been in elk camp for 10 days, and the season neared its close. No one else in camp had killed an elk.

"On the 10th day I went to a spot that Dave had told me about—an old logging clearcut off the beaten path," Chuck says. "There was a small herd of elk in there with three or four raghorn bulls and some cows. I sneaked up and shot, and the bull actually jumped string, and I hit him right in the middle of the ham from approximately 40 yards. He went up on the hill and stood, and I sneaked up on him and finished him off with a heart shot at 60 yards.

"I almost didn't get him because there was another bowhunter behind me who I didn't know about. After I hit the bull, he ran up on the hill. I sneaked up and was trying to get close to this bull that was seriously hurt. I was in position and range-found and took my shot. The second my arrow hit that elk, and he ran 15 yards, there was a whole bunch of cow-calling behind me. I thought, 'What is going on?' And I looked around, and here's this bowhunter. There was a bowhunter stalking my wounded elk, and I didn't know it. And he didn't know I was there. He couldn't see me. He had thought the elk had just run off. He was trying to stop him, and if the timing would have been a little different, I probably would not have gotten that elk and maybe not gotten the first Super Slam. I got that little 4-point bull and I was tickled to death."

With that and the brown bear, it all came down to, of all things, a lion. Those who've never done it, and a few who have, consider turning loose a bunch of hounds and then shooting a lion out of a tree simple, maybe even unfair.

Tell that to Chuck, though, who had hunted lions unsuccessfully before—twice in Arizona and once in Idaho. This would be his fourth trip, again to Idaho, and with the same outfitter, in January of 1990. And for the first time during it all, Chuck felt uneasy, like the mass of all 26 previous hunts and more weighed on him.

It took four mountain lion hunts before Chuck finally got this view—one that all lion hunters imagine—in the mountains of Idaho.

"I didn't really feel any extra pressure the final year beyond just the challenge of the hunt, except for the mountain lion," Chuck says. "And after three unsuccessful tries for mountain lion, I was really wanting to get the darn lion. And if I didn't get that lion in the winter of 1990, I wouldn't be the first Super Slammer. This was my last chance.

"I'd been to Arizona with two different guides. And the bare ground lion hunting didn't work out for various reasons. I had been with Larry Jarrett in Idaho the year before for lion, and everything went wrong like it often does on lion hunts, I found out. I thought it would be easy. It wasn't. It snowed every night on that first hunt with him and covered up the tracks. And it was clear every day, and the tracking conditions were wretched. Larry had a fairly small area, and the lion that we did find walked out of his area and we had to stop because it would have been illegal to go on.

"But I went back in 1990. The conditions were perfect. It snowed the night before, and Larry and I found seven separate lion tracks the first day and we got one of those. And I breathed a sigh of relief. I felt snake-bit on it, I really did."

As this is written, four other archers have since completed Super Slams: Jim Ryan, Jack Frost, Tom Hoffman and Gary Bogner. Though all of them are known in bowhunting circles, the Super Slams that followed the first have received little fanfare. Where would Chuck Adams be today had he not been first?

"I think I'd probably be almost as well known as I am because I'd be reaching so many people with my writing," Chuck says. "I would hope to think that I would be respected as a writer, but the Super Slam was really a turning point. I didn't do one seminar until 1990, but the floodgates were open after I got the Super Slam. But I didn't anticipate all that. That was a pleasant surprise to me that it made as big of a splash as it did. The phone was ringing off the hook to do seminars. Suddenly, my visibility shot way up and made me more valuable to the companies that I was already working with. It was definitely a major spike in my career. Unfortunately, in my opinion, number two doesn't count for much in America."

Hoyt and Easton, the principal companies that Chuck worked with at the time that he completed the Super Slam in January 1990, scrambled to take advantage of the hoopla surrounding the Super Slam. Easton decided to launch a commemorative arrow, and Chuck worked with Jim Easton for nearly a year on a new aluminum arrow with a stronger alloy than had ever been utilized, straighter tolerances than ever, a new camouflage pattern and a new nock system. In 1991 the Easton Super Slam arrow became reality with Chuck's face and signature on the side of it. Hoyt introduced the Super Slam bow, the best-selling bow to date in Hoyt's line.

"We introduced that product in 1992," said Hoyt President Randy Walk. "It was the best year in the history of Hoyt USA in

Chuck took the four wild sheep and all three of the dangerous bears, each on his first attempt. But four hunts were required to bag this lion and the Super Slam with Idaho guide, Larry Jarrett.

the number of bow units sold. The Super Slam helped us get the marketing message out and it had a profound impact on our business."

The marketing and sales successes resulting from Super Slam, however, lead many outsiders to jump to the wrong conclusions.

"I think there's a misconception, though, that Chuck suddenly got rich," Chuck says. "Because that's not true. I was financially involved in those projects, but there's a limited amount of money in this industry. I'm doing well and I'm comfortable, but I'm certainly not rich by any means. I would not categorize myself that way. I still work hard. I'm not on easy street by any means."

As well as Hoyt and Easton Super Slam products have been received by the majority of bowhunters, however, a contingent of archers remains turned off by Super Slam. Some question the means, others question the motives. Still others question the skill that it required compared to the time and the money.

"Skill is number one, time is number two, and money is

number three," Chuck says. "Certainly, you need money to go after some of the animals like sheep and bears. But I'm certain having hunted deer and elk with a lot of people that most of the bowhunters who I know, if they had the money, would still go sheep hunting and probably fail because they're not in good enough physical shape or because they don't have enough experience to be cool when the opportunity arose.

"PSE President Pete Shepley was in a seminar situation one time. Pete and I were in camp together on the Hualapai Reservation and we both shot a desert sheep there. And shortly after that, Shepley was in a seminar, and a sorehead was grousing around about how if he had the money he could go do that, too. And Pete looked him in the eye and said, 'I'll tell you what. I'll pay for a hunt on the Hualapai for you, and you go. If you get your sheep then it's yours. And if you don't, you pay me double.' And the guy backed right off. That's sort of the way I feel about it. It's a combination of things. I could tell you that the other four guys who have the Super Slam certainly have the money to pay for the more expensive hunts, but they're also really hard hunters and experienced hunters, and they put in their time. And it takes all of the above, it really does.

"I wish everybody could have the variety of bowhunting experiences that I've had. I wish everybody could try every species because it's so much fun. I think the backlash from the Super Slam has been negligible, but there have been people who have groused about it. And I only hear a small percentage of the whining and the complaining that there is. But I think most people are impressed with it. There are jealous people everywhere, and bowhunting is certainly no exception.

"Somebody told me last year that there was an article in *Traditional Bowhunter* about the Super Slam and how it didn't mean anything and that it was just a stunt. The same guy was whining about how people like me have commercialized the sport. And, yet, in the same issue, he appears in an ad. I'm sure there's a certain amount of whining, complaining and grousing around. But my impression is that it's mostly by wannabes—people in the industry, people who are jealous, basically. I think it's been very impressive to the average consumer and I frankly don't care about the whiners. I know that it was 23 of the best years of my life doing that. I had fun. If somebody else doesn't want to do it, that's fine.

"My impression is that if they had done it, they'd be the highest proponents of it. It's simply the fact that they didn't do it. So, I just chalk it up to sour grapes. I don't know how you can argue against the end result. Every bowhunter I know is end-result oriented to a big extent. I frankly would contend that the arguments are bogus and that you reverse the roles with anybody who's complaining about it and he'd have a big grin on his face just like I do."

CHAPTER FIVE: **GREATEST HUNTS**

"To have the good luck to see an elk that big, that's so special. I'm glad that I got that elk in Montana because I love the state. I know that part of the state. It's as close to hunting near Chico, California as I can get at this stage of my life."

Asking Chuck Adams to select his five greatest hunts of all time is akin to asking Hank Aaron to pick his five most memorable homers. Still, a few of Chuck's hundreds of hunting adventures leap quickly to his mind. And though as this is written more than a decade has passed since the Super Slam, three of Chuck's top five hunts date back to his journey toward 27. And it's no surprise that the most demanding, challenging hunts provided the sweetest, most memorable successes.

The 15th day, 1,400-pound Alaska brown bear with Brent Jones detailed in the previous chapter is a shoo-in. So is the nine-day Canmore chiller, when Chuck camped in a mountain tent while hunting for a bighorn in minus 30-degree, mind-numbing cold.

"The biggest factor (in making it one of the five greatest) was that it was so cold," Chuck says. "And if you've ever seen the Canmore Bow Zone in Alberta, it looks like the Swiss Alps. It is almost straight up and down. When you cover that with ice and snow, it's treacherous. I fell down hundreds of times on that trip. At that time, resident hunters could hunt bighorn sheep with a bow without drawing a permit, so the single highway through the valley that runs through that bow zone was a parking lot of resident bowhunters with a spotting scope sticking out of every window. When a sheep poked its nose out of the cover up on the mountains, it was a race to see who could get to the sheep first. A legal sheep was four-fifths of a curl, and when one of those guys appeared, if you were on the valley floor, you didn't have time to do the job right. You had to run up the mountain. The fastest guys in the mountains won. And then you just had a few minutes to get the shot before somebody bumbled into the situation."

Chuck and guide Rod Collin put themselves at an advantage during their bighorn sheep hunt by camping on the mountain. That gave them a head start over the hunters below.

Outfitter Charlie Stricker sent guide Rod Collin to partner with Chuck in Canmore. Rod, who still guides hunters in Canada, was in his mid-20s then, mountain tough and sheep savvy beyond his years. "Usually, Charlie, if he got any bowhunters at all, I was the fellow who took them," Rod says. "I was about the only guide who kind of enjoyed hunting with the bow. The rest of them were more concerned with killing something (quickly)."

Rod and Chuck knew what they were up against in terms of hunting pressure. But they also knew that the weather forecast called for a steady diet of brutal, arctic air. Talking over the dilemma, they decided against the conventional wisdom of staying at the motel in Canmore. They'd pitch a tent high on the mountain, live there, and have a two-hour or so jump on all of the hunters starting each day at the valley floor. After a couple of hours of searching the first day on the mountain, they finally found a flat place barely big enough for the two-man tent.

101

For seven of the nine days, Chuck and Rod hunted from that tent in temperatures that ranged from minus 40 at night to highs of around minus 25 midday. Wind chills hit minus 55. The only relief came on Sunday. Since Alberta law prohibited Sunday hunting, Chuck and Rod hiked down Saturday night, savored a warm bed and a few hot meals, and hiked back up Sunday night to be there glassing at daylight Monday.

"We were the only ones who camped on the mountain," Chuck says. "There were four outfitters in the area and umpteen resident hunters. Everyone else stayed in the motel. I guess they're still talking about us up there.

"It was grueling. It was his (Rod's) idea. He said, 'You know, the only way we're going to have a decent chance is to tough it out.' I think that guy was impervious to bad weather. He was tough, like a lot of guides you run into Up North. I had five lower body garments on and seven upper body garments on when I was sleeping at night. I had a goose down sleeping bag from Eddie Bauer rated to 40 below zero and I was so cold I couldn't sleep the first night. So I walked down and got my old square Slumberjack sleeping bag out of my truck and packed it up and had my goose down bag inside my Slumberjack and I shivered all night the whole trip anyway.

"We would wake up in the morning to an ice shower in our tent because all the steam from our breath would freeze to the inside of the tent into little ice crystals. We had to thaw out frozen bottles of water on the fire, just to drink, so we were always on the edge of dehydration."

Despite the fact that they had a good head start on the rest of the bowhunters beginning each day, hunting pressure still caused Chuck and Rod headaches. Early in the hunt the duo went after a big ram that they had spotted. As they were moving in, a look down the mountain revealed three other hunters closing in fast. Before Chuck could work into position, all the activity spooked the ram. On average, Chuck and Rod located two legal rams per day, but even when they'd find one that the other hunters hadn't spotted, it was often in an unapproachable spot. The bitter air made the snow so crunchy underfoot that the sheep invariably heard the approaching danger. Other rams hung out in places that a hunter couldn't go without putting his

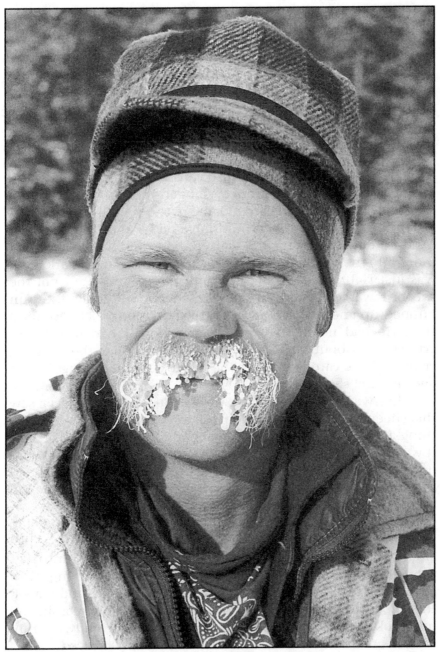

Guide Rod Collin manages a smile during his Alberta bighorn sheep hunt with Chuck. He says that those were the most brutal sheep hunting conditions that he's ever endured.

life in peril because of the steep, slippery slopes.

Finally, they hit pay dirt. Rod and Chuck spotted a huge curl-and-a-quarter ram and worked him all day on an isolated mountainside. No other hunters were in the area; it looked like the perfect scenario. All day they followed the ram's meanderings and attempted to put together an ambush. At some point, Chuck decided to move down the slope with Rod remaining above to keep tabs on the situation. A couple hours later, Chuck had him.

The ram had bedded in a slight depression, giving Chuck enough room to wriggle within 30 yards. The ram had ewes bedded nearby, but Chuck was out of sight and able to range-find the ram's horns—exactly 30 yards. Game over.

"If he had stood up, I would have had a shot," Chuck says. "And if he had stood up and walked, he would have come even more into the open. I just figured, 'I'll wait here until dark.' Rod was just right over the hill and he could see me, but not the sheep. I was concentrating on the sheep. Suddenly, the ram jumped up and just ran away, and I didn't have a chance for a shot. He had heard Rod crunching before I had heard him crunching. About 10 seconds later I could hear the 'crunch, crunch.' Here came Rod over the hill to see what was going on and ran that sheep off.

"That was a 180-plus sheep—beautiful, perfect. I never saw that sheep again. I had him as much as you can say you had anything. He would have stood up before dark. I knew the distance. It was as much of a slam-dunk as it could possibly be. The wind had been consistent for days, and I had the wind right. Rod told me that he thought the sheep were much farther down the hill and that I was just waiting to move in."

Stuff happens. But if you imagine that it might be difficult to sleep in a tent at minus 40, try to imagine what it would be like after watching a golden opportunity slip away. On the ninth day, though, Chuck and Rod were rewarded for their suffering. They found another ram that morning, again a big one, and waited the whole day for him to move out of a sweeping open basin and into broken terrain where Chuck could close in. Finally, the ram disappeared over the edge of a cliff, and Chuck pounced.

"He was in some heavy trees below me about 40 yards, and I could hear him pawing the snow to get to grass to eat," Chuck

The crash site. Despite two arrows in him, the bighorn had enough spurt to make it to the edge of a cliff where he died and then fell hundreds of feet.

says. "Light was failing, and the only thing I could think to do was pick up a rock. So I kicked one out of the snow and threw it beyond the sheep. And the sheep came squirting back toward me, right under me, and that's how I got the 25-yard, quartering-to-me shot. I shot him a second time as he ran uphill and continued around the edge of this cliff and then he staggered and fell, slid right over the cliff and fell.

"Rod said, 'We've got a problem. Nobody has ever found a way into that little canyon that sheep fell into.' It was bluffs all around. I said, 'What about below?' And he said, 'There are bluffs below.' So we had visions that night of having to go get a helicopter or something to try to get it out."

The next day Rod and Chuck circled the canyon perimeter and found two places where sheep tracks were going in and out—both narrow ledges covered with ice and snow. Steep cliffs above and below. With no other choice, they inched out on the "wider" of the two ledges, which was averaging 14 inches wide, and tried not to think about the 100-foot cliff below. A short way in, they realized that they'd have to take their packs off because they were rubbing on the upper side of the slope and pushing them out over the edge. Then, as Chuck gingerly placed his right boot on the trail, the tread failed to grab the ice and he lost his balance. Sprawling, he grabbed a pine tree and regained his footing before tumbling into thin air. Approximately 100 yards out onto the horrible ledge, the trail widened, and they found the ram.

Using a rangefinder, Rod and Chuck figured that the sheep had fallen approximately 450 feet. Its impact with a large evergreen had stripped the branches clean from one side and left a sheep-sized crater in the shale at the base of the tree. After that, the sheep had bounced and ended up against a different tree another 50 yards below. The sheep's spine was broken in five places, and about 3 inches of horn was broken off one side.

"He was frozen solid," Chuck says. "We hacked on that carcass forever just to get the cape off and chunk up the meat, and then we had to carry all that back along the ledge. We used a hatchet; we chopped all the ice off going back. Should have done that to begin with, so we had more level footing to work with.

"That was a horrendously tough hunt. I would not even go so far as to say it was fun the whole time. But it was one of my all-

"That was a horrendously tough hunt," Chuck says about his bighorn hunt. "I would not even go so far as to say it was fun the whole time." Still, he ranks it among his top five. Reward, after all, can be measured in terms of sacrifice.

time most difficult hunts, and I really prize the animal because of how difficult it was."

Later, thrilled to be packing their gear off the mountain, Chuck and Rod encountered another episode like the ones that had played out over the nine days, and one that reinforced again the wisdom of their decision to "tough it out."

"We ran into seven resident hunters on the ridge while we were going back down," Chuck says. "They were all after the same sheep. The first guy was the leanest and the meanest and he was chugging along and he said, 'Did you see that sheep up there?' We said, 'No, we're heading out.' And six more guys were going up the same ridge after the same sheep. It was the foot-race again, and I think the only reason I got a ram without a whole bunch of luck is because we went up there and toughed it out."

WORLD RECORD II

Chuck set aside winter 1988-89 on his hunting calendar to tackle the Coues' (pronounced cows) whitetail for the first time. Again, looking to maximize his odds, he strategized a way to ensure that he'd come out of Coues' deer country only five animals away from completing the Super Slam. And though he certainly hoped to shoot a record-class buck, he never could have dreamed that he'd break the bowhunting world record in the process.

Having heard how challenging Coues' deer were for bowhunters, Chuck decided to maximize his opportunities by purchasing a 1988 and a 1989 Arizona deer tag. He bought a third tag from the San Carlos Indian Reservation. Chuck also relied on the insights of his friend, Larry Heathington, a resident of Arizona, who knew the state's Coues' deer and the country well. "Again, it was a species that I didn't have," Chuck says. "I did what I did, basically, on the brown bear and the sheep. I thought, 'I'm going to really go for it and make sure I allot enough time.

"That world record Coues' deer hunt was one of my all-time favorites because I found Coues' deer to be the most difficult animal in North America to hunt with a bow for a number of reasons. The mountain lions chase them around every day of their life. They're in semi-open country and they're almost always hunted on foot. They are basic whitetails in challenging habitat

The desert Southwest and Mexico, home to the Coues' deer, feature terrain that's right up Chuck's alley when it comes to challenge.

and they're extra spooky."

In December 1988, around Christmas time, Chuck focused his high-powered binoculars on the public land near Graham Mountain in Arizona. And it didn't take him long to realize why he had heard so many bowhunters lament the difficulty of Coues' deer hunting. Seeing the gray ghosts of the desert required retina-scorching diligence. And even while straining his eyes all day through long-range optics, Chuck only managed two or three deer sightings a day. Before he knew it, he was down to December 31st, the last day that his first tag was good for.

"I was tearing my hair out," Chuck says. "I had gotten close to one deer, 10 yards or so, tried to draw my bow and he spooked. I finally started hunting country rather than deer. I started concentrating in areas where there were lots of blind corners and high cliffs. I thought, 'The only way I'm going to get a shot at a Coues' deer is to have solid rock and dirt between me and that

109

bugger until I'm within bow range.' So I started hunting particular areas that were very broken. That's when it started paying off for me.

"The first buck I got, I spotted in a box canyon. He was cruising for does. I basically anticipated where I thought he'd come out of the canyon because most places you couldn't get out. It was high cliffs. So I circled with high cliffs between him and me and I got to the pass where I thought he was going to come out, and he did. I was at full draw when he popped into view. I was peeking through a bush, and he didn't have any opportunity to see me at all. I peeked, backed off, drew my bow, and a few seconds later he stepped into the clear, and I shot him. That was my smallest Coues' deer, but he was still Pope and Young sized."

Some bowhunters in Chuck's shoes at that point might have headed for home, mission accomplished. But all of the Coues' deer frustration was beginning to feel like some kind of sadistic fun. Appealing agony. Ultimate bowhunting challenge. And why waste a perfectly good tag? So Chuck decided to ring in the New Year on the southern San Carlos, but, again, just looking for a good, representative buck that would make the P&Y book.

"The San Carlos Indian Reservation is a mix of easy country and really cliffy country," Chuck says. "The whole time I was there I hunted country rather than deer. I went to places where I thought, 'They're not going to see me until I'm in bow range. That's the only way I'm going to get a deer.'

"I hunted 12 or 14 days. One morning I saw this deer so far off that it was a tiny dot through my binoculars, but I could see a rack shining. He went in a canyon, so I hoofed it across a main canyon and across a side canyon and peeked around a corner and here, bedded in this canyon, was a deer that looked like a standard white-tailed deer—a big 8-point. I about dropped my teeth because I had been seeing all these little deer. I made a big circle and came down above that deer and had him in his bed in this box canyon. It was 63 yards away. I had my rangefinder and I couldn't get an inch closer because there was a cliff. So, I shot him in his bed, and the arrow went right down beside the spine and into the liver. He ran off a little ways and died.

"He was later crowned the new Pope and Young world record (110⅝ inches). After having torn my hair out for a couple of weeks

110

Chuck's 1989 started great with this world record Coues' deer. Because Coues' deer hunting is so much like the often-frustrating deer hunting of his youth, Chuck loves it.

trying to even get a shot, I had a world record. Because Coues' deer are so difficult, that was a really special animal. As a matter of fact, I missed a shot on San Carlos at just a medium-sized 85-inch or so buck, and it jumped the string. I had that deer within 15 yards, and that deer wasn't there when the arrow got there."

Amazingly, Chuck returned to a public land spot during the last half of January and continued Coues' hunting on his 1989 Arizona deer tag. Using the same technique of hunting bowhunt-able terrain, Chuck still-hunted rough country, found a buck 125 yards out and worked his way into bow range from there. Before the day was done, he tagged his third Coues' buck on three Arizona tags in approximately one month's time.

A decade later, during the 2000 season, Chuck went to Sonora, Mexico for his first Coues' deer hunt since the 1988-89 Arizona seasons. On two tags, he killed two more record-class bucks making it a five-for-five sweep on these tiny, elusive whitetails. He attributes his Coues' deer success to the lessons taught to him by the Columbia blacktails growing up around Chico.

"Spot-and-stalk hunting is what I love to do most, and Coues' deer are the toughest animals to spot-and-stalk, so I feel good that I've done as well on them as I have," Chuck says. "There's a strong overlap with Columbia blacktail hunting. That was the best tool sharpener that I could have had for hunting most of the North American species. Most people grow up hunting white-tailed deer from treestands. I grew up in California where there are no white-tailed deer and I hunted on foot because that was the best way to hunt.

"So I learned what I needed to learn in California. I'm glad I grew up where I did or I'd have been behind the curve. I talk to people all the time back East who wonder how you get close to animals on the ground. It's because they don't have the oppor-tunity to do any foot-hunting. You can't hunt whitetails in most places on the ground effectively, so it definitely was a tool-sharpener."

SECOND-CHANCE MULE DEER

The fact that Chuck cut his teeth on Columbia blacktails and prides himself on his foot-hunting abilities makes the mule deer another of his primary targets. Moving to Montana back in the early '80s, mulies were a natural.

So when Chuck received a mule deer hunting invitation in 1998 from his old friend and Alberta hunting guide/outfitter, Gerald Molnar, it didn't take a whole lot of arm-twisting.

"He said, 'You need to get up here. We've had several mild winters, there are some good mule deer up here, and I can guide you personally,'" Chuck says about his conversation with Gerald. "I turned him down the first couple of years because I had other things going on. He finally just talked me into it."

Again, Chuck found himself on public ground and in difficult hunting conditions. The countryside near the Red Deer River where he and Gerald were hunting is wide-open prairie with breaks, but precious little broken ground for a bowhunter to sidle in close to an eagle-eyed mulie. Still, he'd hunted with Gerald enough, including a successful quest for a world record mountain caribou, to trust in his optimistic assessment of the situation. And early in the hunt, Chuck nearly succeeded on a 180-class buck that bolted when the wind switched unexpectedly. The deer were there, and the mild winters, as Gerald had said, looked like they had helped the local bucks maximize their antler potential.

The next day, just before dark, Gerald and Chuck were glassing distant ridges, and Gerald glimpsed the tall rack of a buck just as it skylined and disappeared a moment later over the back side of the ridge.

The following morning, they returned to the spot hoping to lay eyes on the buck again, but dense fog drowned any hopes of hunting for the entire day. The soupy fog hugged the landscape even into the next morning until approximately 9 a.m., when it finally began to clear.

"The fog cleared, and there was that buck within a quarter-mile of where he had been the time before," Chuck says. "The rut was just starting, and he was with some does. I had to cross the Red Deer River to get to the deer. He bedded with a sentry buck—a little 3-point. I got within 40 yards or so crawling on my side. That little buck raised his head. He'd been dozing. The other deer didn't see me. I knew it was the biggest mule deer I'd ever seen. The small sentry buck raised his head and looked right at me. I was lying on the ground motionless, but that deer saw some-

113

thing wrong and jumped up and ran, and the big deer followed him."

Chuck knew the gravity of what had just happened. He'd been within 40 yards of the biggest mule deer he'd ever seen alive on the hoof, and a punk 3-point did him in. He also knew enough about bowhunting big mule deer to know that his 40-yard view of the great buck was likely his first and last. Disgusted, he conferred with Gerald who concurred that he'd never seen a big buck twice during the bow season. Bump 'em once and they're gone.

"The deer ran down into the thick bottom of the Red Deer River which is big—I mean lots of thickets," Chuck says. "I never expected to see him again. We were walking out 20 minutes later, and way off in the distance I saw these two little dots moving. I put up my binoculars and I could tell one was the big buck. They were about two miles away on the other side of the river. They went around a corner into a big draw, and Gerald knew the country. We drove around and looked and we saw that buck again, and Gerald said, 'I think I know where that deer's going. There's a big draw over there, and you're never going to see him again, but we gotta try.'

"I'll be darned if I didn't go over and poke my nose into that draw, and here's that buck in the bottom bedded with the little sentry buck. Just before dark that night, I climbed an almost-sheer dirt bluff, got within about 20 yards of the bedded deer—both of 'em. I could just see their antler tips and I waited. They finally stood up and fed away from me through a 3-foot opening between humps of mud. They were going down into a bad canyon where I never would have gotten 'em. There were does down there. I eye-balled the distance and shot, and killed that deer; shot him right through the heart. It's the biggest mule deer I could ever hope to get. He was 31 inches wide and scored 203⅞.

"I love mule deer. I think foot-hunting for big mule deer is almost as difficult as foot-hunting Coues' deer. When I own a house big enough to put up more trophies, that buck is going to have a prominent place."

'MY BEST ANIMAL EVER'

Still, no matter how long Chuck bowhunts, no matter how

Ever since that Wyoming rifle hunt that he had received as a high school graduation present, Chuck dreamed of arrowing a giant mulie buck. His 1998 Alberta hunt that culminated with this massive non-typical, therefore, ranks among his greatest hunts.

many more trophy animals he tallies, no matter how splendidly invigorating and challenging the hunts, he'll never top what happened in Montana in September 2000.

The bull elk that he shot that steamy September morning embodies everything that Chuck has pursued since he bought that first Ben Pearson recurve back in Chico when he was 13. It is challenge—an old, hunt-wise, call-shy bull on public land. It is diligence—the bull located one year and doggedly pursued the next. It is focus—setting everything aside for a singular purpose. It is historic in antler size and unprecedented as Chuck's fifth bowhunting world record. It is skill in making a difficult shot at the end of a one-year quest. And it is the luck that a bowhunter makes for himself on occasion by being out there more and hunting harder than most anyone else is willing to do. And it is what, on April 27, 2001, earned him the Pope and Young Club's Ishi Award, something that he has coveted like only a boy who grew up scuffing his boots in Ishi Country ever could.

"I've known about the Ishi Award for about 30 years," Chuck says. "I've thought about the Ishi Award, and it's always been the pinnacle for me in my mind. I never thought I'd get an Ishi Award, but I thought my elk had a chance. That's really the pinnacle, I think, of my bowhunting life—shooting that elk and then getting the award. I would not have dared to have hoped too seriously that I would ever get one. I think it's fitting that the best animal that I have ever laid eyes on got the Ishi Award. I mean if there was ever an animal that I bagged that deserved it, it was that elk.

"To have picked up obsidian arrowheads since I was a kid hunting in Ishi Country and then to get an award that is called the Ishi Award with a big obsidian arrowhead on it, ... I mean, that is extra, extra special for me. I'm glad I got that elk in Montana because I love that state. I know that part of the state. It's as close to hunting near Chico, California as I can get at this stage of my life."

Chuck began seriously hunting elk as soon as he and Joanne moved to Montana in 1982. And before he knew it, elk were in his blood. An antler fanatic, Chuck thrilled to the sheer size of elk antlers. And combined with the broad-bodied, belligerent rutting bulls and the grandeur of the September Montana mountains, elk hunting pushed all the right buttons. Especially because the elk won a lot of the time.

"I hunted hard in the Missouri River Breaks in Montana several seasons back in the '80s and never got a shot at a big bull elk," Chuck says. "And I burned my tag at the end of every season. But I learned a lot, and it helped me later on to go back and bag seven bull elk in a row in Montana in very tough hunting situations on public land. Yet I remember the animals that got away at least as vividly as the animals that I've bagged. I savor those memories."

So by the time the 1999 Montana archery elk season rolled around, Chuck knew the drill. He had taken 19 elk with a bow, nine of them qualifying for the P&Y record book. And he knew enough to recognize when public land hunting pressure buggered the elk. Chuck and his outfitter/guide friend, who wishes to remain anonymous so hunters won't overrun his area, quickly decided to pull up stakes and check out some new country. They'd been studying a roadless area on a topographic map. The place looked like difficult terrain that a lot of hunters might shy away from. It didn't take long in the new area for Chuck and his guide to like the looks of things.

Early in the hunt, Chuck arrowed his biggest bull elk ever, one that gross-scored approximately 370 and netted nearly 360. Since the country looked good for mule deer, too, the duo kept working the area for a buck. Four days after killing the big bull and while still looking for a large mulie, Chuck heard an elk growl a throaty bugle approximately 200 yards away. Seconds later, a line of cow elk streamed from the timber, fanned across a clearing and dropped their heads to feed. Chuck sat, locked the 10X binoculars to his eyes and will never forget what happened next.

A great 6x6 bull galloped into view, scattering the cows as he frantically charged headlong through the herd, trying to escape the antlered pursuit of the titanic bull tailing him. Incredibly, the huge bull dwarfed the 370-class bull that Chuck had killed four days earlier.

"I didn't have a tag, and he was in a killing spot for a couple hours that evening," Chuck says. "We just sat there and watched him. I inspected the bull from every possible angle and carefully compared him with the elk that I'd already taken. I came back

117

and told some people about that elk. I called my good friend, Phil Phillips, and I told him, 'I think I saw the biggest elk I've ever seen in my life' and that it could be the world record. I told him I thought it would net at least 415." Chuck put the bull's beam length at close to 60 inches with an inside spread of at least 50 inches and seven long, massive points on each side—including thirds that looked to be at least 17 inches.

"He said, 'If I get this bull, it'll be a new world record,'" Phil said. "I've been around Chuck long enough to know that he's the real package. He knows his animals. Plus, what he told me that made me not question it was that he had just killed his biggest bull and just had his hands all over it and his tape measure all over it so he had that all fresh in his mind. Then he goes out there and looks at the bull in a spotting scope and has the chance to just really critique his rack."

Phil had no reason to doubt Chuck's assessment of the bull's antlers, but plenty of reason to doubt that he'd ever see the bull again. Rifle season was coming. Or the bull could die of natural causes. Or it might just head for greener pastures somewhere else. Chuck prayed that none of that would happen and thought about the bull every day until September 2000. Helping to encourage him was the knowledge that bull elk tend to return to preferred rutting areas season after season if habitat and hunting pressure don't change dramatically.

"I was hopeful because several states have radio-collared elk, and dominant bull elk quite often rut the same place every year," Chuck says. "They'll move 15 to 20 miles from their normal stomping grounds to a rutting area. So, I was hopeful, but I sure wasn't betting on it. Nobody ever found that elk's sheds, so I'm guessing that elk spent most of his time somewhere else. To my knowledge, nobody saw that elk between the time that my guide and I saw him in '99 and when we found him again in 2000."

Nervous anticipation flooded Chuck more than it ever had as he and his guide hiked in the dark toward their morning vantage point opening day of the 2000 season—the same place from where they'd watched the great bull nearly a full year before. Sweltering September heat soaked the hunters in sweat despite the early hour. By 9 a.m. it would be blazing near 90. Then, not long after daylight, a haunting, single-note growl of a bugle echoed like thunder in a steep draw. Chuck's neck hairs prickled with excitement. There could be no doubt. It was him.

Half an hour later, energized with adrenaline, Chuck caught the herd as it crossed the last opening below a doghair-thick bedding hillside. His look was not a good one, but he instantly recognized the bull. The antlers seemed a bit smaller than the year before; instead of seven points on each side, he now had six on one side and a short seventh on the other. But he still looked every bit like a world record contender.

"We saw the elk just before he went into a very broken, steep area, and the winds were notoriously squirrely in there," Chuck says. "I knew that from the year before. So we just backed out and didn't even try him because I was afraid we'd just bust him out of his bedding area and he might not come back.

"I was tempted to go after him. But it's sort of like hunting the Coues' deer in not-broken-enough country. I knew it was such a low-odds deal and there was even more at stake now. I did not want to scare that elk.

"On the Missouri River Breaks where I used to hunt, Fish and Game had some radio-collared bulls. Those elk would hang around in one spot for a few days and then they'd just move 15 miles. Fish and Game said they were sure that every time a bowhunter bumped a big bull, the animal would just pack up his bags and leave. And he wouldn't come back. I was scared to death that this was a one-time-spook-him-and-he's-gone deal.

"On big animals that you might only get one chance at, if you're aggressive at the wrong time, you can screw it up forever. We put it in reverse that day. And I don't know. Every person's different. Every animal's different. You might bump an animal like that, and he might come back because he's got a herd of cows he doesn't want to leave, and the cows want to stay in that area. On the other hand, he might push his cows right out of the country, and you might never see him again. I didn't start out bowhunting knowing all this stuff. I learned over the years. I learned that you handle animals like that with kid gloves and you wait for a high-odds opportunity and then you go for it. If I'm going to err, I'll err on the side of aggression, though. I think when you're foot-hunting being aggressive gets the animal more times than not. But you have to be aggressive at the right time.

119

That's what I've learned. I've gone full-speed ahead at the wrong time. You never know for sure. Even a high-odds situation doesn't always pan out."

So Chuck went with his gut and turned his back on the world record elk the first day of the hunt, leaving him just a few hundred yards away. That evening, Chuck and his guide saw no elk, and the next day they found only 10 cows and one small bull. Yet, though nearly two days had passed since he'd glimpsed the bull, Chuck knew that the great elk lingered somewhere nearby. The bowhunter could feel it in his bones.

And while some hunters might have panicked and chosen a more aggressive approach to locate the bull, Chuck stayed with the program that he had thought about all year since the first time that he had seen the elk—the same program that he had used successfully on other hard-hunted elk.

"I really didn't consider other hunting options because I'm confident in my ability to spot-and-stalk," Chuck says. "I felt for me that was the highest-odds chance of getting that elk. If I had felt anything less than confident in my ability to foot-hunt, there were a number of wallows and watering spots in that area that I could have staked out, climbed a tree, put up a ground blind or whatever. But that would have been a lower-odds chance in my mind. I could have waited all season and I could have blown it. If the elk would have come in from the wrong direction and smelled me, they might have been gone as surely as they might have been gone if I'd blown a stalk. So I felt I was more in control going after him on foot.

"And I didn't call. This elk was later aged at 8½. He acted so spooky and called so little, I didn't think he could be called in. I think some elk are uncallable and I think he was one of them."

Pale, pink shafts of sunlight arched skyward as Chuck and his guide hiked uphill the third morning. Hot, yellow light oozed across the mountains, followed by a blazing, bleached-out sun. Chuck and his guide split to look and listen from opposite ridgelines.

Soon Chuck spotted cow elk emerging from the timber nearly 300 yards distant. Then an antler. The colossal bull crossed a thin gap and nudged a cow. His left, 7-point side flashed clearly for an instant before he disappeared, his dramatic down-sweep-

Bowhunting World magazine dubbed it the "Ishi Elk" when it published the cover photo and Chuck's feature story. This hunt, Chuck says, was the greatest of the five greatest.

121

ing beam identifying him clearly to his pursuer.

Chuck's heart hammered as he hustled crosswind and closed in. The elk pushed rapidly toward the bed ground—the same hillside where they'd vanished two days before. Chuck veered away and loped uphill in a huge half-circle, well hidden by trees. The old bull pushed his herd up a shallow, densely wooded draw. Cows chirped now and then, and the bull growled once. Chuck knew that the ravine took a 45-degree bend a half mile ahead. He eased around a hill, trotted up the next ravine and hooked back over the top at the most likely ambush.

Poking an eyeball over the ridge, he spotted elk streaming past single-file. A split-instant later, the giant bull appeared 50 yards below, swaggering along the same trail as his cows. Chuck ranged the nearest cow and punched the distance button. Thirty-nine yards.

He ducked, drew his bow and eased back up to shoot, crouching, twisting and leaning to clear a low branch. The bull came broadside, and the Easton arrow sizzled on its devastating way. It smashed home, breaking a rib and blowing through both lungs. The bull whirled, staggered uphill and disappeared. Thirty minutes later, Chuck touched the biggest elk antlers that he had ever seen—antlers that later gross-scored 425⅛ and net-scored 409⅞ official P&Y points.

Everything that he had told Phil Phillips and a few other select friends a year before about this bull would prove true. A fifth world record, and a Montana elk at that. Challenge, diligence, focus, skill and luck came together for Chuck on Sept. 16, 2000.

CHAPTER SIX: **THE RAGGED EDGE**

"The wind hit the back of my neck, and the elephant turned and faced us, and his trunk was like a snake. It was going up and down. I'll never forget that, and his ears were spread out. He was trying to get the wind. That trunk was just ... it was evil looking. ... The elephant started walking toward us, and Martin said, 'Run!'"

One who spends a third of his days in the mountains, deserts and forests—often cut off entirely from civilization—is going to witness wild splendor and fury unlike most humans have ever seen. Some kinds of fury will be garden variety, like a dicey bush plane landing or a hungry grizzly raiding camp. Others will put you at the edge of death—so close that you might reach out and touch it.

THE KODIAK QUICKSAND

Chuck's second-favorite place in the world, next to Deer Creek Canyon, is probably Kodiak Island, Alaska. It is a land ripe with Sitka black-tailed deer, Alaska brown bears (often called Kodiak bears there), snow-capped mountains, salmon streams and forgotten lakes. Most years a hunter can go to Kodiak and buy three or four blacktail tags and a couple caribou tags in case he spots some of the feral reindeer roaming the tundra. So much game and so much wild country called Chuck to Kodiak originally back in 1984. After that first trip, he could not resist the island's seduction.

In 1998, Chuck and Pop, his most frequent Kodiak hunting partner, were camped on the island enjoying what had become an August tradition for the duo. Each morning, Chuck would strike out from the tent in a chosen direction for the day, and not until he'd gone four miles would he begin to hunt. That was the agreement between the two. Everything inside a four-mile radius of camp was Pop's to hunt. Chuck had younger legs and a stronger back. And that fact almost cost him his life.

"I was outside the four-mile circle hunting deer and I spotted a herd of reindeer (caribou)," Chuck says. "Pop and I always buy caribou tags. He had two tags, and I had one, just in case we ran into reindeer. I was way up on a mountain, like seven or eight miles from camp, and I spotted the reindeer way out on the flats. There was a huge bull in there. I'd shot two reindeer before with my bow, and one made the Safari Club International record book pretty handily. This one was significantly bigger. Man, I went off the mountain after 'em, and I followed 'em most of the day. They were moving across the tundra flats, and I finally bedded 'em down that afternoon.

"I was 100 yards from the whole herd, trying to figure out how I could get a shot, when I looked over my shoulder, and here comes Pop just huffing and puffing along with his rifle. He's about seven miles from camp! The reindeer had made a big circle. To make a long story short, I said, 'Why don't you go ahead and shoot that big reindeer? He's huge, and you don't have a big reindeer.'"

Charles obliged, anchoring the trophy bull with one shot, and then filled his second tag as the herd scattered. Chuck was already on his feet, hustling around the corner of a hill in the direction that the caribou had fled. Sure enough, some of them clattered past within bow range and he filled his only tag.

But the euphoria of the successful hunt was soon tempered by the glib reality of the chore lying ahead. Three dead caribou seven miles from camp and hungry brown bears all around. One of those bears had made a menace of himself around camp earlier in the hunt and had been back most every evening looking for an opportunity at an easy meal. The sinking sun and the thoughts of that bear raiding camp while the hunters worked on field-dressing caribou weighed on Chuck and Pop.

"We got to talking about it," Chuck says. "It was cold and drizzly, and we figured we could gut them out and salvage the meat without a bear getting on them. So we walked all the way back to base camp after we tagged and gutted the caribou because we were afraid that brown bear was going to raid camp if there wasn't somebody guarding it.

"We walked around the edge of the lake opposite camp, and all of a sudden I heard splashing, and here was a brown bear within 100 yards of camp and heading right for it. I said, 'Shoot one off to the side and scare him away.' And Dad did, and the bear ran off."

Early the next morning, Chuck gathered his gear and readied himself for the seven-mile hike back to the caribou to finish the field dressing and meat hauling. Just as he set out, the bush pilot flew over, and Chuck signaled for him to come in and land. He explained the dilemma to the pilot and told him that the caribou were only about three miles from a saltwater lagoon. The pilot could drop him there, Chuck could haul the caribou meat to the lagoon, and the pilot could come by to pick it up in the next couple of days. Pop wanted to help with the back-breaking work ahead, but the two had agreed that somebody needed to stay near camp to keep the marauding bear at bay.

Two hours later, Chuck arrived at the caribou kills and breathed a sigh of relief that no bears had hit the carcasses. Butchering a caribou is one thing; doing it while looking over your shoulder the entire time is another. An incessant Kodiak rain pelted Chuck as he worked the skin off, quartered and boned out the stiff caribou carcasses. With 80 or so pounds of meat removed and secured to his pack frame, he set out on his first return trip to the lagoon.

"I was walking across a little valley and back up the other side on a deer trail and, all of a sudden, ..." Chuck pauses, remembering the queer sensation underfoot. "I was on that real quivery tundra stuff and I broke through. I went up to my neck and I couldn't feel the bottom. I had that pack with the meat and my dad's biggest reindeer antlers on me. Every time I'd straighten my legs, I'd go under, and I was up to my chin. I was trying to tread water and I couldn't feel the bottom.

"I rolled to the side a little bit and started clawing and I gained a little ground, and the pack's what saved me. I think I would have gone under and never been seen again, if I hadn't had the pack because there was enough buoyancy in that meat. But I couldn't move. I started to get the pack off, but I thought, 'I'm going under if I take the pack off.' So, I struggled and, I don't know, it took me like 20 minutes. I slowly, but surely got onto my side into the fetal position and then crawled and slithered out of there. I almost died right there. It just gives me the creeps because no one would have found me, period, if I hadn't had that meat on my back. It still scares me to this day thinking about it."

Back at the camp that Chuck had pitched at the lagoon, he felt ready to collapse. His struggle to escape the bog and save his life, combined with his cold, soaked body and the three-mile pack had taken their toll. He stripped down, washed off quickly in the frigid lagoon and shivered inside his sleeping bag until sleep enveloped him.

Next day, he plotted a new course, giving the bog a wide berth and keeping his feet on rocky ground. By nightfall, after some 17 hours of labor, all of the caribou meat and antlers were cached at the lagoon, marked and ready for pickup by the bush pilot.

But the misstep gnawed at him. It wasn't something his years of experience and good judgment could protect him from. In the many years that Chuck had hunted Kodiak leading up to 1998, he had heard of people who had disappeared on the island, presumed to have fallen victim to bogs. And he knew what to look for when contemplating travel across the flats. But he had been walking on a deer trail on a slight upslope, in fact, when the Kodiak tundra collapsed beneath him. The unpredictability of the situation haunts him to this day and heightens his respect for wild places that do not allow seemingly minor mistakes.

"That's probably the closest I've come to bagging it, right there," Chuck says. "I never did touch the bottom. Apparently, all of this water was trapped in some kind of pocket there. It scared the heck out of me. It makes me shudder to this day.

"I'm a firm believer that what you think is going to get you probably won't. And some freak thing that you didn't anticipate, if something's going to get you, that's going to be it—like the bog. But I can say I've gotten more cautious as the years have gone by and I steer clear of situations that I probably wouldn't have even thought twice about when I was younger. There is probably still something out there that could get me, but you live and learn."

BAD NEWS BEARS

One would expect that, given the number of days Chuck spends in the company of grizzlies and Alaska brown bears, that a bear, not a bog, would have been his chief nemesis on Kodiak or in other bear country, for that matter. But in all the years that Chuck has wrestled his way through alder thickets and stalked blacktails near salmon streams, only once has a brown bear—or bears—posed a serious threat. And then only because of hunter error.

It was 1986, and Chuck was on top of the world, headed back to base camp with what he believed were the two largest Sitka bucks ever taken by a bowhunter. Three days before, Chuck had left his friend and hunting partner, Jim Clark, at base camp with clear instructions that if he killed a deer he should hang the meat high in a tree at least a half-mile from base camp so that the smell of blood wouldn't lure bears into camp.

The first day out, Jim, a Vietnam vet with shrapnel in his back that limited how far he could hike from camp, killed two large bucks, boned out the meat and hauled it back to base camp arriving right at dark. Spent, he dropped his pack near the tent, crawled inside and went to sleep.

In the middle of the night, Jim woke to the sound of the tent shaking. He stuck his flashlight out of the tent flap and got a close-up look at a yearling brown bear sniffing the deer meat and rubbing against the tent. Jim bailed out when he saw an opening, and spent the next 10 hours on a rock ledge about 200 yards above camp, shivering and watching six brown bears demolish it.

"We were at the mouth of a river in a big tidal flat," Chuck says, "and the bears liked it because there was a lot of food there. And after Jim got through there was more. I came back three days later, packing those two deer of my own, antlers and meat, and I was really tired. It was nine hours in and probably took me nine or 10 hours out downhill because I had more than 100 pounds on my back.

"Jim met me outside of camp packing the .375 camp rifle that he had in case of such emergencies, and he had two shells left out of a box. He had a black and blue spot on his shoulder from the rifle's repeated recoil and he'd been running bears out of camp for all those three days. They'd come back morning and evening looking for meat."

Or whatever they could get their paws on, which included all of Jim's food, which hadn't been properly stowed to avoid detection by bear noses. Chuck had triple-bagged his food in plastic and packed it inside duffel bags. The bears had rolled the bags, but didn't tear them apart. Jim was thankful that Chuck had taken great care to bear-proof his supplies since that was all that was left for him to eat after the bears were through. Jim thought that one of the bucks that he had killed might compare to two world record contenders that Chuck had tagged. But the duo never located even the antlers of either of Jim's bucks despite searching the area on and off for two days while they waited for the bush plane to come in to pick them up. When the plane finally landed at what had been base camp, the two headed for home. "A bad situation," Chuck calls it, but nobody got hurt.

"I've been around bears quite a bit," Chuck says, "and there's always a potential danger, but if you keep a clean camp, keep your food under water or in plastic, I don't think there's any great danger. One of the reasons that I might have been more calm on the hunt for that brown bear in Alaska with Brent Jones is that I'd been hunting Sitka deer periodically for five years before that. I'd been around quite a few brown bears, and that helped calm me down."

Still, it doesn't take a huge grizzly or brown bear to wreak havoc. Growing up in northern California, Chuck also gained a great deal of experience around black bears, which were common around Chico back then. He hunted them with his friend, Dennis Johns, and a pack of hounds. Chuck had killed a number of black bears by the time he and a buddy, Jack Manson, left on a backpack trip into the Yolla Bolly Primitive Area during college. It was July, and the roadless country in the Yolla Bolly was prime for Columbia blacktails.

"I shot a nice little forked-horn buck," Chuck says, "and we hung it up in camp and went out hunting. That evening, just before dark, I was close to camp climbing a mountain, and Jack met me about a quarter-mile from camp, and his eyes were as big as saucers. He said, 'There's a bear in camp!' And I said, 'Aw, no problem.' I had been around bears before. I walked in there, and that bear ran us out of camp. He had that meat and he wasn't going to let go of it. California Fish and Game dumped Yosemite National Park problem bears in that part of the Yolla Bolly, and I'm sure that this was one of those problem bears.

"We sidled up to camp, and I built a big fire. That bear had that deer behind a forked tree, and I could still see his eyes in the firelight. He wouldn't leave. He was crunching bones and eating, and once in a while he'd circle out and run us out of camp. We managed to pack up and take the tent down and douse the fire and got the heck out of there. We spent the night in the Jeep about three miles away at the trailhead. I went back the next day and retrieved the antlers, and the bear was gone."

BOGS, BEARS, ... BUSH PLANES

Though it's hard to, try to forget the bogs and the bears for the time being. If you want to put yourself in peril as a hunter, spend as much time as possible as a bush plane passenger. Eventually, the odds catch up with even the most seasoned, skilled and circumspect pilots in North America. "I don't get into bush planes any more than I have to," Chuck says. "It's like New York taxi drivers. You're putting your life in their hands."

And though one might argue that that's the case any time that you step onto a plane of any sort, 747 or Super Cub, the bush plane pilot faces mountains more uncertainty. Fog or clouds suddenly swallow the land. Random wind currents howling through mountain passes snatch you by surprise. Or, tired from days of hustling to deliver supplies and transport hunters, your desire to get home clouds your judgment and kills you. It happens somewhere in the North every year.

Early in Chuck's career with *Petersen's Hunting*, he received an invitation that any hunter would pounce on like a mountain lion on a fat mule deer. The folks at Redfield Optics asked him along on a Dall sheep hunt in Alaska. Trying to take off at the end of the hunt, the Cessna 185 flipped off the dirt runway in a 50-mph crosswind and rolled into the brush with Chuck and his two hosts inside.

"The guys with me were pilots, and they were white. I was too dumb to know how dangerous the situation was," Chuck says. "We had to get out and wrestle that plane back onto the strip. The next time the pilot didn't take off. The dirt strip ended on the edge of a canyon, and he just flew off the end of the strip into the canyon, 'cause he was afraid the wind would pick him up and slam him into the ground. The two Redfield guys told me later that it was highly dangerous; we almost bought the farm on that one."

Years later, early in his quest to complete the Grand Slam of

129

wild sheep, Chuck got another white-knuckle ride that he hadn't bargained for. He was in British Columbia, Canada with outfitter/pilot Keith Holmes, heading to spike camp to embark on his quest to kill a Stone ram. Holmes owned a slick, well-kept Super Cub, but he owned few hours of airtime, at least compared to a lot of bush pilots. Still, in this case, it wasn't a matter of experience. It was like stepping on quivery Kodiak tundra.

"We flew out of base camp headed for this tiny lake where he wanted to land and hunt out of," Chuck says. "We were circling for the final approach, and the engine stopped. It just sputtered and stopped. Those planes are pretty good gliders without an engine. I looked, and it was just sharp rock spikes under us on the hillside. I looked down and I thought, ... well, I won't tell you what I thought. I looked over at him, but he was too busy fiddling with stuff, and he got that thing going again.

"We came around and landed, and he was white as a sheet when we got out. And I said, 'What was that?' And he said, 'I don't know.' And he finally concluded that there was water in the gasoline. Somehow water had gotten into one of the drums."

Already skittish from peering down through the window of a stalled aircraft, Chuck felt immensely better with his feet on terra firma. At least until he shot his ram and watched where it lay down, near death—a 3-foot-wide ledge above a 100-foot sheer face with rocky crags to catch you below.

"Keith, he was a young guy in his early 20s." Chuck says, "He ran out onto the ledge and grabbed that foundering, dying sheep by its horns and dug his heels in and held him there until he died, so he wouldn't fall and break the horns. And then I had trouble. I was wearing smooth-soled neoprene boots for quiet. He had Vibram. I had trouble even getting out there and helping drag the sheep, and it was scary as hell. He wrestled it. I've got pictures of him grinning with the sheep on the ledge holding the horns. That was a very dangerous situation.

"Keith would not let me fly with him back to base camp. He said, 'I'm scared about this whole gasoline situation.' And he told me how to walk out. It was like 75 or 100 miles if he didn't come back, and I was wondering which was the worse of two evils. He left and then came back with an empty plane, and we went out that same day late. But that scared the heck out of me."

THE DEATH MARCH

Nobody bargains for his Super Cub to turn into a glider, but, as Chuck says, he knows that the odds aren't astronomically in your favor when you buckle yourself into a bush plane. Yet he trusts them more than another popular form of North American hunter transportation—the horse.

"The thing that scares me most in North America is outfitters' horses," Chuck says. "I had a horse slide down a hill on me in Wyoming, and I've had horses almost kick my head off. My dad had a rifle broken in half one time on a moose hunt in Duane Nelson's area. I shot a moose, and Dad came in the day that I was leaving. He had his rifle broken in half the next day when the horse bucked him off and took off, and the rifle jammed between two aspens. I've had horses take off on me several times. You never know what you're getting.

"We were packing out an elk in Montana with a professional packer back in the late '80s. I was walking along behind this horse just a little bit too close. We'd been working on this elk all day, and I was tired. The strap that goes under the tail had

Some hunts that start badly only get worse. Such was the case during the "death march."

131

worked up on the horse and hit that horse under the tail. That horse kicked back; I can still see both those shod hooves come right past my head. That would have killed me. I mean, I could feel the wind, and they went way behind my head. Horses scare me a lot. I prefer to backpack. In fact, my rule is that I won't climb on an outfitter's horse ever again unless I have to in an emergency."

But undoubtedly the most unpleasant "horseback" hunting experience that Chuck endured happened back in 1977 during what he refers to grimly as "the death march hunt."

Easton sponsored a promotion that would send the two national archery champions that year on a bowhunt with Chuck and fellow well-known bowhunter Jim Dougherty—now a member of the Archery Hall of Fame. Someone at Easton booked an outfitter in northern British Columbia for what was supposed to be a memorable bowhunting adventure for moose, caribou and mountain goats. It proved memorable, but not for the hunting.

"We flew in, the bush plane left, and us four hunters discovered a few minutes later that neither guide had been within 200 miles of the area before," Chuck says. "Us hunters had the only map and compass, not the guides. And the horses ... there were 29 horses in camp. The guide had bought them sight-unseen from the neighbor, and the neighbor had screwed him. They were all skin and bones. They had saddle sores all over. Dougherty's horse fell down under him nine times the first hour, and Jim only weighs 150 pounds soaking wet. These horses were so far gone that we walked 60 miles out because the horses wouldn't hold us up all the time. We had three or four horses strong enough to carry our supplies. Nine of those horses died on the trail of malnutrition during the next 12 days."

A snowstorm raged as the hunters and "guides" set out to reach one of the tent camps that the outfitter had assured them would be ready and waiting at various places along the hunting route leading to the pickup point more than 75 miles away. But 12 hours into the first day's hike, and well after dark, there was still no sign of camp.

"Our guide got lost in the snowstorm," Chuck says. "We got him lined out with our compass after we cut our tracks going back. We went in a big circle, and he was adamant until we

One of the death march guides chose to drown his sorrows in the whiskey bottle. Then he fell into the river and almost drowned himself for good.

133

crossed our own tracks. Then he listened to us. We got there, and the tents weren't put up, and we didn't know where the cache was. All we had were tent frames full of snow, 2 feet of snow. We finally got camp in reasonable order as the sun was coming up the next morning."

As one might have guessed, often what starts poorly ends poorly. Nary a caribou was sighted during the 12-day debacle. There were two moose, neither of which were shot; and Chuck and Jim each managed to arrow a mountain goat while their guide watched from halfway down the mountain, refusing to climb any farther.

One of the guides got drunk halfway through the trip. He fell into the river. Luckily, the others fished him out, tied him

Jim Dougherty's horse finally ran out of gas. Nine died during the 12 days.

over a horse face down and got him back to dry land where they built a fire. And then the Humane Society of Canada got into the act weeks after the misery had ended.

"The Humane Society contacted all of us hunters," Chuck says. "They told us that all but one of those horses died before the winter was over and they were pursuing that guy for mistreatment of animals. It was just a total disaster. It was a fiasco. Had we not been in reasonably good shape, all four of us, that could have been a seriously dangerous situation."

Chuck explained that once the bush plane dropped the hunters off and left, there was no going back. The plane would be back to get them in 12 days at Point B, and they had to get there. Given the condition of the horses and the guides' lack of knowledge of the area, Chuck worried for the welfare of the group. But the young horse wrangler helped to calm those con-

The only occasion to smile during the death march debacle came when Jim Dougherty, left, and Chuck doubled on mountain goats.

cerns. After the guide blundered across his own tracks the first night, the wrangler piped up. He had been in the area and knew the route and proved right at every turn.

"I was pretty confident that we'd get out of there," Chuck said. "We had a map, we had a compass, he (the wrangler) knew which direction to go. So I wasn't scared. I don't worry much about getting hurt or sick in the woods. I don't worry about that sort of thing. My main concern was, 'Do we know how to get out of here? Do we have enough food?' There was no going back."

THE LITTLE THINGS

Though Chuck has certainly had cause to worry while trekking at the corners of the continent, it's the world of the little things, sometimes frighteningly close to home, that have proven nearly as dangerous. Twice while rifle hunting in his native California as a teen, he came within an eyelash of death.

"Dad and I were hunting when I was 12 years old in a remote, hike-in area for black-tailed deer," Chuck says. "I was on the edge of a cliff that was probably 200 to 300 feet high. I slipped and ended up with my head and shoulders over the edge. My butt just caught on the edge, and I didn't go over. I thought about that for years. It scared me, because I looked over my shoulder—I would have been dead. That scared the heck out of me."

After Chuck had his driver's license, he and his cousin, Bob Adams, would rifle hunt together for blacktails. Midday with the deer bedded tight in the impenetrable cover, the boys would employ a common tactic to roust a buck. They'd launch rocks into the cover to spook an unseen deer from its bed. But in a blink, a couple of kids out enjoying some good, clean hunting fun got more than they bargained for.

"I stepped out on a boulder that was probably 4 feet in diameter on a steep hillside." Chuck says. "I got right on top and was on the forward part of my rock throw, and the boulder gave way under me, and I went over the top and under it. It bounced over the top of me, cracked my wrist, took all of the hide off of a finger, and came right down on the middle of my rifle which had come off my shoulder, and the rifle went off between Bob and me.

"That could have easily been fatal for one of us. If that rock

136

had landed on me, it would have killed me. And I still shudder when I think about that because the rifle was on safety. But we were poised to flush a deer out of the brush, and I had chambered a round at the very wrong time. So I learned a lesson there. The rifle was ruined."

A couple of years later, with bowhunting taking center stage in his life, Chuck was out enjoying some target practice at his parents' house. The old tube-style quiver strapped about his waist gave no appearance of an accident waiting to happen. But it was, inflicting enough damage to inspire Chuck years later to start his own hip quiver business and build a better option.

"It was one of these (quivers) that clips in two places, and the front clip broke as I was walking back from the target," Chuck says. "It dumped all these arrows out, including the practice Fred Bear broadheads I was shooting, and I walked right into one. And that broadhead drove into my right leg. I was walking at a normal pace. The nock hit the ground, and I walked right into the broadhead. It drove in, hit the bone and glanced out. It was a two-blade broadhead, dull because I was practicing. It glanced out and almost came out the back of my leg. And I reached down and pulled it out and there was a lot of blood. But my mom was in the house, and they got me to the emergency room.

"If the arrow had gone the other way and cut my femoral artery, I might have died. But they got me to the hospital and put stitches in two layers deep. The next day I couldn't even get out of bed. I couldn't walk. And I didn't even hardly feel it at the time. That incident told me, I think, a lot about what an animal feels when it's hit. I think if you kill an animal, he probably doesn't feel much. If he survives until the next day, he probably will be like I was—really stove up. I couldn't walk for a week to 10 days."

THE LARGEST THING

Chuck has had enough close calls with the unexpected to recognize hidden dangers in all of the little things that go into life as a hunter. And he's acknowledged that, in North America at least, the thing that scares him the most is the outfitter's horse. But outside of North America exists a beast whose track alone is enough to singe the back of his neck with electricity.

With the Super Slam behind him and no bowhunting experience beyond the North American continent, Chuck made his first African safari in 1991 with the help of booking agent Ron Oliver. Typical of Chuck, he set aside six solid weeks for the trip, intending to shoot a number of plains game species, but also with the aim of killing one of Africa's Big Five—the highly sought-after and respected Cape buffalo, an aggressive species known widely as "Black Death." Yet, more than two weeks dedicated to finding a buffalo yielded not a single shot opportunity in 1991. So with that unfinished business to attend to, Chuck planned a return for summer 1992. But a wild card entered the deck.

Oliver had spoken to the Zimbabwe government which was in the midst of a difficult decision—whether to allow more general bowhunting for elephants. The number of elephants wasn't the issue, the question of using archery tackle on such an enormous and potentially dangerous beast was. With Chuck scheduling another six weeks to be there anyway in pursuit of Cape buffalo, Oliver figured that he had the perfect man to carry out an experiment on behalf of the Zimbabwe government. Chuck, who knew that elephants had been successfully harvested before with archery equipment, obliged; he figured that his 100-pound draw Hoyt Super Slam bow and custom 830-grain arrow would do double-duty on a buffalo and a 10,000-pound elephant. And during his 1991 safari he had seen several large bull elephants with tusks that would weigh close to 90 pounds. The invitation from the government coupled with the once-in-a-lifetime opportunity at the largest land-walking mammal proved impossible to pass up ... and nearly deadly.

Playing into Chuck's hand was a professional hunter by the name of Martin Naude, in whom Chuck felt supreme confidence. Martin had guided Chuck in 1991 and had proven to be exceptional in every way, especially in handling his .458 Winchester. With Chuck standing witness, Martin deftly swung the heavy elephant rifle and killed a Guinea fowl after it had taken flight. The wing-shooting display with a rifle designed for dangerous game showed Chuck all he needed to see to convince him that he was in capable hands should something go awry. And that's just what happened.

Chuck, Martin, two trackers and the rancher's son, Ed Naude, set out together to search simultaneously for the tracks of buffalo and elephants. As luck would have it, the elephant experiment happened first.

"We were driving down the road, and Martin, who had been on a lot of elephants, came to a skidding halt. He said, 'That's a really big elephant track.' It was heading right across the road, it was fresh, and we got on the track," Chuck said. "A couple hours later we were going through the thick bush and Martin said, 'Stop. I hear an elephant.'"

Martin had heard the elephant's stomach growl from nearly 200 yards away as it digested the huge amounts of roughage that an elephant consumes daily. The next time that it happened, Chuck identified the sound that Martin was referring to. With the wind right, the group—all five of them—eased closer toward the sounds. Then a branch cracked. The old, lone bull was standing in the shade of a tree, feeding on the branches above, now only 50 yards distant. Chuck had seen enough elephants in 1991 to wonder if this bull compared favorably to the best bulls that he'd seen a year prior. But it only took a brief consultation with Martin to convince him that this bull had 60-pound tusks and was a good specimen. Besides, for the moment, everything appeared to be playing out perfectly.

Sneaking closer, just Chuck and Martin now, the distance dwindled to a scant 20 yards in the thick brush. A broad ear covered the elephant's eye, allowing Chuck and Martin a bit more margin. Martin told Chuck to be patient and to wait for the broadside elephant to step its left foreleg ahead, opening the entire chest cavity for a target. Chuck asked Martin for an aiming point on the giant animal's ribs. A 2-inch scar revealed itself in what looked like the perfect location. Martin directed Chuck to place his arrow on the scar.

Fifteen minutes passed with the elephant shifting its 5 tons from side to side, one leg to another, finally stepping ahead slightly with the left foreleg and presenting an opportunity. Chuck's 830-grain arrow—16 inches of 2117 aluminum shaft epoxied inside of a full-length 2317 tipped with a Zwickey Black Diamond broadhead—flashed from the Hoyt bow and slashed the scar where Martin had called the shot. But something went horribly wrong. The impact generated a rifle-like crack, and as the elephant rumbled away, half of the arrow remained exposed on the entry side.

The group reassembled and waited an hour discussing the situation and how it might play out. They had seen enough to know, however, that the first shot would not be the last. They knew that they would be on the trail of a wounded elephant and would have to find a way to finish it as quickly and cleanly as possible. The dry ground ahead on the trail was cratered with deep tracks and scant drops of blood. After a few hundred yards one of the trackers spotted the elephant standing in the brush ahead, still alive, but obviously sick.

"The wind was perfect," Chuck says. "We got to the edge of the thicket and were trying to decide what to do. And Martin said, 'The wind.' And it hit the backs of our necks. The other guy who was with us was the rancher's son. He had a .375 H&H, and Martin had his .458 Winchester. But the wind hit the back of my neck, and the elephant turned and faced us, and his trunk was like a snake. It was going up and down. I'll never forget that, and his ears were spread out. He was trying to get the wind. That trunk was just, it was evil looking the way it was moving around.

"Well, the wind came back in our face. And the elephant was 40 yards away from me, but he was chest-on, and his trunk was covering the soft spot on his throat. There was nothing I could do. Then the wind hit the backs of our necks again, and the elephant started walking toward us. Martin said, 'Run!' And I ran to our right, and Martin ran to the left, and the rancher's son ran straight away.

"That elephant laid back his ears. I looked over my shoulder once. He just laid back his ears and came at a dead run, and I went out of sight from the elephant into the brush. I probably ran about 40 or 50 yards and I stopped and turned around, and the .458 went off, and the elephant dropped right on the heels of the kid.

"He was charging the wind. Now I'm sure he had that kid in his eyesight once he got close. They have these trees called mopani trees there. They were like oak trees and they were thick in that area, and that elephant didn't go around trees when he charged. He mowed them down. We went back, and there were

Professional hunter Martin Naude, left, kept his cool and stopped this wounded elephant with his .458. Ed Naude, Joanne and Chuck still managed to smile after the event.

probably a dozen of these trees that were probably 8 inches to 12 inches in diameter at the base—big, tall trees—they were just flattened all in the same direction. They were catching between his tusks and his face, and he was just dropping those trees. We're talking trees 30 feet high! It was a horrible racket for the first 40 yards, but then it was wide open. He was out on bare dirt, and that kid didn't know that elephant was behind him. It was dead silent. He was not trumpeting anymore. He trumpeted to begin with. But when he laid his ears back and came he was dead silent. He was serious. Several people who know elephants have since told me that when they trumpet they're going to false charge most of the time. When their ears go back and they go quiet is when they are the most dangerous. That's when all the horsing around is over and they're going to try to come and get you."

Meanwhile, Joanne and a driver had taken one of the Land Cruisers and crested a rise about 125 yards from the elephant just seconds before it charged. Spotting the elephant, Joanne reached for her video camera, punched the record button and captured the elephant on tape as it began to charge. The driver panicked, however, and knocked Joanne down trying to bail out of the Land Cruiser. Had Martin failed to stop the bull, the vehicle would have been the next natural target in the elephant's sights.

But Martin managed a shot even better than the one that clipped a flying fowl out of the air. A 10,000-pound elephant in full charge at 15 yards and within steps of squashing one of his party is the kind of insanity that makes a few African professional hunters legendary. Martin had been thinking clearly when he told the others to run. He fled to the side to get out of the wind and to an open place where he could get a clear shot at an elephant that he knew was going to come for them. And when it steam-rolled through the opening broadside at 15 yards, Martin swung his rifle and placed a single bullet perfectly equidistant between the eye and the ear hole, center brain, flattening the elephant instantly.

"He couldn't have walked up and put his finger in a better place than where he put that bullet," Chuck says. "So it was nice to have a professional there. I'm sure he saved the rancher's son's life on that. Martin told me that he had dropped several charging elephants and Cape buffalo before. He had ice-water in his veins, that guy did. You could just tell."

Stunned and dazed, the group gathered at the elephant and tried to make sense of what had happened. From the time that Martin had said, "Run!" to the time that he shot had been less than 10 seconds. Chuck had run 50 yards at an angle, and was 23 steps from where the elephant fell. The young rancher's son was much closer, much too close. At the report of the rifle he had turned sharply. Finding his tracks where he turned and measuring to where the elephant's trunk lay on the ground showed a space of only three yards. Undoubtedly, the elephant's forward momentum made the gap seem closer than it actually had been, but suffice to say that not many people are so close to a charging elephant and survive to tell it.

Chuck, deeply saddened by his failed attempt to cleanly kill an elephant with his bow, went to work to determine what had caused his arrow to penetrate so poorly. The arrow had struck the elephant just in front of the diaphragm, amazing Chuck at how crowded forward the vital chest cavity is on an elephant. The broadhead had caught the rear edge of a rib, killing the arrow's energy and angling it rearward through the chest cavity and into the paunch. With the liver strongly to the right side in an elephant, and Chuck shooting into the elephant's left side, there was no damage to that vital organ, either. With a tractor from the ranch, the team hoisted the elephant up, and Chuck conducted some penetration testing with his 100-pound draw bow and 830-grain arrows that were generating nearly 90 foot-pounds of kinetic energy. The rig proved no match for elephant ribs.

"The ribs were about 2 inches thick, and I'd been told that they were round—that the broadhead would slide off," Chuck says. "And that's not true. They're flat, and the rib cage also curves inward at the front so you actually have a square shot at the rib cage when the elephant is quartering to you. Broadside gives you an even smaller area to shoot at—the ribs just darn near overlap. To make a long story short, when I hit between the ribs during the test shots my arrow disappeared in the elephant. When I hit a rib dead-center it would just go 'thunk' and go in

143

about 2 inches through hide and muscle and stop in rib.

"We cut that elephant in half, and I took pictures. I figured about 30 percent of the actual chest cavity was soft tissue exposed and 70 percent was solid rib. So I figured if you had three elephant tags, you'd probably hit between the ribs one time and kill the elephant. The other two times you'd probably have trouble. In terms of not hurting the elephant, I could have hit a rib dead center, and the elephant would have run off. We would have never found him, and he would have survived. So, I was halfway between a good shot and a horrible shot.

"Unfortunately, the elephant smelled us and charged, and there was nothing that could be done about it. We controlled what we could control. I hit him exactly where the professional hunter said I should. But it's like having a burlap sack over a steel plate with little strips cut in it. You can't see the ripple of the ribs or anything, so it's just a roll of the dice.

"I'm sad that I didn't get an elephant cleanly, but I can tell you that I'll never hunt elephant again because my recommendation to the Zimbabwe government was that it was a one-in-three chance. I had the pictures to back it up. I have the whole rib panel of that elephant at home on the wall. I brought all the ribs back and reconstructed the rib panel, and you can clearly see that a strong two-thirds of the chest cavity is covered by ribs so thick, you couldn't shoot any arrow through those ribs. So I recommended to Zimbabwe that it's a stunt and really shouldn't be done. It's too risky—risky for the personnel who are with you, risky for you, not fair to the animal. And that was my recommendation.

"Now, I still see people hunting elephants with a bow. Some of them get lucky and get between the ribs and they kill their elephants very quickly. But I can tell you that no matter what you read or what you hear, most of the elephants supposedly taken with a bow are not taken cleanly with a bow. Most of them are finished off with a rifle. It happens all the time in Africa with gun hunters, too. They do what they call 'the double-tap,' or they have to finish off a wounded animal."

With the work done, native people from far and wide descended on the carcass and in a few hours' time had removed every scrap of meat and hauled it home to their villages. Chuck kept the tusks, the skull, the hide and the rib panel, taking them home to Montana along with an unpleasant memory and a new-found fear of an animal unlike any he'd ever felt. He'd been toe to toe, after all, with every variety of North American big game including polar, grizzly and Alaska brown bears, and he'd proven himself and his equipment in every case. In the days after the elephant, he did the same when his long-awaited encounter with Black Death, the Cape buffalo, finally came. But the elephant proved out of reach. In the elephant's world, Chuck Adams was no longer in control.

"I kept the ribs just because they're a reminder of how much like an armored truck an elephant is," Chuck says. "And part of me once in a while says, 'You should go try an elephant again.' And then I look at the rib panel and I say, 'No, stupid.' That's my reminder that it's really not something that you can deliberately go do. I think any other animal in Africa you can go and take cleanly. If I can't take an animal cleanly and deliberately with a bow, I don't want to do it.

"And I can tell you. I've been to Africa one more time since, and we saw more elephant tracks after that when we were hunting. Every time I see an elephant track since then, the hair on the back of my neck stands up."

CHAPTER SEVEN:
THE BEST AND THE WORST

"You know, it all balances out. I had a great year in 2000. I got a great elk, though, in '99, and it set the stage for the next year. I really think if you hunt quite a bit, it all averages out. I've never had what I'd call a bad year because I'm always having fun."

A bad day in the woods is still better than a good day at the office. It's an old saying, and one that Chuck Adams certainly won't deny. But there is a price to be paid for making hunting your career and pursuing it with unquenchable desire and determination. And the price is paid in many forms.

There is the microscope under which Chuck operates each hunting season—both in terms of his bowhunting success and his actions while afield. Good or bad, right or wrong, the hunting industry and its consumers mostly measure a hunting expert's "success" by the number and size of the animals that he kills. And a guy like Chuck, who has made a living stressing the end result, must acknowledge his role in creating and sustaining the pervading attitude. In addition, someone who casts himself into the hunting spotlight must deal with a sometimes-vicious world of rumor and innuendo regarding allegations of game law violations or ethical missteps.

Over a 30-year career Chuck has seen his share of good times and bad.

THE BEST OF TIMES

One of the driving forces that led the author of this book to seek Chuck out at the Archery Manufacturer's and Merchant's Organization (AMO) Show in January 2001, to discuss a book about his life was Chuck's astonishing 2000 bowhunting season. The writer had grown to know Chuck well enough and had occasion to speak with him frequently enough that he had been able to keep tabs on what happened almost hunt by hunt. And the

146

Chuck summited Super Slam in 1989-90 with a great season, but 2000 was unparalleled in terms of big animals. This world record fair chase bison was one of many highlights.

successes of 2000 were uncanny.

Beginning in January, Chuck bagged two record-book Coues' deer in Mexico extending his string to five bucks on five Coues' deer tags; something difficult to fully appreciate until you've tried to stalk within bow range of one of these wraiths.

Then in April, Chuck prowled Arizona's Kaibab Plateau looking for a bison that would threaten the Pope and Young world record. After a week of hard hunting, he located a big track and dogged the phantom bull for more than 10 miles before arrowing it and shattering the world record in the process—the fourth world record animal of his career. In May, he shot another bison that also made P&Y.

Add a record-book pronghorn and 30-inch mule deer from his Montana stomping grounds, two high-scoring Central Canada barren ground caribou from the Northwest Territories, and his "greatest hunt ever" for his world record Montana bull elk, and it's no wonder that Chuck considers 2000 the pinnacle, even compared to 1989-90 when he completed the vaunted Super Slam.

"That's gotta be my best year ever," Chuck says. "I shot two official Pope and Young world records in 2000, and nobody's ever done that before. I shot 10 Pope and Young animals in the year 2000.

"In some cases luck plays big because it's luck to ever see an animal like my world record elk. That was the second-biggest elk ever shot in the state of Montana. You don't deliberately go out and see that. I don't know why that happened to me. In some cases you can target an animal like my world record mountain caribou, and if you go back enough times you have, I think, the off-chance of seeing a world record. Same is true with the buffalo I shot. I was pretty sure from the records of gun kills that there was a buffalo in probably both of the fair chase areas in the Lower 48 states—the Henry Mountains of Utah and the Kaibab Plateau of northern Arizona—that would beat the Pope and Young world record. Then the trick is hunting long enough to find the big track like I did that is underneath the big set of horns.

"So maybe there's a little less pure luck in a case like that because the world record is more attainable. I'll hunt the rest of my life and never see an elk as big as the one I got. Finding that elk was pure luck."

Chuck and his close friend, Phil Phillips, concluded a long tradition of pronghorn hunting together in 2000 by tagging old "Flare Prong."

A quick count above reveals only nine of the 2000 record-book animals. The 10th, even though it wasn't close to a world record, deserves special mention.

In August, 2000 Chuck was hunting with outfitter and long-time hunting pal Phil Phillips on what had become his traditional summer antelope hunt in Colorado. Most years, Chuck and his dad made it a father-son vacation, and every year they looked forward to the trip because of the camaraderie of getting together with old friends in a familiar camp that they had grown to love. Adding to the anticipation that August was the hope of spotting an antelope that had become like an old friend, too—a buck that had turned Chuck inside out with fruitless frustration for 17 days a year earlier.

"There was an antelope at Phil's camp that they called Flare Prong," Chuck says. "Phil and I had seen him for four years

149

straight, and he was huge. Nobody had ever seen him drink at waterholes, so I tried to stalk him a number of times. And I finally killed Flare Prong in 2000. I stalked him and shot him, and he was old and he was smaller, but he was still Flare Prong. That was really special."

Making it even more significant, and bittersweet, was the fact that the hunt marked Chuck and Phil's last hunt together at the traditional antelope camp because the state of Colorado no longer allowed Phil to renew his leases. A 10-year tradition had ended.

"Chuck said, 'I didn't even go over to him Phil,'" Phil said, recounting the day that Chuck killed Flare Prong. "He said, 'I shot, I watched him run and tip over, and I never even went over there. I wanted to come back (to camp) because I wanted you to be in on this deal because it's our last year and it's a buck that we've been after.' And all the guys in camp who had their tags filled had to come along. That's what's neat about Chuck that a lot of people don't understand. I mean he was happy to have the whole crew come along then and get in on the fun of the recovery and the story. It was really neat."

REALITY CHECKS IN

Every season can't be like 2000. A year before, it seemed as if nothing would go right.

"1999 was a pretty thin year," Chuck says. "I chased Flare Prong around for most of August. That's the one year that I didn't get an antelope at Phil's. I had a terrible time trying to find a mule deer in Alberta to shoot with my bow. The year before I had taken that monster. In 1999 I hunted extra days, a total of almost two weeks there, and ended up with kind of a consolation buck that made Pope and Young, but not by very much.

"That year was also the only time I've shot a mule deer in Montana that didn't make Pope and Young. I couldn't find one. I shot four Pope and Young animals in 1999, and that's the thinnest year I've had in many years. And some people say, 'Wow, that's great!' But for the amount of time I spent, ... I went to Quebec with the guys from Easton, and the caribou migration was thin when I got there and went to almost zero during our six-day hunt. I had two caribou tags in my pocket and only saw one bull that I went after and I killed. He barely made Pope and Young.

"You know, it all balances out. I had a great year in 2000. I got a great elk, though, in '99, and it set the stage for the next year. I really think if you hunt quite a bit, it all averages out. I've never had what I'd call a bad year because I'm always having fun."

And though Chuck loves bowhunting more than anything else—even when things are going badly on a hunt—he realizes, too, that some of the successes to come can never be so sweet as the ones gone by. Like the musky fisherman who casts tens of thousands of times with the dream of boating a 40-pounder; what is left for him when the dream is realized?

"Elk are special," Chuck says. "If I had to pick one animal to hunt the rest of my life, it could very well be elk. I'm going to love elk hunting just as much as I ever did, and I'm going to take the biggest one I can find every year, and I'm going to enjoy it. I'm not going to get depressed. It's just the opposite. I feel incredibly blessed that I got a chance at a world record elk and I don't think that I'll let anything take away from elk hunting in the future for me. If the biggest bull I can find next year scores 280, I'm going to try to get that 280 elk and keep dreaming about a big one. But I know in my heart of hearts I'll never again see another elk that scores over 400. The odds are just so astronomically against it that you just take it and go on.

"I got just as excited shooting a doe white-tailed deer in the Bitterroot Valley of Montana a number of years ago as I have on any animal because the season ran all the way from September through mid-January and I was hunting in January at the end of the season. I hadn't shot anything in quite some time and I was in an area where the deer were pressured. I hunted for two weeks to get one shot at a doe whitetail for the freezer. I killed that deer and I was doing cartwheels. So it was the immediate challenge that got me on that. My adrenaline was flowing as much on that whitetail as any animal I've ever shot."

Even when Chuck might be enduring a tough string of hunts, he says that he's always excited about the writing aspect of the job—something that continues to grow and reach millions of bowhunters. He currently writes regularly for *North American Hunter, Buckmasters, Bowhunter, Bowhunting World, Bow & Arrow Hunting, Bugle, American Hunter, Insight* and *Outdoor Life.*

"I've published nearly 4,000 articles in major magazines during the past 25 years," Chuck says. "I've written six books on bowhunting and archery, plus a book on waterfowl hunting and major sections of several other hunting books. There is never a shortage of work."

Despite the criticism that comes with any high-profile job, Chuck strikes a chord with readers who enjoy his down-to-earth style and mastery of the subject matter. As evidence, *Bowhunting World*, which Chuck has written for since the beginning of his career, has presented him the "Reader's Choice Award" as the most popular writer in the magazine every year since that program began more than a decade ago. The honor is voted on by a large readership. And editors from the other magazines that Chuck writes for point to the high volume of positive reader mail that comes in addressed to Chuck.

Additionally, Chuck's "Bowhunter's Digest" is the best-selling book in the history of modern archery.

THE WORST OF TIMES

Though there are no statistics to back it up, one could make a strong argument that men who attempt to carve out a career as outdoor communicators, the way Chuck did, deal with an above-average rate of divorce. Hunting is a passion that has flowed in the very blood of man for thousands of years. Millions of us love it because we had to love it to survive. We had to be driven to hunt with the same zeal that we were driven to reproduce. Hunt well—survive. Hunt poorly—die. It remains at the core of our being, and to those of us who know it to its fullest, hunting can pull with great strength even up against the loves of our lives.

This inner strife is especially difficult when one's livelihood is also dependent on hunting and communicating the outdoor experience. Your wife or loved one knows that you love what you do. The office is the woods. The business calls are hunting conversations. The travel is to the mountains in Alaska or some other faraway wild land. The man is conflicted. The woman feels cheated.

So that's what some onlookers suspect happened to Chuck and Joanne after 12 years of marriage ended in March 1994. Just when Chuck was riding high, his career cresting after Super Slam in 1990, his world crashed down around him.

But Chuck won't pin the blame for the divorce on his hunting time away from home or his drive to complete his Super Slam.

"A lot of people assume that because I'm gone so much it was a marriage breaker, but that was not even an issue," Chuck says. "Most people don't realize that Joanne and I hunted and traveled together a lot, including two of the trips to Africa. Joanne went on more than half of my hunts with me and she genuinely loved it. We just grew apart, and half the adult population in the U.S. knows about that first-hand. People break up. But, fortunately, Joanne and I are still friends to this day, and I'd do anything for her and I'm sure she feels the same way.

"1993 and '94 were the low point of my life. I was pretty darn depressed because I was splitting up with the love of my life. It was hard, but I had some good family and friends to support me. Anybody who's been through that knows how tough it can be. And I really think Joanne and I had a closer bond than most married couples that I've known. We knew we were drifting apart for a couple of years, but it was very difficult.

"And then, though it's less important in my mind, we financially split what had happened during the years after Super Slam, and that's one of the reasons I'm saying I'm not a rich guy. When you get a divorce it sets you back financially, and I don't begrudge that; Joanne was a part of that. But, you know, that was a financial set-back that I haven't recovered from yet."

You don't have to count the number of filled or unfilled archery tags to know the worst bowhunting seasons of Chuck's career. They came in the seasons surrounding the divorce when even the thought of bowhunting couldn't rescue him from the ordeal.

"The year coming up on my divorce, '93, I had a general Montana big game tag," Chuck says. "I didn't hunt Montana that year. That's the only year that I can remember since I started hunting Montana that I didn't hunt elk or anything else in Montana. And I basically moped around in September when I normally would have been out there chasing elk all over the place. It was partly because I didn't have Joanne to hunt with and partly because I didn't feel like hunting. And that tells you how down I was. We were living in separate places, and I wasn't in any mood.

"I went back to bowhunting hard in 1994 and I was back elk hunting. But they say the average person takes about a quarter of his total married life to heal up from a divorce, and my case was much worse. I've thought about that a lot. I'd say it took me almost until 2001 to get over it, to quit feeling sad about it a significant number of times a year and to really heal up. I've only felt really whole again for about a year and I think that's just a reflection of how close we were."

Charles said that he worried more about his son during the divorce than during any other time in his life. "There was a time when I really thought he might come unhinged. In fact, I explored the possibility of taking a leave from the university so that I could be with him for a while because he just seemed to be so low. Those were tough times."

Today, Chuck has managed to put the most difficult time in his life in perspective.

"I think maybe bowhunting since the divorce has been even more of a highlight because I've had more downtime. So I regard the bowhunting as more 'up' time—it's therapy in a way. When I'm doing seminars, if I'm sitting there signing autographs or talking to people, my mind will wander to the time when Joanne and I were sitting there together. We went to a lot of sport shows together in the early '90s, so I won't kid you that it hasn't been difficult. But I think anytime you go through adversity you come out the other side stronger, and I think I'm tougher-minded and probably more impervious to hardship than I was before. I always try to look at my cup as being half-full, not half-empty, and I wouldn't change a thing. I mean, I learned so much from being married and sharing things with somebody. I value that. If I ever get married again, which I honestly hope will happen someday, I know I'll be a better man and a better husband because of my relationship with Joanne. I don't look back bitterly on any of it."

THE UGLY

Though Chuck's divorce wasn't headline news, it sparked enough gossip, within the industry at least, to make it even more painful for a guy who values his scant privacy. And, since Super Slam, Chuck's celebrity has created a rumor mill churning out chatter. It's another price to be paid for being the most recognized hunter alive today. And the rumors probably bother Chuck more than anything else that life can throw at him.

Unfounded allegations gnaw at his core. Each time that he gets wind of a new one, he stresses over it, attempting to decipher how it could have started. He looks at it like this: Work hard, play by the rules, and you give no one any reason to level an accusation of wrong-doing. Still, the accusations fly, often in the face of reason. And while most are nothing more than second-hand, obviously false, far-flung claims from unknown corners of the hunting community, others come from prominent people in hunting circles.

"There was a tremendous investigation in Alaska regarding wanton waste with Sitka black-tailed deer," said former editor of *Petersen's Hunting*, Craig Boddington, during an interview for this book. "I don't think charges were ever made, but there are a lot of people there who would shoot (Chuck) if he set foot on Kodiak again."

Boddington is one of the most highly respected hunting and gun writers in the business. He served as editor of *Petersen's Hunting* for more than a decade, is a prolific book author and writes today for many of the hunting and shooting magazines on the market. Yet, while he praises some of Chuck's achievements like the Super Slam, he carries with him this Kodiak contention that, were it true, would soil Chuck's reputation and possibly threaten his career. And when someone like Boddington speaks, people listen.

What's more, scandalous words like these tend to spread through the hunting world like a Montana wildfire. Yet it appears that the accusation is patently false. An investigation conducted for this book reveals that, in fact, there was no investigation like the one that Boddington suggests. A trooper with Alaska Game and Fish confirmed that Chuck has never been charged for a game law violation anywhere in the state. The trooper also said that he found no record of any investigations of any kind.

"He's full of crap on that one, and Craig is the only one I ever heard about this from," Chuck says. "Back in '86, I went with Jim Clark. I hired an air taxi to take us into the hunting area. Dean Andrew took us in and out. The guy who owned the air taxi kept trying to get me to give him deer meat in return for flying. And I told him that's not legal. I told him 'I'll give you some deer meat at the end of the hunt, but I'm paying you full cabin.' So, we did the hunt, I gave him a $200 tip to his flying service and the meat from one or two deer at the end of the hunt, and we were done with that.

"The next year, '87, I went back by myself, and another guy with the same air taxi service flew me in. Meanwhile, this owner was asking for deer meat again. That year I shot three deer and I took all the meat home. He said, 'You got any deer meat?' I said, 'It's in my bags, and I'm taking it all back with me.'

"After that the owner of the air taxi service and this other pilot wrote a letter to Craig, who was editor of Petersen's at the time, saying that they knew that I had shot deer both years and not salvaged any meat. That's a bunch of bullshit. I submitted to Boddington the meat locker bill back in Montana for the processing of these hundreds of pounds of deer meat. The only investigation was Boddington. Fish and Game never contacted me. There never was an investigation."

During an interview, Dean Andrew confirmed that he's unaware of any wanton waste investigation and said that, in his experience, Chuck has done a good job of venison field care.

Jack Lechner operates Cub Air on the island and has flown Chuck in and out of hunting locations on numerous occasions.

"All I know is I've probably dealt with him for the last six or seven years, and he's overboard with regard to taking care of every bit of meat," Lechner says. "And making sure that there's no spoilage. They (Chuck and his dad) do an excellent job. I'd rank them right there at the top of anyone I've dealt with. I've hauled a lot of meat out for them and usually they set up a schedule of about every three days for me to come by and take care of the meat that they have. They're excellent."

Bowhunter Jack Frost is an Anchorage, Alaska resident who frequently hunts on Kodiak and is heavily involved in some of the state's hunting organizations.

"I've never heard a whisper of anything (ethical or game law violation)," Frost says. "I've got a little bit of sensitivity about game law violations. I've been investigated twice for questionable wanton waste and I go out of my way to do everything as legal and by the book as I can possibly figure out how to do it. The game laws during Chuck's career and my career have gone from fairly simple to so complex that you almost need an attorney with you. Alaska's got the most stringent wanton waste laws that you can imagine and they enforce them like it's the Holy Grail. I have never heard any scuttlebutt about (Chuck) doing anything wrong."

In fact, Chuck says that he's never been cited for a game law violation anywhere, anytime. Still, every once in a while, another rumor crops up out of nowhere ... or directly from left field.

"My world record elk is an example," Chuck says. "There was a game warden in Montana who got a call, and somebody said, 'You know what? There was a huge elk shot this year by a bowhunter, and I want to tell you, it was poached on private land. He was there without permission, and it's supposed to be the new state record.' The game warden said, 'Well, who did this?' And the guy said, 'Well, Fred Bear.' And the game warden said, 'Well, now excuse me, but Fred Bear's been dead for a number of years.' And the guy immediately backed off and said, 'Well, I'm not sure who did it, but I heard it was Fred Bear.' ... I mean talk about dumb."

Chuck said that another rumor circulating on the internet claimed that Chuck had hired 100 people in Montana and that each of these people had scouted extensively for two years to find Chuck's world record bull for him. He said that as the conversation gained momentum, the rumormongers complained that nobody should have such an advantage. "I laughed my head off at that rumor," Chuck says. "I'm broke now," he adds, sarcastically thinking of what 100 people on a two-year payroll might have cost.

Yet, rumors have a way of attaching themselves to world record animals. Something similar happened soon after Chuck killed his world record Coues' deer in Arizona in 1989.

"The Arizona state record book people wanted to enter my big San Carlos deer as the state record, and this was in 1990," Chuck says. "They received a report from somebody in Arizona that the person had seen me shoot the deer, leave the area, go into the headquarters in San Carlos on the reservation, buy a deer tag and then go back the next day and tag the animal and get it out.

"The head of the records organization for Arizona called me and said, 'We'd like some documentation on your deer.' Well, I had received my tag with a date on it several months before the hunt. I had arranged to get my tag a year before the hunt. So all of that was bogus and could be documented as bogus, but they wouldn't tell me who was complaining. I seldom, fortunately,

157

throw anything away. I had the original tag, both the stub and the tag, that had gone on the deer. I had all that, photocopied it, sent it to Arizona, and they put the buck in the book. And I told them to tell that guy to shove it.

"Now I, frankly, have not heard many rumors like that. Those are the highlights of my whole career. There probably haven't been half a dozen rumors I've heard of law-breaking by me in my whole career, and they quickly go away because they aren't true. And I can't even imagine how they start."

Doubt. Doubt combined with a dash of jealousy is a recipe for rumors in the hunting world. "How can anyone be that good?" That question is one that is asked by bowhunters in and out of the bowhunting business. Consider a conversation Chuck says he had with *Bowhunter* magazine founder M. R. James in the late 1980s.

"M. R. said, 'There are a lot of people who think your profile is too high and they're wondering when the other shoe is going to drop.' That's exactly what he told me," Chuck says. "And I said, 'What do you mean?' He said, 'Well, a lot of people don't think anybody can be as good as you and that you must be doing this illegally.' Now he didn't say he believed this, and I consider M. R. to be a friend. He was just telling me what he had heard as editor of the country's biggest bowhunting magazine."

Doyle Shipp, Chuck's hunting buddy from Montana, wishes that some bowhunters would lighten up on his friend.

"I talk to a lot of hunters, and all of them who know Chuck seem to really respect him," Shipp says. "But, well, then there are those other guys who are constantly shooting rubber blunts at somebody they don't even know. And if Chuck ever screwed up in the slightest, they'd switch from blunts to broadheads in a heartbeat and try to take him down. I never realized what a pressure cooker Chuck was in until we started hunting together. It's not fair, but I guess it's part of being Chuck Adams."

"I've heard that comment relayed back to me a number of times: 'Nobody can be that good,'" Chuck says. "I'm in a fishbowl. And I make darn sure—as sure as I can possibly be—that I know the game laws. One of the downsides of my job is I travel to different states with numerous laws. I read the game regulations cover to cover before I go anywhere. I'm very careful about that. Then, to hear the rumors; it used to bother me more than it does now.

158

"I've learned more about human nature on this job than I knew about the first 25 years of my life, and I've grown fairly thick-skinned about things. But I must tell you, it still bothers my soft center a bit when things like that happen."

The differing game laws from state to state and the complexity of those regulations, as Jack Frost also pointed out, can be daunting to someone who travels as much to hunt as Chuck does. He pointed to an Illinois whitetail hunt that he went on where a stamp was required in addition to the bowhunting license. Chuck went in to buy the license, but the vendor never mentioned the stamp. Chuck had read the regulations and asked about it, and the guy behind the counter said, "Oh, yeah, I forgot about that."

"Had I not known about that and gotten checked, I might have lost my whole career right there over a $5 stamp," Chuck says. "And those are the kinds of things that I'd be crucified for if I made one little mistake."

Though Chuck says he frets about knowing the game laws inside and out, he's never felt like conservation officers have targeted him because of who he is.

"I've been checked repeatedly by game wardens," Chuck says. "In 1984 in Alaska I hunted barren ground caribou, and my two hunting buddies and I were checked three times by game wardens in bush planes during a two-week period. And they came and they looked at every cut of meat we had on the meat tree and they looked at our licenses. But they weren't doing anything because it was me, it was just coincidence. I've never been singled out.

"I do a lot of remote backpack hunting and I might go a year or two and never see a game warden because I'm so far back that nobody's even going to know I'm there. But I've been checked dozens of times over the years by game wardens, and the *t*'s are always crossed and the *i*'s are always dotted, so I don't worry about it. I've had my meat checked for wanton waste in Alaska probably a dozen times over the years for Sitka black-tailed deer and caribou, and I always take every speck out. I figure if you don't break the law, you don't have to worry about it."

Still, Chuck knows that he hasn't heard the last of the rumor mill. But he seems resigned to live with it because in the final analysis, the best days on the job outweigh the worst that this business can throw at him.

CHAPTER EIGHT: **WHAT THE GUIDES AND OUTFITTERS SAY**

"I've hunted all the guys who finished (Super Slams) behind him. I've hunted Tommy Hoffman and Jimmy Ryan and Jack Frost. I finished all their Grand Slams as well. And in my opinion Chuck is the finest bowhunter I've ever seen."
—*Arizona hunting guide,* **Larry Heathington**

Short of being there with him glassing the mountains, hiking the tundra and stalking the fields, talking to the men who've hunted alongside Chuck is the best barometer we have to measure Chuck the hunter. And these same people certainly offer valuable insight into Chuck the man as well.

Remember, too, that most outfitters and guides aren't the least impressed with "outdoor writer types." In fact, the prevailing attitude among guides and outfitters is that writers write, guides hunt. A writer is a wreck waiting to happen. They don't care if you've had a byline in *Outdoor Life*. They don't care if

"You would not want him hunting you. He just seems to have a sixth sense about him. He knows how to use cover as good as a coyote or a wolf; every depression. He's just unbelievable."—Canadian outfitter/guide Duane Nelson.

you've been on a hunting show on TNN; probably never even heard of it. They don't care if you're on the pro staff for some hunting equipment manufacturer. In fact, if anything, those credentials will only make them doubt you even more than they would have if you were some regular Joe from Pennsylvania.

It takes a lot to impress your average guide or outfitter. Most of them have seen it all while making a living out there where it counts—where self-reliance, a strong back and a love of the land pay the bills. In the real world where these men and women live and work, only the strong survive because Mother Nature still rules.

Chuck will tell you, as he has earlier in this book, that he prefers not to hunt with an outfitter unless it's legally required. He enjoys the challenge of doing all the legwork on his own and points out that most guides and outfitters prefer to do the same when they go hunting. And while one might expect that Chuck's perspective on this point would offend most of the outfitters and guides who he's hunted with, it appears that it's more of a common bond between them.

PHIL PHILLIPS, PHIL'S BOWHUNTING ADVENTURES

"He called me and said, 'This is Chuck Adams with *Petersen's Bowhunting*,'" Phil says. "And I said, 'Yeah, I know who you are Chuck.' And he said, 'Well I'm real interested in coming out and doing an antelope hunt with you.'

"You never know with a phone conversation or somebody who's that high-profile, so I never try to form an opinion until you actually get a chance to meet him. When we did finally get a chance to meet, I was pleasantly surprised at just how genuine and down-to-earth a guy he was. He hunted with us 10 years straight after that."

Phil became famous for his summertime antelope hunts near Maybell, Colorado, where he offered bowhunts on Ranching for Wildlife tags. A strong antelope population, good genetics and Phil's knack for setting up perfectly positioned pit blinds for his hunters combined to earn him a solid reputation. Chuck got wind of Phil's track record early on and saw the opportunity to extend his bowhunting season by being able to start in July.

"The first two or three years it was a great opportunity for

161

Chuck to come out before his big seasons started," Phil says. "Then we started to become pretty good friends. So his dad started coming with and made it an annual thing for the past seven years."

Yet, during that time Phil rarely hunted side-by-side with Chuck. Instead, Chuck would stake out a pit blind or head out on foot slinking through the sage, trying to corner an eagle-eyed "goat." Both Phil and Chuck knew that in a spot-and-stalk situation, one man was better than two.

"Chuck's pretty much of a loner when it comes to the hunting side of it," Phil says. "I've been out on the recoveries and seen the situations and the sites after the fact a number of times. He hunted with us three or four years before he ever got in a blind. It wasn't because the conditions were bad, it was just the challenge he was looking for.

"But last year (2000) he stayed a couple of extra days. He was after a particular buck (Flare Prong). We hadn't seen the buck, and I just said, 'I don't think he's here Chuck.' The last day he was packing up to leave, and we took a little tour around and danged if we didn't find him. There was no question when we spotted him. He was by himself for the first time. He didn't have an entourage of does with him. When Chuck had been trying to stalk him in previous years he had all these extra eyeballs to contend with. I said, 'Well, you've got no excuse to leave now.'

"We watched the buck for a little while with a spotting scope, then made a big circle around and let Chuck off. I had to make a trip into town to pick up my truck which was in the shop. And by the time I got back, Chuck was standing on the front porch of the hotel. I got out of the truck and I said, 'I suppose you got him already.' And he said, 'Well, I forgot something. I had to come back.' I said, 'What did you forget?' He said, 'My gutting knife.' Chuck had sneaked around, tried four or five different approach routes and had about a 30 mph crosswind and he drilled him."

Earlier during that August antelope hunt, Chuck and Phil had a lot of time to talk as they searched for Flare Prong. And the conversation often turned to an elk that Chuck had first told Phil about a year before, the elk that he thought had the chance to break the Pope and Young world record and, therefore, couldn't get off his mind. In antelope camp Chuck bounced elk strategy off of Phil. A month later, Phil's wife, Leslie, relayed a voice message from Chuck who had called in from Montana with a report.

"We talked about that elk at length," Phil says. "We talked about it shortly after he saw the elk (in 1999), too. That's what just blew me away is that at camp we were talking about his bull. We talked about a lot of different things, strategizing. He left a message as soon as he got to a phone and he said, 'Phil I got that bull, but, believe it or not, he's smaller than he was last year.' And he goes on to say, 'But he grosses 428.' And Leslie told me this over the phone, and I said, 'Well, that poor bastard!'

"Actually, I wasn't that shocked when he said he killed it. If it had been anybody else, I would have said, 'Well, good luck.' But I told Leslie, 'It doesn't really surprise me.' There are a few things that I think made all that happen for Chuck. He's got a knack for finding the right places. He does his homework. And he can afford to get on places if he knows they're good. But it really doesn't matter. There are a lot of guys who annually spend a lot more than Chuck does on hunts, and they can't hold a candle to what Chuck's done on a year-to-year basis. So I think it's more that once he gets out there, and the animal's there, he gets himself into the right position and then he's able to close the deal where so many other hunters will just take a lesser animal."

Though Phil has formed a strong friendship with Chuck during the past decade and has gotten to know both the hunter and the man behind the bow, he's also heard the naysayers. Phil is well connected in the bowhunting business. If there's a Chuck Adams rumor or complaint out there, he's heard it.

"All the negative things I hear bug me," Phil says. "The only downside is that if you get enough negative, it can't be good for anything whether it's true or false. Like how's he really doing all this? And the claim that no hunter alive can find a bull like that, go back the next year ... can you really find him again and get close enough to kill him with a bow?

"I think tons of it is jealousy. And guys who don't bowhunt for a living, I just don't think that they can believe that anybody is that good at his craft. And it just kind of grows from that. If a bad rumor starts, people start feeding on it.

"I think he's going to be legendary. It's unfortunate that they're always appreciated more when they're gone because

163

then all the other stuff gets forgotten—all the rumors. I think he'll probably be, if it's possible, even more famous then than he is now. He's got a tremendous following, but it's unfortunate that it is a mixed bag because it should all be positive, and it's not. You're not going to find anybody more dedicated. He will put everything that he's got into it. I know a lot of the outfitters he's been with, and all of them who I've talked to think the world of him."

DUANE NELSON, MILK RIVER OUTFITTERS, ALBERTA
(FORMER OWNER NWT OUTFITTERS, NORTHWEST TERRITORIES)

As Chuck prepared for his Grand Slam of wild sheep back in the early '80s, he soon settled on Duane Nelson and NWT Outfitters for his Dall sheep adventure. He could turn the trip into a combination hunt and have the opportunity to take his first mountain caribou as well. As it happened with Phil, Chuck and Duane became friends on the first trip, and Chuck returned multiple seasons for mountain caribou, sometimes for moose and once for another Dall ram. Duane ran NWT Outfitters for 24 years and saw a lot of hunters from all over the world come through his camps.

"Yep, I'd say Chuck and I are friends," Duane says. "And as a hunter, he's unbelievable. You would not want him hunting you. He knows animals extremely well, knows when to move, when to hold still. He just seems to have a sixth sense about him. He has tremendous eyesight, so that he can see things happening. He knows how to use cover as good as a coyote or a wolf; every depression. He's just unbelievable. And he's patient. He knows when to go and when not to.

"I wasn't with him, but to back it up a little bit, he was camped not very far from our base camp hunting Dall sheep (during his second sheep hunt). And the Dall sheep were there, but the wind was never right. He and the guide stayed in the tent with the sheep within a quarter mile for two days. And the guide said, 'I don't think you even want to hunt.' And Chuck told him, 'When the conditions are right, we'll go.' And the conditions changed, and within 45 minutes he had a 39-inch Dall sheep. Some guides have the philosophy, 'Well, let's do something even if it's wrong.' But Chuck has hunted enough to know when to make the move

"There are not very many hunters who I think have been tougher than me backpacking, and Chuck took a bigger load than I did."—outfitter Duane Nelson, right.

and when to lay off.

"To meet Chuck and to talk to him and to look at him, you don't think that he possesses all these hunting qualities that he does," Duane continued. "But he's tough! There are not very many hunters who I think have been tougher than me backpacking, and Chuck took a bigger load than I did and he was right there."

Duane said that in the 24 years that he and his family operated NWT Outfitters they hosted a number of different writers. He said that no one provided a more accurate account of the hunt than Chuck consistently did in his articles. And Duane said that when he asked Chuck for a favor in return, there was no hesitation.

"Well, I was a scout group committee chairman and twice he came up here and did presentations at no charge," Duane says. "I noticed that when he did these presentations, it didn't matter who was asking him questions or anything. He was very good to explain and answer questions whether it was a 12-year-old kid or an 80-year-old guy. He respected everybody."

ROD COLLIN, HUNTING GUIDE, YUKON TERRITORY

Rod Collin is one of those rare men with guiding in his blood. Despite low pay and long hours, he has made it his life's work and is well known in many parts of Canada for his quarter century of experience. Early in his guiding career, he drew the assignment of guiding Chuck for his bighorn sheep in Canmore, Alberta (Chapter Five).

"I thought we got along really well," Rod says, looking back on the frigid adventure with Chuck. "When Charlie told me that I was going to have him, of course, I had heard of him before then. I had read some of his articles, but I hadn't really paid a lot of attention to him. So when I heard that I was going to be guiding him, I started digging out old hunting magazines and stuff, and reading articles and whatever I could find on him. And I thought to myself ... I kind of got the impression that he was a little proud of being Chuck Adams. I was wondering if I was going to find a fellow that was a little arrogant. But I was pleasantly surprised. I didn't find him arrogant at all, and I enjoyed the hell out of hunting with him.

"I thought Chuck was probably one of the best if not the best bowhunter that I had guided. And not just bowhunter, but hunter. He was serious about it and he was about half-deadly, you know. I'd have hated to have had that man after me with a bow. I enjoyed watching him. He knew how to go about hunting something with that bow. He was good."

BRENT JONES, AAA ALASKAN OUTFITTERS

Sometimes an outfitter doesn't know what to expect out of a bowhunter. Back in the 1980s a lot of outfitters, especially those operating in the Far North for expensive big game like dangerous bears and wild sheep, never had a client willing to spend big bucks on a lower-odds bowhunt. Well-known outfitter Brent Jones was one of them when Chuck called to try to arrange his 1989 Alaska brown bear hunt.

"I'd never met him," Brent says. "He was the first bowhunter I had. I had talked to him on the phone a few times, and he decided that he was going to bring another guide with him, Larry Heathington. So he and Larry came on the hunt together. I told him if he would bring someone else along who paid full price on the hunt, just like Chuck did (Chuck paid the full price of approximately $9,000), that I would guide them both myself for a 21-day hunt, so that's what we did."

Brent said that, though the hunting conditions that fall were tougher than during most seasons because of the poor salmon run and ugly weather, Chuck maintained the proper focus during the 15-day adventure (which was detailed in Chapter Four, Part II). And Brent said that by the time Chuck arrived in October 1989, he knew of Chuck's Super Slam quest and the fact that other bowhunters were in hot pursuit. Yet, he said that none of it seemed to affect Chuck.

"If the wind is blowing the wrong direction, you just can't hunt up the creeks because it'll run the bears right out of the country," Brent says. "So we had to wait for the wind to switch to get the wind in our favor. That's critical. These big boars are even more spooky than a sow or a younger bear. If they even smell your tracks where you walked around, they'll take off. So you have to be very careful. You just cannot go barging up there because you're just going to run 'em out. You'll never see those bears.

"Chuck had a tremendous hunting attitude. On the days where the weather was really bad and blowing, and pouring down rain, we would just stay in the tent and rest and get ready. Then, as soon as we would get a good day, we were out from daylight 'til dark. And that was really good because you can go out on those bad days when the wind is blowing and pouring down rain. Man, you can sit there and watch and watch, and the chance of even seeing a bear is so slim you're almost wasting time. So basically he just rested on days like that. And that really worked out well.

"There was never one complaint from Chuck the whole hunt about weather, food, tents, lodging or anything. He was there for one mission and that was to get a brown bear. And it didn't have to be a big bear. All he asked me (for) was a bear without any bullet holes in it. And that was all. I mean he didn't care if it was a 7-footer, an 8-footer, a 10-footer, he just wanted a brown bear without any bullet holes in it. That was our mission. It was, I would say, the most fun hunt I've ever had. You couldn't ask for anyone better to have in camp."

And on the good days when Brent and Chuck were able to hunt, Brent says it didn't take long for him to realize that, given the chance, Chuck could make good on an up-close-and-personal encounter with a salmon-eating machine.

"I mean he is a very hard, serious hunter," Brent says. "He was in great condition. Half of the hunters we get couldn't go after (a lot of) bears if they wanted to. But he was in good condition, and that's what's fun. He's such a good shot. We'd practice all the time. We'd be walking along, he'd say, 'How far is that spot?' I'd say, 'Oh, 35 yards.' He'd get out his rangefinder. And we'd shoot at little mud spots on the bank. He never misses, I'll tell you. It's right there. He had it all figured out."

When the chance that Chuck and Brent had been waiting for finally arrived, it burned the images to Brent's memory with crystal clarity. And he recalls the final moments of the hunt again in extreme awe of the way that the experience unfolded.

"A big flood had washed out some big clumps of alders, so there was one of those between us and the bear. And the bear came down that side to that clump of brush and then the bear turned and started across the creek. Chuck was ready, and when that bear came up out of the water, walking, that's when he got the shot.

"The bear let out a big roar, he jumped sideways about two or three feet, and stood right up and looked at us, and I'm ready to shoot. We knew it was a good hit, so we just let the bear go. And, of course, man we were excited. We were jumping up and down hugging each other. We knew we had the bear, so we packed up our stuff and walked back to camp.

"Most of the time when you walk up on a bear, they get smaller as you start getting up on 'em. This bear started getting bigger. We walked up to this bear, and this thing was huge. We had at that time a bunch of horses we used for guiding. They were like 1,000-pound horses, and this bear was bigger than any horse we'd ever had. So we were looking at this bear and just couldn't believe how big it was."

For AAA Alaskan Outfitters, it remains one of the biggest brown bears in terms of sheer body size ever taken from that guiding territory. And for Brent, that 15-day hunt is more than enough for him to judge Chuck the hunter and Chuck the man.

LARRY HEATHINGTON, ARIZONA GUIDE

Most of hunting's upper crust knows Larry Heathington. Larry's home state of Arizona is home to some of the most sought-after big game tags on the continent. A single coveted elk or mule deer tag in the right unit might bring tens of thousands of dollars at auction. A desert sheep tag can fetch hundreds of thousands. And after some well-heeled hunter drops a fortune on a tag like this and begins his search for professional guiding help, Larry's name usually comes up.

That's because he's also known by hunting's more common folk as a guy who gets the job done. His reputation has kept him busily guiding hunters since 1978. And in that time, he says that he's seen most of the foremost names in the hunting business, including Chuck. The first time was in 1986 as Chuck inched to within one step of the Grand Slam of sheep.

"I finished his Grand Slam," Larry says. "I had the hunt concession on the Hualapai that year. And I was involved in training the Indians how to guide. At that point (the day that Chuck shot his ram), we were all hunting together—me, and the two Indians and Chuck. I actually found that sheep on that contour and put (Chuck) down off the wall on a rope to get to the sheep. And he got him killed, and then the sheep fell off a 150-foot cliff."

Of course, that first hunt set the stage for Larry to join Chuck on the brown bear hunt with Brent Jones. From there, Larry helped Chuck get set up to go Coues' deer hunting on the San Carlos Reservation. Larry said that he provided Chuck with marked maps of the area and did some of the logistical work, and left the rest to Chuck.

"You don't need to guide Chuck Adams anyway," Larry says. "With Chuck, pretty much, you just go hunting with him."

The two hunted together again when Chuck bagged his world record typical tule elk in California. "Yeah, I've hunted with him a lot in a lot of places," Larry says.

"I've hunted all those guys," Larry continued. "I've hunted all the guys who finished (Super Slams) behind him. I've hunted Tommy Hoffman and Jimmy Ryan and Jack Frost. I finished all their Grand Slams as well. And in my opinion Chuck is the finest bowhunter I've ever seen."

At that point Larry pauses and thinks on his lofty assessment

169

for a moment, leading one to wonder if he's questioning it. Instead, he broadens it. "He's probably the finest hunter I've ever seen. And I've hunted lots of 'em. I mean lots of 'em."

Coming from someone who has spent so many days afield with so many renowned hunters, this high praise begs the question: Why? What puts Chuck on a different level?

"Ability to read the critter," Larry says without hesitation. "He has a better ability to read than say some of those others. He gets a better feel for what the animal's going to do. And he goes and gets it done in a shorter amount of time. Bowhunters generally take too much time to get there because they're just slow. They think they need to be slow. And Chuck and I kind of have the same attitude. Put yourself totally out of sight, cover as much ground as you can, and don't give (the animal) time to change position on you. And Chuck is probably the finest shot I've ever seen. Watching him shoot is a thrill in itself."

GERALD MOLNAR, ALBERTA, CANADA GUIDE

Another guide who has observed his fair share of bowhunters is Alberta guide Gerald Molnar. He has also guided Chuck more often than anybody else has. Gerald and Chuck met during a mountain caribou hunt in Duane Nelson's territory in the '90s, and Gerald guided Chuck five consecutive seasons there until Chuck achieved his goal of a new Pope and Young world record bull. The two men have also hunted together for moose and in Alberta for mule deer.

In more than 12 years of guiding, Gerald says he's seen more animals shot by bowhunters than any one bowhunter has seen, including Chuck. And based on his experience, he says that Chuck ranks in his own league.

"I get lots of archery hunters coming in, and all of them or most of them have a strong suit of some type," Gerald says. "There are some really good shooters. And there are some who are good at stalking and then you get some who are pretty good with a pair of binoculars. But with Chuck, he's got it all.

"He's a tremendous shot, very good with a pair of binoculars, phenomenal stalker, but if I had to say anything, his strongest suit, which is probably what puts him out front, is that he has the tenacity of a pit bull. He just never quits. Never quits. I've tagged

"It's just that there are some people who seem to be born or destined to be great at what they do, and I do believe that he was."—Alberta hunting guide, Gerald Molnar, right.

along chasing caribou with him for hours, trotting to keep up, and he just keeps dogging them whether he gets them or not. We chased a big bull right around a place called Divide Lake one time and I watched him get on top of that bull no less than four times, and on the fourth time he actually passed him up. He just decided he wasn't going to take the bull. I think that's what really sets him apart from all other hunters. Just that unbelievable drive that he's got to succeed.

"And I'm not belittling the other hunters. It's just that there are some people who seem to be born or destined to be great at what they do, and I do believe that he was. There just seems to be no stopping him. He's just a killing machine. The average bowhunter pales. I don't think I've ever run into an archer who can kill at will. We've been on very few animals that he really wanted that he didn't take. It's really hard to be up on that pedestal, but he is the best in the world. It's that simple."

Gerald says that Chuck always treated him really well and that the two of them got along because they share a common bond as serious trophy hunters.

Yet, he can understand why some might perceive Chuck to be rather aloof as a person.

"He's hard-driven," Gerald says. "Once you get to know him, he's a good guy. He's fairly reserved and meticulous. I think that to sum it up, he is exactly what he has to be to be in the position that he's in. You couldn't be the type of guy who hunts for two or three hours and then goes and has cocktails and be in the same position. He's not the jovial guy next door who's handing you beers and slapping you on your back and is your buddy. That's not the makeup. He's what he is and that's hard-driven. They don't make a perfect man. You can't be loved by all. It's an impossibility. He's gotta have that drive, and it never seems to end. It still surprises me. The drive is still there."

CHAPTER NINE:
THE DARK CONTINENT

"Africa just has a different feel about it. I've never seen such abundant wildlife. I could go to Africa and just look at the birds for a week or two, and listen to the insects and the frogs. I don't know why, but there is more life in Africa, of every sort, than in North America. But just the sounds, the background sounds ... they're always there. That was actually more important to me than the hunting itself."

With the Super Slam completed in 1990, Chuck achieved singular success in North American bowhunting history. He had answered for himself every question about each of the continent's species.

Free to relax his focus, Chuck began to imagine international bowhunting pursuits, and the Dark Continent of Africa leaped immediately to mind. His boyhood idol, Fred Bear, had hunted there numerous times, bagging everything from an elephant to warthogs. Curious to experience any bowhunting challenges that he hadn't already encountered in North America, Chuck immediately began coordinating plans for his first African safari to occur in October 1991.

CAPE FEAR

Chuck's friend and booking agent, Ron Oliver, set up the trip to Zimbabwe with the primary goal of targeting Black Death—the Cape buffalo, one of Africa's renowned "Big Five." Along with that goal, Chuck planned to pursue various plains game. So, as he had done throughout his treks across North America, Chuck allowed himself plenty of time to do it right—a full six weeks.

Another part of doing it right involved finding the best professional hunter for the situation. With the help of Ron Oliver, Chuck teamed up with Martin Naude. Martin's experience guiding hunters in Africa ran decades deep, but the hunt with Chuck in 1991 marked his first with a bowhunter.

"About half the trip was devoted to his learning about bowhunting," Chuck says. "Martin was like some North American outfitters who haven't had bowhunters. He was openly skeptical to begin with—curious, but still skeptical. When he started to see what an arrow could do to animals he got very respectful of the equipment. And he was really digging it toward the end."

Martin enjoyed it so much, in fact, that after the hunt Chuck decided to send him a bow. Martin set it up, practiced and proceeded to arrow African game with it.

The two primary trackers assigned to the 1991 hunt were members of the Shangaan Tribe—a tribe that fashions its own primitive bows and arrows, but whose people are not allowed by the Zimbabwe government to hunt there. Chuck said that the two native trackers were so amazed by his modern equipment and Chuck's accuracy, that they began calling him "Number One Shot."

And though the waterhole hunting in 1991 proved fantastic because of the historically dry conditions, Chuck, Martin and the trackers toiled mightily trying to close ground on a Cape buffalo.

"I found Cape buffalo incredibly difficult to spot-and-stalk because lions chase them, and we were after a trophy bull," Chuck says. "We were trying to find a big one. We were in an area where most of the buffalo were kicked-out, old, single or bachelor-buddy bulls. There weren't many herds of buffalo, but there were some really big ones.

"It's really tough to sneak up on anything with more than one person," Chuck continued. "We not only had Martin and me, but we had two trackers with us all the time. Between the four of us, we just kept bumping buffalo. We'd find tracks coming off of water. I think the largest herd of buffalo we tracked was six—all bulls—and we'd track from one to 15 miles during the course of the day, trying to come up on the buffalo and see them before they'd see us. It was flat as a billiard table and pretty open. It was difficult. So I did not get a buffalo that trip. We hunted for buffalo 15 or 16 days, and I never got a shot."

Persistent as always, Chuck shrugged off the failed Cape buffalo quest. Instead of dissuading him, it inspired him and added to the African intrigue. Shortly after returning home from his 1991 adventure, he spoke again to Ron Oliver, and they began making plans for a second trip in 1992.

A Cape buffalo took precedence again in June and July of

It took two trips to Zimbabwe and three solid weeks of effort for Chuck to finally take one of Africa's "Big Five," the Cape buffalo otherwise known as "Black Death."

175

1992, but the elephant hunt outlined in Chapter Six factored significantly. Therefore, Chuck chose the same 100-pound draw bow for both the elephant and Cape buffalo. His personally customized 2317 Easton arrow included 16 inches of a 2117 shaft epoxied inside and a two-blade Zwickey Black Diamond broadhead on the front for a total arrow weight of 830 grains.

Finally, after six more days stalking Black Death—a combined 22 days of hunting in 1991 and 1992—Chuck found an opportunity to strike.

The only buffalo that Chuck and his guides were able to find consistently were traveling near the edge of the ranch between watering areas and then bedding occasionally in a small range of rocky hills. And the buffalo seemed even spookier than Chuck had remembered them being in 1991. Several mornings he and his companions heard lions roaring in the area where they looked for buffalo, and Martin surmised that the buffalo were being regularly harassed by the big cats. Locating the tracks of a herd of six bulls one morning, Chuck and Martin knew where the buffalo were headed. Sure enough, the tracks lead to the rocky range of hills.

"We got up in these big boulders, and the tracks started meandering around and they turned 45 degrees into a big rock pile to our left," Chuck says. "And then Martin saw a buffalo horn sticking up above the rocks about 100 yards away, and we all dropped to the ground. The trackers stayed back, and Martin and I circled to get the wind just right. I crawled up between boulders that were about the size of Volkswagen bugs. It was really boulder-strewn, and I peeked up over this line of boulders and I could see four buffalo feeding about 30 or 35 yards away. So I range-found the nearest one, ducked down, drew my bow and then came up on my knees at the edge of a boulder and shot him.

"I shot that buffalo angling away through both lungs. My broadhead was eight inches outside the other side of the buffalo. And I centered a rib on each side, and their ribs are big. He went about 300 yards, lay down and died.

"They don't call Cape buffalo 'Black Death' for nothing. Martin and the trackers were impressed with the job the broadhead did. But I will tell you that that buffalo lay down and died, but he didn't die quickly. That animal was double-lunged but took the better part of an hour to die. I was blown away.

176

Evolution is alive and well in Africa. The animals alive today are designed to withstand all kinds of damage imparted by big cats."

A DIFFERENT BREED

Twenty-two grueling days in pursuit of a Cape buffalo, and Chuck's hair-raising elephant encounter detailed in Chapter Six, left an indelible mark on his bowhunting life. In Africa, this talented human predator found prey supremely adapted to survive the fiercest of predators—the big cats.

Another example is the eland. These moose-sized animals proved incredibly wary. And though Chuck pursued eland from the beginning of his 1991 safari, it took him until the final week of his hunt in 1992—a full 12 weeks—to tag one. In hindsight, Chuck says that he considers the eland the most intelligent and wary African species that he hunted.

Then there's the tiny duiker, another animal that, for other reasons, tied Chuck in knots at the outset of his safari.

"I missed the first seven duiker I shot at," Chuck says. "They started calling them 'Adams deer' in the area where I hunted because I could not hit one. I was shooting a Super Slam bow that I had helped Hoyt design earlier that year, and it was deadly accurate and very quiet. But duiker are at the bottom of the food chain. They're little, dog-sized antelope and they'd come to waterholes, and you could see their sides twitch constantly. They're always wound up to jump to get away from predators.

"We were in treestands to begin with, which I found to be less effective on string-jumping animals because all the noise goes right down to the animals. We started hunting from ground blinds in 1992. Ground blinds encapsulate the noise of your bow a lot better. Animals don't jump the string as much.

"In 1991, the average duiker I shot at was probably six feet away from where the arrow hit, from distances averaging 20 yards. I never saw animals jump the string like that in my life. And I'm not making excuses. I think I was pretty much on target every time. I just couldn't hit one of those suckers. I finally decided that the way to get a duiker was to only shoot a duiker beyond 30 yards where they weren't so intimately threatened. I killed four in a row between 30 and 40 yards. That was interesting."

As Chuck mentioned, lions, leopards and cheetahs cause

177

plains game to be justifiably jumpy. Over thousands of years this has helped those species to evolve stronger hides, muscles and bones so that they might survive wounds inflicted by a superficial attack. This evolution, Chuck says, also requires that bowhunters closely scrutinize their gear before planning an African safari. Chuck took his 100-pound draw bow for the elephant and buffalo, and didn't back off dramatically in his equipment choices for plains game.

"In both '91 and '92, and again in '99, I had a bow that was drawing about 80 pounds and shooting about a 600-grain arrow," Chuck says. "I was getting about 65 foot-pounds of kinetic energy with the longer finger bow in those cases. The same gear that would take elk would easily take any plains animal in Africa, including a 2,000-pound eland. They are big, but if you hit an eland behind the shoulder, 60 or 65 foot-pounds would do it. I've been in African camps, particularly in '99, with other bowhunters shooting what are considered now to be conventional setups with very light arrows, 350-grain to 450-grain arrows, and expandable-blade broadheads. And the difference in penetration in animals was dramatic in Africa.

"In one of the camps, two of the bowhunters were shooting Easton's really fine A/C/C arrows which were mainly designed for tournament shooting. They were getting very high speeds, 280 to 300 fps, and shooting small fixed-blade broadheads or, in one case, mechanical broadheads. Those guys, between the two of them, probably shot 25 to 30 animals, and I can't think of a case where the arrow went all the way through. They were shooting draw weights heavier than mine with kinetic energies higher than mine.

"By comparison, I was shooting heavier arrows and a more friction-free broadhead with a cutting nose, the Super Slam, and I shot through the majority of my animals. It was a dramatic comparison about what penetrates best and what doesn't. I'm not saying that those guys weren't bagging their animals, but their animals were going farther with less blood on the ground to trail. And they were videotaping their hunts, so we could watch and see. One guy shot a really nice sable antelope, which I think was probably a 500-pound or 600-pound animal, broadside. Half the arrow was still sticking out the entry side. The only problem with my sable was finding my arrow in the mud on the

This huge 58-inch kudu is one of 16 species and 69 individual animals that Chuck collected during three separate trips to Africa in the 1990s.

other side of the waterhole after it zipped right through.

"It's advice that most of the bowhunting consultants and booking agents also give. Shoot heavier equipment—both heavier arrows and higher kinetic energy—and don't shoot mechanical broadheads over there. I think every booking agent I know recommends against mechanicals in Africa. The average animal over there is twice as big as a deer."

WHY AFRICA?

Whereas Chuck embarked on Super Slam as a quest toward variety and credibility as an outdoor writer and bowhunter, he didn't need Africa for the same reasons. Instead, it harbored legend and intrigue that he desired mostly for personal motivations.

Sure, other notable bowhunters had been there, and Chuck's absence from the African hunting scene could have been regarded by some as a question mark on his credentials. But Chuck regarded Africa as an escape; a place where he could reflect on and savor Super Slam far from all the attention surrounding it. And, most of all, he could bowhunt in a place that offers unparalleled opportunity.

During his first two African safaris in 1991 and '92, Chuck bagged 52 African big game animals. Hunting with his father in 1999, he added 17 more for a total of 69. More than 20 of those were impala antelope that had become overpopulated on the particular ranch where Chuck hunted. The ranch managers culled approximately 3,000 impala annually in an attempt to control the numbers. By the time that he left for Africa, Chuck had already arrowed a lot of North American game. But the African adventure helped to hone his skills even further.

CHUCK'S AFRICAN SAFARI SPECIES

duiker antelope	klipspringer	bush buck
impala	(antelope)	gemsbok
warthog	kudu	hartebeest
zebra	tsesebe	water buck
wildebeest	bush pig	eland
sable	Cape buffalo	

In 1999 Chuck took Pop along to experience the African adventures that he'd fallen in love with in 1991 and 1992.

"I don't know that many bowhunters who've shot 69 animals with a bow in North America in their whole life," Chuck says. "To shoot that many animals taught me even better to pick a spot and aim. It certainly calmed my nerves. I think every time that you shoot an animal, you get calmer when you're close to the next animal. You can aim more steadily and be more clearheaded about it. I learned a lot about equipment, too.

"My favorite form of hunting is not stand hunting, and I had the good fortune to shoot about a third of those animals on those trips from the ground. Because Martin was not very adept at the bowhunting game, he wanted to stay back behind me a bit. I would sneak along the Chiredzi River where there was some relief to the ground. I shot my second-biggest kudu, a nice bushbuck and a number of other animals on the ground. That made it really rewarding for me because I like to hunt on foot."

The implications of shooting so many animals should not be underestimated. While it is true that the shot itself is a fraction of the entire bowhunting equation, the successful culmination of any hunt ultimately rests there. Yes, you must know the game. Yes, you must plan your stalk or your ambush perfectly.

But without the shooting experience gained through encounters

181

on live game, all that comes before might be for naught. A measure of control during the moment of truth comes only after a bowhunter has been there many times. Africa helped do that for Chuck.

TRACKING TRAINING

Africa also set the stage for Chuck's introductory training in the art of tracking. The two trackers assisting Chuck and Martin had practiced this skill all their lives. In Africa, children are responsible for finding individual animals from their parents' herd of goats or cows. When the animals wander off in different directions, it's their responsibility to recognize each individual track, track those animals down and get them back to the corral at night so that the lions or hyenas don't nab the valuable animal.

When you grow up with that, the way Chuck grew up with hunting, you get incredibly good at it.

"I learned so much in Africa about tracking," Chuck says. "It's not something that's really practiced much in North America—partly because of the nature of the soil. In Africa, the soil's almost always soft and trackable. In a lot of places in North America, like the average whitetail woods, the ground is covered with leaves and grass, and tracking is virtually impossible. But if you work at it, in a lot of places you can track animals, both arrow-hit animals and healthy animals.

"My world record buffalo from the Kaibab Plateau of northern Arizona that I shot in April of 2000 is an example. I tracked that animal, as near as we could calculate, more than 10 miles from the very crack of dawn until just before dark. I could never have done that if I hadn't tracked buffalo with my professional hunter in Africa. It was very similar. The tracks were similar, the techniques of telling what's fresh and what's not are similar. When I went hunting buffalo, I would have been a total duck out of water if it hadn't been for Africa.

"The tracking advice that I would give applies to all of bowhunting, and it is this: Become the animal if you can. The best trackers I know try to get inside the head of the animal and look at more than the evidence on the ground. They try to anticipate where the animal is going the same if you were trying to figure out the end of a mystery novel. Animals are somewhat predictable.

"Then learn how to read tracks. Learn what a fresh track looks like in a particular area. An area like where I hunted buffalo, where the wind blows all the time and where the soil is sandy and soft, the tracks get soft-edged within a few hours and don't have any sheen to them in the bottom of the track. In other areas the difference between old tracks and new tracks is largely how much debris has fallen in them, whether there are little insect trails in the base of the track, and whether the color of the track is the same as surrounding soil.

"Those are all real valuable things to learn. I'll never be as good a tracker as the trackers in Africa. But I bowhunt as much or more than anybody I know, and that experience makes me a better bowhunter."

AFRICA REMEMBERED

Despite the practical experience that his African hunts have yielded, Chuck maintains that he did not go there to utilize it as a proving ground. He also asserts that he returned to North America with much more than the many trophies.

"I fell in love with Africa," Chuck says. "What I like most about Africa is not the hunting. It's the wildlife and a culture halfway around the world. I went and saw the Great Zimbabwe Ruins and had a great time bartering with native craftsmen at roadside bizarres. It is a wild and free place compared to North America.

"Africa just has a different feel about it, and I've never seen such abundant wildlife. I could go to Africa and just look at the birds for a week or two, and listen to the insects and the frogs. I don't know why, but there is more life in Africa, of every sort, than in North America. But just the sounds, the background sounds. They're always there. That was actually more important to me than the hunting itself. And it's less expensive per animal taken than if you hunt with an outfitter in North America. Joanne went with me on both trips (1991 and 1992) and she want-ed to move to Africa, she loved it so much.

"I would highly recommend Africa. But I also tell people that I prefer to hunt North America. I would rather hunt one animal for 10 days than shoot 10 animals in 10 days. Now, if I lived there and had the chance to concentrate on specific species, like a big kudu, or if I could hunt a giant impala or something, then I'd probably be on the same track that I'm on in North America."

183

CHAPTER TEN: **THE RECORD BOOKS**

"In my experience, I regard the detractors as coyotes. They're slinking around the edges. They don't have the balls to do it to my face because they know their arguments don't hold water. So they're just sniping when they can take a free shot."

A round 1980, just about the time Super Slam became a twinkle in Chuck's eye, he faced an ugly, no-win situation. He'd been writing for outdoor magazines for nearly a decade and had shared with readers numerous accounts of record-class big game animals that he had taken with archery gear.

Many of the animals were large enough to qualify for the Pope and Young (P&Y) Club's record books. But Chuck hadn't bothered to enter any. At the time, he didn't see any need. He hadn't ever met anyone at the club and didn't really consider P&Y entries necessary for his career. Chuck knew that he'd taken the animals fair and square, and figured he didn't require a listing in a book to legitimize the kills for everyone else.

His naivete was revealed, however, when Pope and Young Club members began to approach him occasionally making snide comments like, "Where are all these big animals you've supposedly shot?" The assertion, a position that pervades the club's ranks today, was that if it's not in the book, it's not real. Of course, the club charges a fee for every animal entered. So entries satisfy their financial peace of mind, too.

Chuck finally caved in to the pressure, seeking to quash any debate about whether he should be taken seriously. In one fell swoop he entered every contending animal—dozens of them— that he'd ever taken. But instead of resolving the issue with the doubters, it caused a backlash that remains today—a stigma that Chuck will never shake. The same people who had whispered veiled disbelief about whether Chuck was legit and deserved the recognition that he was attaining, later attacked him as an egotistical hotdog for having the gall to enter so many record-book animals. How dare he rub their noses in it?

The perceived attempt to make a mockery of the venerable Pope and Young Club made Chuck an instant target for some club members. The club couldn't refuse his entries without proof that he'd violated a game law or fair chase ethic, but they certainly didn't have to embrace Chuck as one of their own.

RE-COUNT ACCOUNTS

In 1993, *Bowhunter* magazine published an article quoting P&Y President Fred Asbell, challenging the number of record entries that Myles Keller and Chuck were claiming in press releases issued by the companies that they represented at the time. Chuck says that an innocent transposition of numbers—a 45 mistakenly turned into a 54—in the press release caused all the fuss. He adds that he never had the chance to review the release before it was mailed to a number of hunting publications. *Bowhunter* seized the error and published "Pope and Young Hyperbole" in response to the erroneous press releases.

"*Bowhunter* took me to task without ever calling or writing me," Chuck says. "They basically said, 'We think this is terrible. These people should be more responsible.' And it pissed me off. They never bothered to contact me, and I've always thought that they should have been more professional about that. Since that time, I've told everyone who I work with that those kinds of things, I suppose, are inevitable. But it smelled of sour grapes to me."

In 1996, *Outdoor Life*, the magazine that Chuck had revered and read religiously as a young boy, accepted and published one of Chuck's articles, a feature titled, "In The Grizzly Zone." Curiously, the magazine went out of its way to publish an editor's note that on the surface appeared to offer readers an account of Chuck's impressive credentials. Below the surface, however, it inexplicably called those credentials into question.

Again, the issue revolved around the number of official P&Y animals that Chuck owned. Chuck had counted his P&Y certificates and forwarded that number to *Outdoor Life*, which later turned around and called club headquarters to confirm the number. When P&Y told *Outdoor Life*, however, that the number of animals actually listed in the book was less than the number given by Chuck, *Outdoor Life* played on the discrepancy and then insincerely dismissed it by saying something like, "Who cares?"

185

The damage had been done, and the *Outdoor Life* editors knew it.

Again, instead of calling Chuck to ask about the difference, the magazine's editors assumed that he was exaggerating. Apparently, though, they didn't realize that record-book minimums increase from time to time and that some animals, like velvet-antlered entries, are placed in one book and not published again. The animals still count. Chuck had the certificates to prove that he was right, but it was too late.

"That irritated me," Chuck says. "It was like an intentional slam. I don't know why they did that. They were wrong. I was right. But they cast a doubt on my integrity, I thought, in that article. It almost was like they were thinking, 'Let's take this guy down a peg or two.' I never did quite understand what that was all about."

'ELITE' COMPANY

Asbell, president of P&Y for approximately 18 years beginning in 1984, presided over the adversarial relationship that Chuck has had at times with the record-keeping organization since his first entries more than two decades ago. Far from being friends, Chuck and Asbell are about as far apart philosophically as two bowhunters could be. And there is the fundamental reason for the record-book rift. The club accepts animals taken with compound bows—it knows that it must to survive—but Asbell and a few of his fellow members are stickbow shooters who openly disdain compound bows and any other "high-tech gadgets" that they deem unfit.

Chuck recalls a telephone conversation that he once had with Asbell. Chuck claims that during that conversation Asbell openly opined that stickbow shooters are more skilled than those who choose compound bows.

In the Summer 2001, issue of the club's newsletter, Asbell's "President's Column" offered a defense for prior comments that he had made about bowhunters being an "elite" group compared to hunters who choose to hunt with firearms. In the article, he didn't draw distinctions between bowhunters, but he clearly conveyed his belief that one way, his way, was more honorable than other hunting methods. When asked about the telephone comments that Chuck claims, Asbell laughed and categorically denied them.

"That's absolutely not true," Asbell says. "Chuck and I had an argument about some things. First off, I would never say that because it isn't true. In some way, it could be what he thinks he heard. I would say at this moment, and I'm sure that what I would have said in any conversation with him, is that I know many very, very talented bowhunters who shoot traditional equipment. I also know very many who shoot compound bows. If anything like that has been taken out of context, the only thing I can say is that's not true. I would never have said that, period.

"I think that a lot of people have assumed that because I've been a traditionalist for a long time, that I'm completely opposed to (compound bows) and that's completely untrue," Asbell continues. "I don't care for them, personally. The problem is that it seems to be an item that can be improved almost to infinity, and that I don't think has been good for us. When equipment gets to the point where human effort is almost eliminated, then you have to start saying, 'Hey, I don't know if this is really what we ought to be doing.' But whether a guy is shooting a bow that I think is pretty or not is sort of silly. So it really is a philosophical thing."

Asbell, hunting editor of the magazine at the time, also says that he wasn't responsible for the news piece in *Bowhunter* that attacked Chuck over his number of record-book animals.

"There were a couple of people, including Chuck, who were spending an awful lot of time advertising that they had more animals in Pope and Young than anybody else," Asbell says. "The (P&Y) board of directors, for whom I work, decided that what we should do is write a letter to those people and say that what you're saying is not true. ... And, so, I wrote them a letter. And, again, I'm not trying to step out from under it, but it was at the direction of the Pope and Young Club. Chuck took great offense to it.

"The editor of *Bowhunter* magazine (M. R. James) took that (letter)—unfortunately, he was on our board of directors—and made a news item out of it which was really totally unacceptable. And he sort of tied it back to me with the statement in the article that said, 'Not so, says Fred Asbell.'

"The letter to Chuck and the other bowhunter (Keller) who were kind of arguing about who was the greatest, was intended to be private. ... So all of it fell back on me, and they decided that I was the evil guy. I guess that comes with the territory.

187

"I have never suspected that Chuck was anything but a really tremendous bowhunter. I understand advertising hype, but, you know, the guy who's killed the most, I don't know, there's something that sort of gets caught in my throat about that. ... I don't think anyone's intention was ever to say Chuck Adams is a bad guy, but the numbers and things that they were saying at the time, as well as I remember, were inaccurate."

Chuck and Keller both deny arguing about anything, particularly who is best with a bow. "Myles is clearly the white-tailed deer king," Chuck says. "Who can dispute that?" Both men also say that they never received a letter from Asbell or anyone else about the numbers in the press releases. The first time that they say they saw the complaint was when it was published in *Bowhunter* magazine.

One could dismiss all of these antics, were the jealousy among these grown adults not so painfully obvious. Consider the fact that, regardless of the accuracy of the number in the press release, P&Y needed Chuck Adams, and Chuck needed the club. Both parties have benefitted immeasurably from one another. What should have been a powerful partnership—one aimed at growing and celebrating bowhunting—instead deteriorated into a power struggle.

In any other business, in any sport, Chuck would have been placed on a pedestal in an effort to garner support from the general public. Instead, P&Y sought to discredit him over petty jealousies. And without the complete support of P&Y, others began to take pot shots.

POSING A THREAT

Chuck shared a piece of mail that he received from a fellow bowhunter. The envelope included the first Easton ad in which Chuck appeared. The person had drawn a bull's eye on Chuck's forehead with an arrow sticking in it and attached a nasty note filled with name-calling and profanity.

"I got worried for Joanne," Chuck says. "We were living in Montana at the time. This was right after I got the Grand Slam (of sheep). I took this to the FBI. They considered it a death threat. But later the FBI said, 'You know, we think this guy is a harmless nut.'" Chuck says that he knows who the person is—a

Here's the photo from the first Easton arrow ad in which Chuck appeared during the late 1980s. The ad helped Chuck's stature but also made him a target.

former P&Y senior member—and that he's another guy with a compound bow-sized chip on his shoulder.

Yet another "traditional" archer cornered Chuck at about the same time at the Cantina La Cocina restaurant in Montana where Chuck used to go to get a bite to eat and unwind after long hours writing in his office.

"I was in there, closed my briefcase, went out the front door, and somebody behind me said, 'Are you Chuck Adams?' And I said, 'Yeah, how you doin'?'

"He just walked right up and got right in my face and said, 'You SOB, you've done more bad for bowhunting than anybody in the industry. You commercialize our sport, and that's bad for our sport. You high-profile guys are prostituting yourselves and making money on our sport, and it should be pure. We old-guard guys stand for pure bowhunting.'

"And it was one of the few times in my life where I was startled and I said the right thing. I said, 'Who do think you are to interrupt a peaceful evening that I'm having? ... How dare you get in my face! I'm making a living like anybody else and I have a right to do what I do and I really don't care what you think.' And I said, 'Who are you anyway?'

"Finally, he fled back into the restaurant. He threatened later to burn down the restaurant. He kept drinking with his friends, and my friend, Carole Dickson, who owns the restaurant told me they had him thrown out. But it ruined my day. That's the only time in my whole career that one of my detractors has said anything negative to my face, and I doubt that he would have if he had been sober.

"In my experience, I regard the detractors as coyotes. They're slinking around the edges. They don't have the balls to do it to my face, partly because I don't think their arguments hold water, and they know that. So they're just sniping when they can take a free shot."

CONFLICTING AGENDAS

Particularly puzzling is another strange ingredient at the center of the conflict between Chuck and some of those people with Pope and Young.

While the archery industry is focused on increasing participation and is spending millions of dollars to fund initiatives toward that end, some P&Y members believe that less is more. Wanting more animals and more space for themselves, some of the traditionalists disdain compound bows, crossbows and other equipment that increases enjoyment and helps to bring more people into the sport. They think that since technology is the antithesis of tradition, it must be bad.

Similarly, some of these same people dislike suburban archery-only deer hunts. They believe that if archery is perceived as an effective big game management tool that it will cease to be regarded as the ancient, ultimate hunting challenge. And if that happens, they argue, liberal access to archery tags and long bowhunting seasons might be tightened.

It is a difficult rationale to follow, and, to be fair, it is not the type of logic that all P&Y members and leaders subscribe to. Many, in fact, are attempting to bring P&Y more in line with the times. However, it is apparent that some "old guard" traditionalists still wish to separate themselves from the general bowhunting population. They think that they are different, better, elite.

"I read a really good article a while back in a health magazine about aggression," Chuck says. "The author said that everybody's always thought that the people who are insecure are the most aggressive. But he said that he's convinced that people who are most aggressive have superiority complexes. They're elitists. He said that he's not talking about confident people. He said that confident people are less aggressive. But he said that the people with the highest opinion of themselves are the most aggressive. And I immediately thought about the elitist bowhunters who are always sniping at other people. I really think that they feel that they're superior.

"Some people who I know in the archery industry regard Pope and Young as severely behind the times and almost irrelevant at this point. And I don't think some of those folks in the club even realize that. The older guard, they regard themselves as the elite. And the rest of the archery world has just buzzed by them. Some of the elitists don't want anybody else in the woods, but don't realize that without numbers we're in trouble. Fred Bear told me, 'I've been hammered by the same people, a number of detractors in Pope and Young.' When he quit being a threat, then he was put on a pedestal. It's Papa Bear. Now he's idolized."

THE ISHI AWARD

One wonders why, given the animosity from some quarters, Chuck would continue entering his animals in the P&Y books and supporting the organization financially and through the endless promotion that he has provided in magazine articles. He knew, however, that despite the discord, he couldn't afford to turn his back. Super Slam had proven the value of confirmed, legitimized big game trophies. Much of Chuck's status as a hunter, and thereby his career, rested on his trophy hunting accomplishments.

There was another, perhaps more important reason that Chuck continued to send in his annual P&Y membership dues and tout the club in his writings.

"Some of the best people I know belong to Pope and Young," Chuck says. "Some have had or still hold leadership roles. And I think that people like them actually comprise the majority of the membership. When I thought about good friends like Jim Dougherty, M. R. James, Dr. Dave Samuel, Randy Byers, Stan Rauch, Glenn Hisey, Kevin Hisey, Billy Ellis, Dwight Schuh, Larry D. Jones, Neil Summers, Myles Keller, Judy Kovar and others who I'd come to know and admire, I simply could not turn my back on the club."

And there was another purpose for all the entries, a dream that he kept deep inside—one every bit as big as the Super Slam.

While wearing out the pages of *Outdoor Life* reading about his hunting heroes, Chuck had learned about Ishi, the last of the Yahi. Fred Bear had talked about him. Chuck knew that Saxton Pope and Art Young had applied many of Ishi's teachings to modern archery. And when Chuck finally entered all of those animals in the P&Y book early in his career, he learned about the club's Ishi Award. But as he learned more about the prestige surrounding the award—the fact that an Ishi Award wasn't even presented at every convention—Chuck knew that the odds of him ever holding one of his own were slim. He might as well dream about killing a new world record typical elk.

In 1986, Chuck attained his first Pope and Young world record with one of the many Sitka blacktails that he'd eventually tag on Kodiak Island. When the P&Y convention rolled around the following year, the one that would recognize the deer as the new world record, Chuck didn't attend, throwing gasoline on the fire. Chuck says that he had a business conflict crop up late in the game and that his absence from the banquet couldn't be avoided. Yet, the perceived snub infuriated some P&Y members.

Chuck went to three conventions after that one and says that

The new world record mountain caribou that Chuck tagged in the Northwest Territories in 1995 failed to earn an Ishi Award at the 1997 P&Y convention in Edmonton.

the chill was unmistakable.

"I felt shunned at all three by some members," Chuck says. "Friends who attended felt the chill, too, and asked me why I bothered. And after Edmonton (1997), I said, 'I'm not going back.'"

In 1995, Chuck had tagged his third world record animal of his career, a huge mountain caribou from the Northwest Territories that easily eclipsed the previous world record which

193

had stood since 1978. The 413% bull had been the result of dili-
gent discipline to set a new benchmark in that category. For 10
years, Chuck went to Canada's Northwest Territories seeking to
break the world record. He turned down countless record-book
animals searching for that special bull.

So, to that point in his career, Chuck was staring, at the 1997
Edmonton convention, at his best chance ever to achieve what in
his mind was bowhunting's highest honor—the Ishi Award.

"The Ishi Award description says that it's given to an outstanding animal," Chuck says. "I was told that I had a good crack
at getting an Ishi Award at Edmonton. They didn't give one. And
they don't give one every time, but they had at almost every convention up until then. And it (mountain caribou) was a record
that had stood for 17 years, and a lot of my friends grumbled
about that."

Chuck skipped the 1999 convention as he vowed he would,
but something happened in 2000 that made him realize that
he'd have to swallow his pride and risk defeat in front of his
peers again. Against all odds, Chuck found the huge bull elk that
had haunted his dreams since September 1999. Several months
after shooting it on Sept. 16, 2000, official P&Y scorer Stan Rauch
painstakingly taped the bull at 411% typical, giving Chuck almost
8 inches of margin over the standing record of 404%. The incredible elk, his fifth world record, made his world record Arizona
buffalo, taken in spring 2000, almost an afterthought.

The P&Y convention was scheduled for April 26-28, and a couple of weeks before the convention, Chuck still wondered if he
ought to risk showing up despite the nationwide buzz about the
elk. Doubling the risk was the fact that he had succumbed to the
urging of some P&Y members like his friends Glenn Hisey, M. R.
James and Jim Dougherty to finally apply for regular membership into the club. Each application for regular membership is
put to a vote. Chuck didn't consider the membership nor the Ishi
Award a shoo-in. In fact, he held serious doubts.

"My big elk has the very best chance of any animal I've ever
shot," Chuck said in early April 2000. "The animal is the most
qualified for an Ishi Award for an outstanding animal. Then they
take into account the hunt and the situation, and the hunter.
And I'm betting that I'm not going to get the Ishi Award again.

Young Chuck takes a break from bowhunting to search out Ishi arrowheads in California's Deer Creek country.

Maybe I'm preparing myself for disappointment. In my mind looking at all the Ishi Awards over the years, this thing should be a slam-dunk given the fact that it's an elk. I'm betting that I'll be passed over. I hope I'm wrong."

If not?

"Suspicions confirmed," Chuck said. "I'm not going to sweat it. The Ishi Award would be really neat because I grew up in Ishi Country. And it's a big, long obsidian arrowhead on a beautiful plaque. And that would be nifty to have. But, considering the source, I'm not going to worry about it. And if I get it, I'm going to consider it a triumph of good over evil. And possibly the fact that I finally applied for regular membership could be a factor."

Maybe it was appropriate that Chuck's mountain caribou didn't earn an Ishi Award in 1997. Seated at the 2001 P&Y convention in Salt Lake City amongst 30 or so friends, many of them from Hoyt and Easton, Chuck calmed his nerves by telling himself that the Ishi Award probably wouldn't happen. He'd used the same technique in the field when tailing the Montana elk herd like a wolf. Full-speed, fully focused, fully attuned to everything happening around him, yet cooling the anticipation with a dose of doubt. It had worked throughout his bowhunting career, calming him when the moment of truth arrived, as if unexpected.

Asbell stood at the microphone. Chuck's elk and bison were two of five world records being recognized at this convention. The other three included a desert sheep, a pronghorn and an extraordinary bighorn sheep that Chuck considered his stiffest competition for the coveted obsidian arrowhead.

Asbell started to speak about the Ishi Award revealing that the 15th Ishi Award ever bestowed would be in one lucky hunter's hands within minutes. ... "And we're giving it to the big Yellowstone elk that scores 409⅞," Asbell announced.

"It was truly special because I had a cheering section of friends from Hoyt and Easton," Chuck says. "There was a bighorn sheep taken in Alberta that was also a truly exceptional animal that beat the old record by eight or nine points. And I guess the debate, I found out later, was between my elk and that sheep. I would not have wanted to make that decision. So I was shocked."

"He is living up to the people he looked up to," Chuck's sister Becky says recognizing the impact of the Ishi Award on Chuck and his family. "I mean, he read everything he could from Fred Bear, and Ishi was just amazing to Chuck. So for him to get that Ishi Award, I just started crying because I thought, 'Wow, that just really means something to him.'"

The membership? Approved. Four years after swearing off Pope and Young conventions for good, Chuck went two-for-two and is now a regular member of the club that in some ways was his arch rival for many years. M. R. James, a member of the Pope and Young Club, talked to Chuck leading up to the convention and knew that the application for membership was making Chuck especially uneasy.

"Chuck wanted to support the Pope and Young Club for some time, but he didn't apply for regular membership because he was worried about being turned down," James says. "He said that he just couldn't in his mind handle that kind of rejection from America's prestigious record-keeping organization. And I said, 'I don't think that's going to happen.' There were a few dissenting votes, but I told him there's no one who applies for regular membership who doesn't get some 'no' votes."

Chuck with his own Ishi Award—something that he dreamed of holding since his first P&Y entries decades ago.

ISHI AWARDS HISTORY

Non-typical white-tailed deer, 279⅞; 4th recording period (1963-64); taken in Nebraska by Del Austin (1962).

Typical white-tailed deer, 204⅘; 6th recording period (1967-68); taken in Illinois by Mel Johnson (1965).

Bighorn sheep, 176⅜; 7th recording period (1969-70); taken in Montana by Ray Alt (1968).

Barren ground caribou, 446⅝; 8th recording period (1971-72); taken in Alaska by Art Kragness (1970).

Alaska-Yukon moose, 248⅝; 9th recording period (1973-74); taken in Alaska by Dr. Michael Cusak (1973).

Columbia black-tailed deer, $172\frac{2}{8}$; 11th recording period (1977-78); taken in Oregon by B.G. Shurtleff (1969).

Black bear, $22\frac{4}{16}$; 12th recording period (1979-80); taken in Colorado by Ray Cox (1978).

Mountain lion, $15\frac{11}{16}$; 13th recording period (1981-82); taken in Idaho by Jerry James (1982).

Typical mule deer, $203\frac{1}{8}$; 14th recording period (1983-84); taken in Colorado by Bill Barcus (1979).

Dall sheep, $164\frac{5}{8}$; 15th recording period (1985-86); taken in the Northwest Territories by Gary Laya (1986).

Non-typical Yellowstone elk, $419\frac{5}{8}$; 16th recording period (1987-88); taken in Arizona by James L. Ludvigson (1985).

Non-typical Columbia black-tailed deer, $194\frac{4}{8}$; 17th recording period (1989-90); taken in Oregon by James Decker (1988).

Canada moose, $222\frac{1}{8}$; 18th recording period (1991-92); taken in Quebec by Charles Roy (1988).

Pronghorn, $90\frac{6}{8}$; 19th recording period (1993-94); taken in Oregon by Roger W. Clarno (1993).

Typical Yellowstone Elk, $409\frac{2}{8}$; 22nd recording period (1999-00); taken in Montana by Chuck Adams (2000).

FORGIVE AND FORGET?

Now that Chuck is officially part of the Pope and Young Club's upper membership, it's difficult for him to detail the long-standing feud that he had with the organization. He's more careful and calculated in his P&Y portrayal compared to the weeks leading up to the 2001 convention. He knows who to avoid within the organization. And instead of resigning himself to P&Y being irrelevant, he holds out hope that he can effect positive change.

The same goes for his relationship with *Bowhunter* magazine. Despite the checkered history, Chuck pursued a columnist position with the publication for nearly 10 years, due in large part to his friendships with founder, M. R. James; publisher, Jeff Waring; and editor Dwight Schuh. As of early 2000, he hadn't gotten anywhere.

But a year later, he began writing "Huntin' Big Game," finally landing a regular gig with the magazine. *Bowhunter* staffers say that the column is quite popular with readers and that they're thrilled to have Chuck on board. Incidentally, Fred Asbell is no longer affiliated with the magazine.

For someone who the traditionalists say is consumed by pride and ego, it's surprising that Chuck's been able to put the past behind him and to move forward with what's best for his career. Some high-profile hunters would have scorned P&Y and *Bowhunter* forever, even if they came crawling to have the world record elk in their book or the column in their magazine. Instead, Chuck realizes that there's more to be gained by setting philosophy and grudges aside.

As it stands now, he says, "Things are changing with P&Y. Some of the best people I know are in Pope and Young." Chuck certainly means that about some of his friends in the Club. The others? Well, if you don't have anything good to say about somebody, don't say anything at all.

Life in the record books is more civil today than it used to be for Chuck. But a valid question begs to be answered. Asbell raised it earlier in this chapter, wondering why it's important who killed the most. And that raises even more questions. Does P&Y animal number 112 really matter at this point to Chuck's career? What's left to prove? Why keep entering? Is it only to bolster his ego and to put more space between him and second place? If record-book entries become one's prime mover, then is the animal devalued and disrespected?

Chuck, of course, doesn't look at it that way. He is proud of his record-book animals, but he insists that the entries are an afterproduct of his hunting ambition and passion. He is moved to bowhunt, he says. He admits that he is also moved to heighten the challenge by pursuing the finest trophy representatives of the species. He makes no apology for entering 111 animals in the books, for planning to enter number 112 someday soon, and for continuing to shoot for huge animals. He says that he eats wild game year-round, gives a lot of it to family and friends and then empties his freezer annually donating what's left to charity.

"I believe in record books and setting a benchmark," Chuck says. "I love to look through the list and see where the biggest mountain caribou came from. I've suggested to a couple of people at Pope and Young to take the hunters' names out of the book. Well, that didn't go over well at all. Everybody wants his name by the animal. It's to my advantage to have my name in there, too.

ANOTHER BOOK, ANOTHER 189 RECORDS

The other large record-keeping organization for bowhunters is Safari Club International. Chuck says that he has had no political problems with that group and supports it for the same basic reasons why he supports P&Y.

Chuck has more animals entered in SCI than any other archer in history—189 at last count. These include African species and categories like javelina and non-native imports to North America like wild boar, blackbuck and auodad.

In 1993 Chuck was inducted into the SCI Bowhunters Hall of Honor, joining a select few that include Fred Bear, Jim Dougherty and Chuck Saunders. The 47-pound bronze and walnut trophy commemorating that induction sits beside his Ishi Award in a prominent place in his office.

"I know that anti-hunters are down on trophy hunting. But I don't make any apologies for it," Chuck says. "Why should I apologize for not shooting the first critter that walks by when I can wait and run a much higher risk of not filling my tag? It makes no sense to me to knock trophy hunting when all I'm doing is limiting myself. And then when I do take an animal, if it's a trophy animal, that animal has already bred a bunch of cows or does and has left his genetic imprint on the population. So I think it's an honorable thing to do. And I do it for challenge. I trophy hunt not to hang something on the wall and brag about it. It goes back to why I started bowhunting. I can hunt more and kill less."

CHUCK'S POPE AND YOUNG CLUB ENTRIES

Columbia black-tailed deer (typical)
1977, 90%, California
1979, 93%, California
1982, 106%, California
1982, 104%, California
1983, 94%, California

Columbia black-tailed deer (typical velvet antlers)
1970, 99%, California
1977, 109%, California

Canada moose
1976, 164%, British Columbia

Alaska-Yukon moose
1978, 173%, Alaska
1990, 186%, Northwest Territories
1993, 195%, Northwest Territories

200

Mule deer (typical)
1979, 153 3/8, Montana
1996, 158 0/8, Montana
1997, 150 1/8, Montana
1998, 157 0/8, Montana
1999, 148 1/8, Alberta
2000, 152 5/8, Montana
2001, 167 3/8, Montana

Mule deer (non-typical)
1998, 203 0/8, Alberta
2001, 175 6/8, Alberta

Rocky Mountain goat
1979, 44 4/8, British Columbia

Yellowstone elk (typical)
1982, 349 0/8, New Mexico
1985, 277 0/8, Montana
1990, 282 1/8, California
1991, 309 1/8, New Mexico
1994, 331 5/8, Montana
1995, 304 4/8, Montana
1996, 305 2/8, Montana
1997, 282 6/8, Montana
1998, 316 6/8, Montana
1999, 357 4/8, Montana
2000, 409 2/8, Montana
2001, 367 7/8, Montana

Black bear
1982, 18 2/16, Montana

Barren ground caribou
1983, 392 2/8, Alaska
1984, 396 6/8, Alaska

Sitka black-tailed deer
1984, 77 2/8, Alaska
1984, 94 7/8, Alaska
1986, 91 4/8, Alaska
1986, 92 0/8, Alaska
1986, 107 6/8, Alaska
1986, 108 4/8, Alaska
1986, 97 2/8, Alaska
1987, 107 4/8, Alaska
1987, 103 5/8, Alaska
1987, 93 3/8, Alaska
1994, 89 3/8, Alaska
1994, 89 2/8, Alaska
1994, 76 7/8, Alaska
1995, 99 2/8, Alaska
1996, 102 1/8, Alaska
1996, 80 7/8, Alaska
1996, 89 0/8, Alaska
1996, 89 0/8, Alaska
1997, 93 2/8, Alaska
1997, 94 1/8, Alaska
1997, 89 3/8, Alaska
1997, 86 1/8, Alaska
1998, 89 2/8, Alaska
1998, 86 7/8, Alaska
1998, 98 5/8, Alaska
1998, 89 4/8, Alaska
1984, 71 3/8, **Note:** Below current minimum, but qualified and earned a P&Y certificate. Published in P&Y 4th edition book (1993).

Mountain caribou (velvet)
1985, 374 7/8,
Northwest Territories

Mountain caribou
1990, 373 2/8,
Northwest Territories (NWT)
1992, 328 3/8, NWT
1993, 347 1/8, NWT
1995, 413 6/8, NWT

Dall sheep
1985, 141 5/8, NWT
1995, 151 1/8, NWT

Stone sheep
1985, 152 3/8, British Columbia
Bighorn sheep
1985, 171 7/8, Alberta
Bison
1986, 106 6/8, Utah
2000, 118 0/8, Arizona
2000, 102 2/8, Arizona
Desert sheep
1986, 141 2/8, Arizona
Shiras moose
1987, 144 3/8, Utah
Woodland caribou
1988, 286 4/8, Newfoundland
Grizzly bear
1988, 20 10/16, British Columbia
Coues' deer (typical)
1988, 67 4/8, Arizona
1989, 110 5/8, Arizona
1989, 75 2/8, Arizona
2000, 82 2/8, Mexico
2000, 97 6/8, Mexico
Quebec-Labrador caribou
1989, 359 3/8, Quebec
1991, 339 7/8, Quebec
1996, 363 6/8, Quebec
1996, 343 2/8, Quebec
1999, 326 7/8, Quebec
1989, 309 2/8, Quebec, **Note:** Below current minimum, but qualified and earned a P&Y certificate. Published in P&Y 4th edition book (1993).
1990, 322 7/8, Quebec, **Note:** below current minimum, but qualified and earned a P&Y certificate. Published in P&Y 4th edition book (1993).

Alaska brown bear
1989, 27 1/16, Alaska
White-tailed deer (typical)
1992, 130 5/8, Texas
1993, 147 3/8, Texas
1994, 134 6/8, Texas
1997, 128 6/8, Texas
1997, 142 2/8, Texas
1997, 130 7/8, Texas
1998, 136 5/8, Texas
Pronghorn
1993, 72 4/8, Colorado
1994, 70 2/8, Colorado
1995, 70 0/8, Colorado
1996, 71 2/8, Colorado
1997, 74 0/8, Colorado
1997, 76 0/8, Montana
1998, 67 6/8, Colorado
1999, 72 0/8, Montana
2000, 71 0/8, Colorado
2000, 74 2/8, Montana
Central Canada barren ground caribou
2000, 316 7/8, Northwest Territories
2000, 358 6/8, Northwest Territories

***Note:* Current and former world records in *bold*.**

CHAPTER ELEVEN:
A GIFT FROM GOD?

"I can honestly say that I don't ever doubt my ability to do it. I mean, I started out doubting when I first started bowhunting. But I can honestly say now that I practice so hard in the off-season and get my gear so right ... I know I'm fallible, but I don't have insecurities floating about in my head. ... I'm very confident."

How can anyone be that good? It is a central question in this book because it is asked almost every time that Chuck Adams is mentioned in conversation. But at this point, if you believe what the guides and outfitters have said in Chapter 8 about Chuck's hunting ability, and accept the facts of the record book entries and world records all being legitimate, the question takes on new meaning.

Chuck regularly checks his equipment to make sure that it is perfect. From there, he can concentrate fully on the job at hand.

It's then not a question of "Is he really that good?," but "*Why* is he so good?" Are Chuck's talents God-given, as the talents of other athletes are so often described, or did Chuck take average physical tools and train himself to become the bowhunting predator that he is?

"I think hunting is deep in my genes and I think I'm extremely lucky that I was blessed with good eyes, good ears and good hand-eye coordination," Chuck says. "And I'm lucky that I was born into a family with a strong hunting tradition so that I could refine my basic God-given talents, I suppose. But it's got to be a combination of the two—plus, a lot of luck in being in the right place at the right time. You get steered along so many random paths in life, and who knows what would have happened if Ken Elliott hadn't hired me? I might have gotten a better job and been further along in my career than I am now. I might have suffered serious setbacks. A lot of it, I believe, is random.

"But I think there's a strong genetic component. I think it's definitely genetically built in to me. It's strong. And it was brought out. I think it was brought out by the traditions of my family. I know that I'm a natural predator, and that's genetic. And I bet if I hadn't grown up in that tradition I would have been a predator in the business world or someplace. It would come out in some way, but I'm happy that it comes out in the most natural, basic way. I'm not sublimating. I'm doing what I'm designed to do.

"And I would bet that it varies from human to human. We're not all created equal. There are those of us who have a stronger predatory instinct than others. And that was naturally selected for in a lot of areas, I would bet you 1,000 years ago. Now it's not. So maybe there are fewer people with that strong genetic drive now. It stands to reason, if you believe in evolution, because those without a strong predatory drive can survive pretty nicely these days. They might not have way back when. They might have needed that edge to survive, if they had to put meat on the table. I know I've got it very strongly."

As Chuck says, being born into a hunting family gave him the chance to become the hunter he is. The genetic drive existed and so did the physical traits. From there, his dad started taking him hunting at a young age. Living in what at that time was rural

California allowed Chuck to be outdoors and among wildlife almost constantly. By the time he entered college, Chuck had as strong a hunting foundation as any person could build in 18 years. From there, it became his career choice that allowed him to distinguish his bowhunting talents.

"I think that what has made the difference has been the opportunity to really refine what I've got," Chuck says. "I think it's the weird combination of being able to write and being able to hunt. Being able to write has, ultimately, allowed me to hunt maybe more than just about anybody with a bow. And one confidence builds on another, and your skills are already refined. You get calmer the more you do it. You're more able to make the critical shot. My writing and ability to structure my schedule have also allowed my abilities to mushroom.

"There are two things that people in the industry commonly call me when they're putting me in ads and other promotions— one is 'America's best-known bowhunter' or the 'world's best-known bowhunter,' and the other is 'America's most successful bowhunter,'" Chuck says. "I allow those to be said, but I've never allowed anyone to say, the 'world's best bowhunter' because I don't think that's necessarily true. I think anybody in any particular situation could be the best bowhunter. Somebody might be the best bowhunter in his neck of the woods for whitetails, elk or whatever. I don't think 'best bowhunter' is a fair statement to make. The combination of an ability to write and an ability to bowhunt has put me where I am.

"Had I stayed a college teacher and grabbed my two to four weeks of bowhunting time every summer and at Christmas time ... if I'd hunted every bit of vacation time I had when there were bowhunting seasons going on, I still wouldn't be, I don't think, nearly as adept as I am now. I would not have put in the time over the years. I wouldn't have learned from as many mistakes and wouldn't have become as confident. Confidence is important in every sport, and bowhunting is certainly no exception. The more you bowhunt, the better you get, and it just compounds.

"I firmly believe that a lot of folks out there with the raw God-given talent could be as good or better than I am. But they're either strapped by their job or they made the decision to have

205

kids and got nailed down and for whatever reason weren't able to fully develop what they had. It's the same with any athlete—top athletes in their field, they have the opportunity to fully develop what they have."

As Chuck said in Chapter Three, he made his life choices knowing that there would be a price to pay. He acknowledges that he reflects on the sacrifices, especially in terms of family life, that he's made and that they are significant. For these reasons, he points out that his path is out of the ordinary and probably not one that most people would *want* to take for many important reasons.

DELIVERING IN THE CLUTCH

Still, phenomenal athletes come into professional sports every year heralded as the next Ted Williams, Michael Jordan or Walter Payton. And every year many of them fail or wallow in mediocrity.

Unrealized potential. It happens all the time to people who are blessed with the rarest of physical skills but who, for whatever reason, cannot completely capitalize on them. The great ones, on the other hand, make the tough shot, deliver the clutch hit or snare the acrobatic catch when everything is on the line. And they do it consistently over the long haul.

Granted, bowhunting is different. It is not a professional sport that you can try out for and earn a living from exclusively. Nor is it played in front of an audience. But hunters are athletes in every sense of the word, even if hunting is not part of their profession. To hunt well, especially for a variety of big game under a gamut of hunting conditions, requires superior physical and mental toughness as well as the savvy that comes with experience in the field. It also requires drive and dedication to make your sport your life's work.

For the great ones, there is no off-season.

Chuck could have failed in his quest for the Grand Slam and the Super Slam. He could have failed to put himself into the proper position to strike. Or, when the opportunity came, he could have blown key shots. And a string of failures during those crucial hunts back in the mid-'80s could have destroyed his confidence and changed the course of his life.

Even being the first to Super Slam, he could have later struggled to maintain that edge. He could have slacked and rested on that accomplishment. He could have been dynamite on targets, but incompetent on animals. Instead, year in and year out since he turned on the switch nearly three decades ago, he's delivered the clutch shot under the toughest of circumstances.

How? How can anyone be that good?

"I can honestly say that I don't ever doubt my ability to do it," Chuck says. "I started out doubting when I first started bowhunting. Those first three years I hunted without shooting a deer with a bow. I couldn't imagine actually seeing an arrow go into an animal. I didn't think it would ever happen.

"Then after I shot a few deer, I was still not all that confident that it would happen. But I can honestly say now that I practice so hard in the off-season and get my gear so right ... I'm confident that I can get the job done. I know I'm fallible, definitely fallible. But I don't have insecurities floating about in my head. I'm very confident.

"And I've always been a pretty confident person," Chuck continues. "I think the academic successes extended into other successes in my life, and my confidence in general has grown. I don't believe I'm cocky. But I do feel very calm and confident when it comes to bowhunting."

Like most good athletes, Chuck says that he spends equal time conditioning his mind and body. He knows that without the mental focus dialed to precision, he cannot perform at his peak. In fact, Chuck referred to a quote made famous by legendary golfer and avid hunter, Jack Nicklaus, who once said, "I've never made a bad golf shot in my mind."

"I wish I had used Jack Nicklaus' quote first because I think it does apply," Chuck says. "When I watch the winter Olympics on TV and I watch the athletes with their eyes closed—like the lugers—they're going through the whole course in their mind. I do that a lot, year-round. I visualize that when I'm shooting targets. I often pretend that it's a really big animal and I have one chance: 'There's the vital zone, don't blow it.' I practice those things in my mind: Pick a spot, pick a spot. I do that a lot.

"I know a lot of bowhunters lack confidence, and I've hunted with a few of my friends who are beginning bowhunters. They

207

go out there and they're not sure that they're going to be able to make the shot. Even some of them who shoot well on a target range lack that confidence out in the field. I think if you have successes, you can build on those successes."

LOW-IMPACT APPROACH

Although Chuck is constantly immersed in bowhunting, he does not train physically as much as one might expect. At age 50 as this is written, he is guarding against wearing down his body and shortening his bowhunting career. So he shoots just enough to stay sharp. And he thinks that less is sometimes best.

"I start seriously shooting at least two months before any hunting season occurs," Chuck says. "I shoot twice a week and I don't believe in shooting every day. I think you wear yourself down physically and mentally. You can overdo it, and I have overdone it at times in my past.

"I've gotten tired, particularly right before hunting season when I was having an off-day. I'd push it and just keep flinging arrows. I don't do that anymore. If I'm having an off day, I just put the bow away and come back a couple of days later and try it again.

"I used to shoot year-round virtually every week of the year. I don't do that anymore, partly because the doctor told me that I'd probably be better off not to shoot year-round because I might develop bursitis in my shoulder. And when seminars hit me in 1990, I suddenly found that I didn't have much time in the winter and spring anymore, and that's the off-season when I used to shoot a lot.

"I don't know what to say about physical conditioning," Chuck continues. "I cross-country ski a little bit in the winter, but not a heck of a lot. I live in a mountainous area, but I don't hike a lot before season. I'm too busy. But I seem to display the same basic trait that my dad still does at age 74. When Pop was my age, he could sit behind a desk as a college professor and just stand in front of classrooms and never do any physical labor to speak of. And then he could go out opening of hunting season and walk all day long. And I seem to have the same trait. Both my grand-dads had that. I certainly toughen up as the season goes by, but I don't do a lot of (physical) preparation.

"I try to stay healthy and I try to eat right—a low-fat diet and all. I don't have any really bad habits health-wise. I try to lead a healthy lifestyle. At age 50, one of my resolutions is to get on a year-round exercise program because I'm sure at some point I'm going to notice a difference. But it hasn't happened yet. I still feel like I'm 25. And I don't know why that is. Maybe I'm just blessed.

"I've always been able to go and lift pretty heavy weights. I had a doctor tell me that he thought that I did this enough months a year that I never got that far out of shape. So even when I took off to do seminars in the late winter and early spring, I wasn't totally out of shape when the hunting season came around again."

PRACTICE REGIMEN

How exactly does Chuck practice when he shoots? He doesn't have a structured shooting regimen or system. In fact, at this point in his career he's most concerned with *how* he's shooting versus *where* exactly the arrow ends up. Like all good shooters, he knows that if his technique is down-pat, the rest will follow automatically.

"At this stage of the game I don't worry about the target I'm shooting at," Chuck says. "I concentrate almost exclusively on my muscle tone and my form. I normally shoot spots. It's almost like I feel that my mind is already trained to shoot and all I have to do is get in physical shape and I'm there. It's been that way a long time.

"I shoot multiple sight pin setups that are very similar to what I shot even 20 years ago. I don't even think much about my sights. I almost shoot sights instinctively, particularly on animals. If I'm in top physical shape from twice-weekly shooting and sharpened up on the basic skills like following-through, for me, it doesn't seem to matter whether I shoot at spots or an animal target. I always pick a spot on an animal and pretend that it's a bull's eye. And that's worked for me a long time.

"The first few years I started bowhunting, I shot cardboard silhouettes a lot. We didn't have the great McKenzie targets that we have now. But I shot paper animal targets a lot and learned to pick a spot. I think that was essential back then.

"When I was pulling all-nighters early in my career to get

everything done before going hunting, it took me a few days to slow down and not make mistakes because I was just too revved up. But today it's almost an instant thing. It's not like the gears are rusty and after a while they get well-oiled. I feel pretty well-oiled as soon as I step out of my truck and go into the woods."

SOME SAY IT'S THE GEAR

Some bowhunters who favor traditional bowhunting gear will argue that Chuck couldn't be as effective with a recurve or longbow, something discussed at length in Chapter Ten. Yet, as Chuck pointed out earlier, he doesn't believe that modern equipment has made him the bowhunter that he is today.

"I heard through the grapevine that one of my detractors said a few years ago that my animals didn't count and that the Super Slam didn't count because it wasn't done with a recurve or a longbow," Chuck says. "I snort at that kind of talk because I shot a recurve bow for a number of years before compounds came on the scene. I shot indoor leagues with recurves and compounds and I shot within about a half a percent of the same score indoors with my old Wing recurve bow as I do with compound bows today.

"And I really believe it's more the person behind the bow than the bow itself. I would even get a bit cantankerous and say it's all sour grapes and that person is hiding behind his equipment a little bit and saying, 'I can't do it because I shoot primitive gear.'

"For me, there are two main advantages of the compound. The average compound stores a lot more energy, so I think it's a much better penetrating machine on bigger animals. But I still think if you hit 'em in the right place that's not an overwhelming factor. The other thing is that it's easier on my body to shoot a compound. If I were still shooting a recurve, I probably would have to be shooting twice a week, 52 weeks a year to stay in shape and hold that thing at full draw. But if I'm strong enough to hold it steadily, a recurve and a compound in my mind are equally accurate. If you put them in a shooting machine, they're going to group the same. So if I'm the shooting machine and I'm strong enough to aim it, it doesn't matter.

"Everybody draws his line in a different place. I have enough challenge for Chuck Adams with a compound bow. The animals kick my butt a lot of the time anyway, and most of the big animals I see get away from me. Often, I never get a shot, even when I'm chasing them for days and days and days. There are many notable examples of that. I think everybody should hunt with whatever they're having fun with that's legal to hunt with. And that's the end of the story."

NIT-PICKING

A better argument about how gear separates Chuck Adams from the average bowhunter would focus on what Chuck does to the gear to give him every possible advantage.

His bow is not simply a compound bow. It is a perfectly tuned machine. His arrows are not simply a dozen aluminum shafts grabbed from a barrel in an archery shop. They are sorted for straightness to the thousandth of an inch. His broadheads are not torn from the package, screwed into the shaft and hunted with. Instead they are subjected to serious testing and scrutiny. When he's done, it's true: Chuck Adams' gear might be better than the gear that the average bowhunter hunts with.

"You could probably accuse me of being obsessive-compulsive about tuning my gear and that would be right," Chuck says. "My stuff is probably more perfect than it has to be. But I don't worry about it after I've set a standard and met that standard. I check my aluminum arrows periodically if I think there's any chance that anything got bent or that a nock might have been damaged because I fell down or whatever. But I don't think I'm unreasonable once everything is set up. All the connections on my bow are glued down with Fletch-Tite so they won't move, and then I move on. I know it's right. I can put it out of my mind.

"But I am nitpicky to a fault. I have never known anybody anywhere in any bowhunting situation who paid as close attention to detail in his equipment as I do. I can honestly say that. People who I hunt with just shake their heads and say they've never seen anybody spend so much time with their gear. I won't even have an arrow in my hip quiver that isn't at least twice as straight as the Super Slam standard. I sort my Super Slam arrows, and they are so straight that I don't even know how you would measure it."

Any wobble in an arrow shaft or broadhead spun over rollers

211

eliminates it. Chuck fletches his own arrows and sorts bags of vanes by one-fourth of a grain to make sure that they weigh exactly the same. He says that when he's finished, he knows what each of his completed hunting arrows weighs to within one-fourth of a grain. And he points out that if you take the best arrows on the market, grab and glue on the best fletches, and screw in the best broadheads, you're looking at plus or minus 3 grains from one arrow to the next. That means that Chuck's arrows at plus or minus one-fourth of a grain are 12 times better. He also keeps a close eye on his bowstring, checking it weekly for any sign of stretch. If it's one-32nd of an inch long, he twists the string to get it back to the precise length.

"I admit I go overboard on everything. But I do it so that when I'm out there, the main variable is me and the animal, and not the gear," Chuck says. "I've been in camps where people aimed down from a treestand and their bowsight fell off their bow ... more than once! I've been in camps where guys threw their bows in the backs of pickups and let them bounce around! I'm on top of all that stuff because I know that it can make a difference, *the* difference. And I always err on the overboard side. I want everything to be exactly right so I know that if there's a mistake made it's not the equipment, it's me. And that actually builds confidence."

Confidence. Not superstition. Chuck says that he doesn't get so attached to a "lucky" bow that he's afraid to start from scratch and set up a new one.

"I know quite a few hunters who even name their rifles," Chuck says. "I don't get that wrapped up in hardware. I know that I can take a half dozen bows off the rack within a particular model, and they might vary slightly. But I have confidence that I can work with any of those bows and get them to shoot just fine. So I never worry about that."

Chuck says that he shot five or six different Hoyt ProVantage bows back in the late 1980s when he was in hot pursuit of the Super Slam. If ever there had been a time when he would have feared changing anything, that would have been it. But Chuck needed different tools depending on the game. He didn't want to take a 70-pound bow that he'd use for mule deer and put it up against a polar bear.

Here Chuck checks an arrow shaft spine during the mid-1970s. If Chuck's equipment is better than that of the average bowhunter, it's because he makes it better.

"It worked out that I could tune up those individual bows, get 'em right with all the nit-picking that I do, and then go out and get the job done," Chuck says. "So, no, I don't have any bows named Betsy or Fred or anything like that.

"It's only hard because I know how much effort will go into setting up the next one. And I'm not going to set up another bow unless I need a bow with more draw weight or a bow with a different camo pattern on it. Once I get a bow dialed in, I love that bow and I'm reluctant to let go of it—but it's only because of all the effort I put in to get it the way I wanted it."

213

And unlike some archers who derive great pleasure from building their own arrows or tinkering with their gear, it's business to Chuck.

"All that equipment preparation is just a means to an end for me," Chuck says. "Fletching arrows is fun. But it's fun because I'm thinking ahead to the time when I'm going to see one of those arrows go through an animal. I take a great deal of pride in having perfect equipment. But standing alone, the process wouldn't mean that much to me.

"The most important thing to me is hunting ... and knowing that when I do get a shot everything is likely to fly right and penetrate well. I am the kind of guy who would tie a trout fly better than I really thought it needed to be to catch a trout because I like the aesthetics of the fly. But the fly also has to be right to catch the trout. That's the most important thing."

QUIVER COUNTING

Chuck says he's not superstitious enough to carry any lucky charms with him when he bowhunts, but four items are with him every time that he goes—binoculars, rangefinder, a hip quiver and a spare arm device. The spare arm is simply a hook that hangs from his belt and allows him to hang his bow while glassing or rangefinding. From there, the rest of the gear is selected months in advance of any hunt, and most of it is the stuff that has proven itself over time.

Of all of it, Chuck's signature hip quiver is the most recognizable and the item that people pay closest attention to in photos where Chuck is posing with an animal. The "how can anyone be that good?" attitude has lead people to count the arrows in that eight-arrow quiver.

"People look at the number of arrows in your quiver closely," Chuck says. "For example, I killed my polar bear with a single arrow in the chest. But I knew it was going to be a rough ride on the dogsled. I modified a case so that I had to set my quiver in on top of the bow, and then the lid closed down and locked the quiver in place by the hood, and by the rubber gripper without touching the arrows inside. I could not put eight arrows in my quiver without an arrow grinding on the bow. So I left one arrow out of the middle of my quiver. So when you see a picture, it's an

Chuck's nearly empty quiver in this photo led some bowhunters to wonder if Chuck had been off the mark in attempting to down this muskox during the Super Slam.

215

eight-arrow quiver with six arrows in it. And I can't tell you how many people have said, 'Now tell me the truth, how many times did you shoot at that bear because there are two arrows missing.' People count!"

Another example is the muskox that Chuck shot multiple times through the lungs until it dropped.

"I had three arrows left in my quiver and had shot five into the muskox," Chuck says. "People assume that there was a disaster. All the arrows were in a 5-inch group on the same side of that muskox, yet people look at that and assume the worst."

Steve Cooke, Hunting Editor of *Ontario Out-of-Doors* magazine, was on the muskox hunt with Chuck and there watching when Chuck shot his bull: "It was extremely cold; we never saw the sun, and at that time of the year there's only four hours of daylight anyway. We wound up wearing these heavy caribou skin outfits. What really impressed me was the first day when the rifle hunters went out, he (Chuck) stayed in camp and he practiced taking the parka off and shooting, just practicing to make sure that he could shoot under those conditions.

"He plunked that bull perfectly," Cooke continues. "It was dead on its feet after the first arrow. But it didn't go down, so Chuck shot it again, and the arrow hit about two inches from the first one. He hit it in practically the same spot with all five arrows."

HOW FAR IS TOO FAR?

By all accounts, Chuck is "that good." No one interviewed for this book would say that he's not. But some of them and many others take issue with Chuck publicizing the distances at which he's shot some of his trophies. Chuck's never been shy about mentioning successful 40-, 50- and 60-yard shots in print. And while no one will come out and call him a liar, many criticize this approach, contending that it will encourage bowhunters to shoot beyond their effective range.

It's certainly true that the average bowhunter is not capable under field conditions of hitting a deer's vital 8-inch chest cavity every time at 40 yards. Yet, a lot of above-average bow-shooters are. One need only to attend a 3-D archery tournament and watch the professional-level shooters hit a heart-sized circle 20 out of 20 times at unmarked distances out to 50 yards. With properly matched equipment, practice and skill, this level of accuracy is possible.

"It depends on the exact situation," Chuck says when asked how far he'll shoot at a big game animal. "I'll shoot as far as I know for almost certain that I can hit the vital chest cavity.

"I say, 'almost certain' because I don't think you can be totally certain about anything. You might be more tired than you thought, a gust of wind might come up. But, in general, I shoot as far as I think I can hit the vital chest on the animal virtually every time. And that varies with the animal. I can shoot archer's minute-of-angle with broadheads (1-inch groups at 10 yards, 2-inch groups at 20 yards, etc.) and I reduce the chest size of the animal by 25 percent. I have done this with every animal I hunt or that I can get statistics on. For example, the average whitetail has a chest cavity that's 8 inches deep, so I wouldn't shoot at a whitetail, ever, beyond the distance I thought I could put all my arrows inside a 6-inch group.

"But I take other factors into account, too. Obviously, I want a clear shot—no obstacles in the way. And animal attitude is very critical. If I think that the animal is going to move before the arrow is going to get there—either because it jumps the string or because it seems to be tense—I won't shoot, even at very close range.

"For example, my former world record Coues' deer was 63 yards away and I could not get one yard closer. A Coues' deer has a vital chest area of about 7 inches top to bottom, and I could shoot 6-inch groups. He was angling away from me, and I figured I had a slightly larger target area to shoot at because he was presenting more of a cross-section of the chest. I didn't run all that through my head deliberately on that deer, but I just felt I could kill that deer because he was bedded, relaxed, looking the other way. So I ranged him and I hit him the first time and killed him.

"Some of the old bowhunters—Howard Hill and Fred Bear and some of the others—used to say you could kill an animal as far as you could cast an arrow with a recurve bow. Some of those guys shot at extremely long range. Art Young and Saxton Pope openly talked about shots at 60 and 70 yards."

217

Chuck warns here, as he has often in his magazine columns, that the old, "don't try this at home" disclaimer applies.

"I think the average person might try to emulate it and botch it," Chuck says. "You have to factor in your own ability coupled with animal attitude and how clear of a shot you have and how comfortable you are. And then on animals like dangerous bears, I wouldn't shoot past 30 yards because you have the additional factor that you might put somebody else in danger."

Again, Chuck has probably shot more big game animals with a bow than most people alive today. This experience, coupled with his own innate talent and the years of honing that ability on target ranges and in the field, make him the exception rather than the rule when it comes to shot distances. He keeps shots within his own personal ability and says that every bowhunter should do the same.

"Err on the side of caution to get closer to the 100 percent factor," Chuck says. "Theoretically, I could say that if I could group all my broadheads inside 6 inches at 60 yards, that if I had a pin, I could kill elk at 120 yards. But when you get out at distances like that I think the chance that the animal might move before the arrow gets there goes up exponentially. And the fact that we all screw up and don't shoot as well under field conditions comes into play. And I would never say that I could hit 6 inches at 60 yards in all field conditions, absolutely not. There are too many factors."

Chuck says that the average shot distance during his career has been right at 30 yards. And it might be because 30 yards is his favored distance, too.

"I don't like critters too close because I think that they're intimately threatened by the noise of your bow. Plus, the chances of string-jumping and other problems go up," Chuck says. "There's also the chance they'll see you draw. I would say 30 to 40 yards is my ideal distance; except on whitetails. I like to be a little bit closer. And on whitetails I am usually in a treestand."

Despite the serious flack that he's taken for writing the truth about the distances at which he's shot some of his animals, Chuck says he doesn't plan to change his approach.

"I think somebody should not be apologetic about his shooting ability," Chuck says. "If he works hard at it, I feel he's earned the right to shoot farther. I believe I'm doing the general public a disservice if I lie about the distance because I think I'm encouraging mediocrity. I want people to practice at longer ranges and test the limit of their ability in practice. They'll be better shots at 20 yards as a result."

HEADED DOWNHILL?

Chuck is defying the odds, according to Pope and Young statistics. Based on the numbers, bowhunters between the ages of 30 and 40 take the most record-book animals. After 40, record-book entries tend to decline, and they plummet after 50.

Yet, Chuck calls 2000 his greatest season ever, when at age 49 he tagged 10 Pope and Young animals and two Pope and Young world records. Is he getting better with age?

"I'm hoping that I'm going to beat the curve," Chuck says. "I think I am better now than I've ever been as a bowhunter. I shoot as well or better than I ever have, partly, I think, because bows are getting better and because I know how to tune a bow perfectly.

"So my shooting is at its best. I'm physically as capable as I've ever been to hike and carry loads. I think I'm wiser about hunting than I've ever been. Hopefully I am. I can assess situations more quickly and make better decisions in a pinch.

"There's certainly going to come a point where the body goes or the eyes go. Then the overall shooting ability goes downhill. I don't know when that point will come. I'm not worried about it. Hopefully, to a certain extent, knowledge and experience will overcome some of that. I'm going to be frustrated if I'm not physically able to go do the things that my knowledge tells me I can do mentally. You can't go and hunt Kodiak Island and shoot three or four record-class Sitka deer unless you're physically capable of backpacking and bivouac hunting. I would not have gotten that big elk this past year if I had not been able to hike 10 miles a day. So I think it all works together. I'm enjoying the peak."

CHAPTER TWELVE:
THE BOWHUNTING BUSINESS

PART I: MIXING BUSINESS WITH PLEASURE

"I would say my strongest allies are clearly the people with whom I've hunted and shared campfires. It seems almost without fail that when we go into a hunting camp and spend quality time hunting together, those people really understand me, I understand them better, and we get along."

Chuck has survived and thrived in a business where if you seriously step out of line, you are shunned like a bowhunter wearing blaze orange.

Though the hunting industry is an outwardly friendly place to work, anyone trying to make a name for himself as an "expert" hunter faces intense scrutiny. It's not like hunting camp where your partner slaps you on the back and offers support even when you make a mistake. And if you think that you know some bowhunters around home who have a little bit of an ego problem, walk around one of the hunting trade shows for a while and you'll encounter ego so thick that a Zwickey broadhead can't penetrate it.

Chuck's old hunting buddy, Richard Long, has known Chuck for more than 30 years. He offers keen insight on the uphill battle that a hunter faces when trying to distinguish himself in a world of hunters.

"For men in general, ego is a very big thing," Richard says. "Ninety-nine percent of all fights don't start for any rational reason. They start because of ego. There are a lot of people who just can't be comfortable with someone greatly excelling over what they have accomplished. Yet, that's all Chuck does. Chuck hunts very hard. He works about three times as hard as the average hunter is willing to work, including a lot of the guys who bitch and moan over his accomplishments."

So you won't see Chuck welcomed with open arms every-

Chuck's long-time friend Richard Long of Chico, California has hunted with Chuck many times, including a drop camp hunt in Alaska for caribou.

where that he walks within the hunting industry. It's a team thing. High-profile hunters who use a certain manufacturer's gear are sometimes bad-mouthed by the competition. The kind of camo you wear, bow you shoot, and optics you tote determine, sadly, your friends within the hunting business.

And though Chuck certainly has his allegiances like Reflex, Hoyt, Easton, Realtree and others, he bristles at the suggestion that these friendships cloud his judgment and objectivity. He believes that he can give everyone a fair shake. And team colors aside, he likes to think that there's more that makes the world go round in the hunting industry.

"I would say my strongest allies are clearly the people with whom I've hunted and shared campfires," Chuck says. "Some of those are folks who I work with every day like Erik Watts, the CEO of Easton, and Randy Walk at Hoyt, Bill Jordan at Realtree and others. But it seems almost without fail that when I go into a hunting camp like I did with Jim Kinsey at Kinsey Archery, Bob Mizek at New Archery Products and Pete Shepley at PSE Archery, and we spend quality time hunting together, those people really understand me, I understand them better, and we get along. So those are my greatest allies.

"To go hunting with somebody, I think, is to get to know that person and to realize that he or she shares the same enjoyment that I do. I mean, there are people I've hunted with who I wouldn't want to hunt with again, but they're rare. They really are."

Watts has hunted with Chuck and wishes that the industry and consumers had the same opportunity to get to know him.

"The analogy I use is when John Elway was going into the NFL he got a lot of bad press because he was so good and a bit cocky," Watts says. "I had the opportunity when we had Elway under contract to meet John personally and I realized that here's somebody who is not at all like his press persona. If people could have the opportunity to meet Chuck and realize what a great guy he is, he'd have no PR issues at all. People think that he gets opportunities that the rest of us don't. He creates the opportunities. He creates his own luck and his own success."

The competition between manufacturers is just one of the dynamics at work within the industry. "Expert" hunters are a dime a dozen. And the expert hunters know it. So, much of their

Easton played on Chuck's signature stocking cap during its ad campaign announcing the release of the Super Slam aluminum arrow in the early 1990s.

success rests on image. If manufacturers want to tout a particular hunter in their advertising, he will quickly gain a reputation as an expert and thereby garner acceptance among consumers. This is key to any expert hunter who hopes to command top dollar for seminars, magazine articles, product endorsements, etc.

But advertising and promotional budgets in the hunting business can't hold a candle to say, NASCAR, or other professional "sports." Thus, competition among the "experts" is heated. In public they'll glad-hand with one another and put on a show of solidarity. In private some of them will resort to rumors, backstabbing and other attempts to grab a larger piece of a paltry pie. From afar it might appear glamorous to be a hunting personality. Up close and in reality, it's a tough way to make a living.

"My most vocal enemies are people I don't know in the industry who resent the fact that I'm competing with them in their mind or in reality on any level," Chuck says. "Or they resent my success as a hunter. And I don't think those are valid reasons to be my enemy, but I think those facts remain. Bowhunters are really independent people by nature. The average bowhunter is an independent person. And I think that tends to draw lines between people when they don't know each other.

"I never worry about somebody who I've met and gotten to know because I get along well with almost all of those folks. But people who don't know me sometimes are detractors. I think that one of the strongest human emotions is jealousy. And I never really fully realized that until I got into this business.

"But I don't think it's just this business. In any competitive environment, anyone who is successful is going to have detractors. It just goes with the territory. My philosophy is that if you're not in the front, they won't be biting your butt. And I don't worry about it. If somebody knows me and has a bone to pick with me that's real, I'd be concerned about it. If somebody's upset with me for some imagined reason, I don't worry about it. I don't lose sleep about it."

For example, a few hunters have gagged over Chuck's trademark toothy grin that leaps from every "hero shot" ever published of him. Still, Chuck claims that it's not an affectation—that it's the same smile he's been smiling since he was a toddler. He hears about it once in a while, but he says he's not going to quit grinning.

At an Archery Manufacturer's and Merchant's Organization (AMO) show years ago, a guy told people at the Easton booth that he didn't like how Chuck grinned so much. Chuck says that the same guy showed up at the Xi booth and told the representatives of that bow manufacturer that he didn't like the fact that bowhunting personality Myles Keller never smiled. "You can't satisfy some people," Chuck says.

"I've found it kind of odd that a handful of people over the years said I shouldn't grin as much over animals. I mean, I'm proud of 'em, and it's just a natural thing to do. I mean, I worked my butt off and here's what I shot and I'm happy about it. That is my smile. That would be my smile if I never bowhunted again in my life."

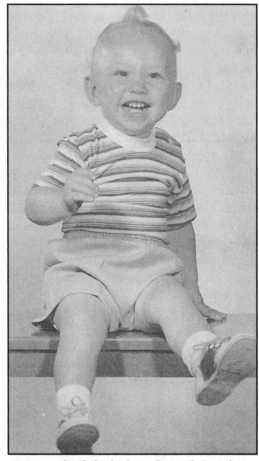

Some wonder if Chuck's hero-shot smile is real. He says it's always been that way. It certainly was at age 2.

Or the signature stocking cap.

"I'm asked about that so much," Chuck says. "My shooting style, the way I hold my head when I shoot, cocks my face down forward a bit. And for that reason I've never been able to shoot while wearing a hat with a bill on it because it collides with the bowstring with longer finger bows. Coupled with the fact that it seems like the majority of my bowhunting is in nasty places like Kodiak Island where it's cold or wet, I've just found the stocking cap to be the most versatile headwear. I don't always wear it, if I'm in really hot weather. Over the years, it just became one of the signature items. I've had people tease me about that saying, 'What a goofy thing to wear,' but I think that it has actually worked to my advantage because it became so recognizable over the years."

WHO'S WHO?

As Chuck has said, the kind of nit-picking that he has to endure comes with the especially enviable turf that Chuck calls "work." Being the most recognizable hunter alive today brings the highest level of scrutiny. And by all appearances, it seems as if Chuck's reputation stands up to all of it. So let's put the shoe on the other foot and get Chuck's take on some of the other major players in the business. Does the guy who's regarded by many as the best bowhunter ever hold other bowhunting experts in high regard?

"There are a number who come to mind, some who concentrate on specific species like white-tailed deer," Chuck says. "I don't know him well, but Myles Keller, I think, has more Pope and Young whitetails than any bowhunter in history, and my hat's off to him. He's a treestand hunter and he puts in his time. He hunts thousands of hours to shoot those big whitetails and he's pretty much king of that particular game.

"The other guys who have taken the Super Slam—Jimmy Ryan, Tom Hoffman, Jack Frost and Gary Bogner—all have my respect because they've hunted every kind of North American animal and, obviously, have done the job in a wide variety of circumstances. I don't know all of those guys well. None of them would be considered hunting buddies of mine. But I do know all of them, and they also are very nice guys.

"There's a long list of good bowhunters in the industry, people like Randy Ulmer who are superb target shots and carry that over into hunting. In his case, he specializes in big Western animals like elk and pronghorns and mule deer. Phil Phillips is one of the best bow shots I've ever seen, and he has taken animals on several continents. Jim Dougherty is deadly and he's a barrel of laughs in camp. Frank "Gus" Addington Jr. is an incredible trick shot with his recurve bow, shooting aspirin out of the air in front of crowds. But the list is too long to try to go through all of them. There are many good hunters in and out of the archery industry."

Next to Chuck, probably nobody in the hunting biz gets as much grief as Ted Nugent.

Talk about love him or hate him! Like Chuck, Ted thrusts himself front and center, though in a very different way and with a different purpose in mind. The Whackmaster, the Motor City Madman ... by whatever nickname you know him, Ted makes the bowhunting biz buzz. Like with Chuck, some people swear that Ted's way is dead wrong. Others would follow him to the bitter end.

"Ted is the polar opposite of me, I believe," Chuck says. "I've had dinner with Ted. I've talked with Ted numerous times. I've never hunted with Ted, but I think he brings visibility to hunting. But he's as off-the-wall as I'm not. He certainly reaches a segment of the market and an audience that somebody like me doesn't, so we're both drawing people into the sport and that is important. Anybody who says we should go back to the good old days when we could hunt all day and not see another bowhunter is totally wrong. You need strength in numbers."

By all accounts, Ted and Chuck are part of something that's working. Latest estimates put bowhunting participation somewhere in excess of 3 million, signifying a steady climb in the face of stagnant overall hunter numbers. The present is bright, the future uncertain, and Chuck is quick to point to the past and offer credit to those who laid the foundation for where bowhunting and the bowhunting industry are today. And when you mention bowhunting's past, the first name that pops to mind is clear—the same man whom Ted wrote a tribute song for; a song which has become a hit in the man's home state of Michigan.

"I idolized Fred Bear," Chuck says. "I grew up reading about Fred Bear and had the good fortune to interview him shortly after I signed on with *Petersen's Hunting* magazine. I flew to Grayling, Michigan, and actually sat in his office and talked to him with a tape recorder and wrote an article about Fred Bear for the magazine. And that's one of the highlights of my life, just to actually meet him.

"And I had the good fortune after that to have dinner with

Fred a couple of times at sport shows, and he turned out to be just as genuine and just as nice as he seemed to be in magazines. He was a genuine person with everybody. He was a true role model, and I was happy that he was the way that he had seemed to be from a distance. But I couldn't call it a friendship. I didn't know him that well. I never hunted with him.

"I have had people say, 'You're the next Fred Bear,' and I always just shrug and say, 'There's nobody like Fred Bear,' and I still believe that. I don't think you can compare folks like that. Every era's different. He was humble, and I think that was one of his secrets of success. He had it all together. He had good products. Obviously, he was a sharp businessman. He promoted himself well. He always wore the same clothes and hat in all those bowhunting films, and that was sharp business. But I think the fact that he was the genuine article had to play large in his success. Like Fred was Fred, I just try to be myself."

But Chuck's list certainly doesn't begin and end with Fred. To Chuck, bowhunting's success is as much about bringing first-rate gear to market as it is about personalities or anything else. Make great equipment that is easy and fun to shoot, and make it affordable to the average hunter, and you are on your way to expanding and popularizing a lifestyle.

"Certainly Doug Easton and his son, Jim Easton, and now Greg Easton the third generation in that company ... they've been on the cutting edge of arrow technology since Doug started it all. I've had the good fortune to hunt with Jim and Greg, and they are both fine people." Chuck says. "Tom Jennings certainly was a pioneer when it comes to compound bows. He was the first one to successfully market the compound bow and really put it on the map.

"Duke Savora was an icon in the replaceable blade broadhead market. I don't think Duke really gets enough credit because his Savora broadheads were the standard in replaceable blade broadheads in the late '70s and early '80s.

"Earl Hoyt was important in bows. Earl was just a task-master at bow design. He largely designed the handle on the old ProVantage compound that I loved so much. Everybody to this day agrees that was the most accurate fingers bow ever produced.

"I think Andy Simo at New Archery Products has done a bang-

Chuck holds a 1982 Savora broadhead in comparison to some of the Ishi arrowheads he found as a kid. He considers Duke Savora a pioneer in broadhead technology.

up job. Andy is an absolute nit-picking perfectionist, and so am I, so I guess I admire that. But it really shows in his products.

"Craig Dougherty at Satellite Archery is a long-time friend. I believe he's one of the sharpest marketing gurus in the industry, and he's also a nice guy. We've hunted together several times, and I can tell you he's the luckiest bowhunter I know. I mean, how many archers shoot a 350-point bull elk their first time out?

"When it comes to scent control products, Scott Shultz at Robinson Labs is tops," Chuck continues. "Here's a first-rate 3-D shooter, avid bowhunter, and product innovator all rolled into one. From carbon scent suits to liquid scent eliminators and lures, Scott's always at the forefront of innovation.

"Cabela's has a well-deserved reputation for selling excellent hunting products. From Dick and Jim Cabela on down the management ladder, most of the people are real hunters. I believe that makes a huge difference. I've personally hunted with Ev Tarrell, Pat Snyder, Tom Gallagher, Doug Zingula and others from this biggest-of-all outdoor mail-order outfits, and those guys know their stuff.

"Some people might think I'm biased because I do business with a few of the folks I just mentioned. But my respect for them came long before we signed contracts or collaborated on products. I won't work with someone I don't hold in high regard."

CHUCK AS PRODUCT INNOVATOR

Today a bowhunter can likely find an archery pro shop within an hour's drive of his home. There he can purchase state-of-the-art equipment and arrows perfectly matched to his setup, then get the whole rig tuned precisely over his lunch hour. Once he steps into the field, the degree of difficulty hasn't changed a great deal from bowhunting's earlier days. But imagine what it must have been like back in the 1960s and '70s—before the compound bow had gained a foothold, before the Eastons had perfected aluminum arrow technology, and before bow accessories like sights and rests were engineered as integral bow components.

Back then, a successful archer, much more so than today, needed to possess a clear understanding of how to make a bow and arrow setup work efficiently. Thus, most bowhunters built their own arrows or modified equipment to make it work in concert with their personal shooting style. The equipment side of the bowhunting equation required almost as much diligence as the actual hunting.

Some aspiring bowhunters might have been turned off by the difficulties of making those more crude bow-and-arrow setups perform. But Chuck relished the challenge. He's enjoyed working with his hands since his childhood. And if he could tweak his bow or his arrows and produce positive results, it brought a smile to his face, knowing that he'd have an even better chance against the blacktails next time out.

Chuck had a fletching tool set up in his archery workshop where he fletched full-size, 5-inch turkey feathers to his arrow shafts and then burned the fletches to shape.

In the very early days of his bowhunting endeavors, he experimented with Port Oroford cedar shafts, tapering the ends with a tool similar to a pencil sharpener. Glue secured his broadhead to one end and a nock to the other. It didn't take Chuck long to realize what a God-send Easton aluminum arrows were!

But he modified equipment all the time. He hand-carved the wood handle on his Wing recurve bow, modifying it so that a Bear Archery arrow rest would fit better. He took an old Fred Bear quiver design and revamped it in an attempt to make it more sturdy and quiet. That began the process that eventually made the Chuck Adams Arrow Holster a reality during the late 1980s.

While working as a consultant for Easton early on and then later with Hoyt, part of Chuck's job entailed product testing and input on designs. One of the things he enjoyed was using automotive Bondo to form and file a better-feeling bow grip. Some of that detail work turned into designs that eventually were mass-produced on Hoyt bows and Easton arrows. Though his name didn't appear on those product improvements, he was working toward the day when it would.

After completing the Super Slam in 1990, Easton released its top-of-the-aluminum-line Super Slam arrow. Not only did it have Chuck's name on it, but for approximately five years his image appeared on every XX78 Super Slam shaft. In fact, Chuck says that Easton's Super Slam arrow is probably the product, out of everything that he's had a hand in designing, that he's most proud of today. The shaft is constructed from Easton's 7178-T9 aluminum alloy providing 100,000 psi strength and straightness of .0015 inches. Combined with the Super UNI Bushing system and Super Nock, the Super Slam continues to be touted by Easton as the "most trusted hunting shaft of world-class bowhunters."

"There were probably thousands of hours put into testing nock design on the Super Slam, with the first nock that double-snaps on the string so that it can't fall off," Chuck says. "I helped to conceptualize the camo pattern. I can't take credit for the Super Uni system, but that arrow has been very popular and successful, and I was one of several people who worked on that. Jim

231

Easton was directly involved. But I shot one nock 1,000 times out of my bow just to test the material to make sure that it was not going to get loose in the Uni bushing. So I worked very hard on that project."

"I think he's really a perfectionist, and I guess I am too, so I think we got along fairly well," Jim Easton says of working with Chuck on the Super Slam arrow. "The Super Nock has been a major breakthrough and one of those products where it was the right place at the right time. At that point, we were so pleased with the relationship that we were willing to put his name on an arrow."

In the late '90s, Chuck confided in his old friend, Craig Dougherty, then vice president of Golden Eagle/Satellite Archery. Chuck had been thinking about bringing to market his own signature line of bowhunting accessories. In fact, he'd already thought through many of the product designs in his head or sketched them on paper. But Chuck needed to partner with an established company that had the production capacity, the distribution channels and the marketing wherewithal to make the products a success.

During a bear hunt in Quebec, Chuck and Craig brainstormed. Shortly thereafter, the Chuck Adams Super Slam line of bowhunting accessories became a reality with a broadhead, stabilizer, arrow rest and arrow rollers.

"If you ever saw Chuck work with archery equipment and work with engineers, you would say, 'My goodness, he knows more than most engineering teams and design teams that he works with,' and that's true," Dougherty says. "Chuck is a perfectionist. He understands the underpinnings of how the gear works and what you have to do to make it work. On the products that we developed with him, he was very, very demanding of our engineers. At times it challenged everyone to meet his standards."

Chuck says that he originally approached Satellite with 25 products that were reviewed under a non-disclosure agreement. It's likely that some of the 20 or so products still on the drawing board will be brought to market bearing Chuck's name at some point.

"I feel that all of them are unique and either superior to the existing products or completely unique," Chuck says. "I get asked a lot, 'Did you really help design this product or did you just put your name on it?' And it's usually kind of a skeptical question. I've never put my name on anything that I wasn't instrumental in designing or testing."

SELLING STUFF

Some skeptics question Chuck's endorsements of various bowhunting products. He has had an alliance with Easton since leaving Petersen's back when he was 25. Similar long-standing relationships exist with Hoyt and Reflex bows, Realtree camouflage, Robinson Labs, Cabela's and others.

Everyone knows that Chuck is paid for his affiliation with those companies and the particular products that he endorses for each. So, again, the assumption is that paid-for endorsements are necessarily tainted.

But that assumes that when Chuck is asked to endorse a product his primary interest is financial gain and that the quality of the product is secondary. He insists, however, that the reverse is true— that he first determines if the product is worthy of his endorsement. Only then does the discussion turn to compensation.

"I do believe 100 percent in everything I endorse," Chuck says. "I'm not saying everything's perfect, that things can't be improved upon. But I think that everything I endorse is better than what was out there before that product came along.

"I will tell you that I'm approached regularly by people who just want me to promote something in return for money. I turn those folks down. I won't prostitute myself that way because my main obligation, I feel, is to bowhunters and readers of my magazine articles. If I ever betray those folks by promoting something that I don't believe in, I wouldn't be true to myself or to them."

One of the products that some bowhunters point to, though, is camouflage. Early in his bowhunting career, Chuck hunted primarily in blue jeans. In fact, he went out of his way in his writing occasionally to say that full-body camouflage was unnecessary given the poor vision for detail and color that most big game animals possess. He stressed instead that stealth ruled the day when it came to avoiding detection by an animal.

Today he is a member of Bill Jordan's Realtree camo pro staff.

"I did used to hunt in blue jeans because camouflage pants weren't durable enough for me," Chuck says. "I'd wear 'em out. Things have gotten better. I always would have rather had camouflage, but I didn't think it was necessary. And, obviously, I shot a lot of critters with blue jeans on mostly because I learned to be a spot-and-stalk hunter. Ninety-five percent of my hunting is on the ground. And I figure if I'm doing my job right, the animal should never see me below the waist anyway. I'm using terrain and foliage to hide, so I could probably be wearing white painter's pants and get those animals anyway, the majority of them. Now we've got great fabrics in addition to great camo patterns."

At the end of the day, what lures companies to Chuck isn't necessarily the Super Slam. After all, that's old news. Instead, according to Hoyt's Randy Walk, it's the visibility and ambassadorship that Chuck generates through his widely circulated articles and his personal appearances. And, according to Walk, Chuck doesn't owe any apologies for accepting a paycheck for a job well done.

"Chuck has created that value himself," Walk says. "That's not been handed to him. He earned it. I mean he touches a ton of people, and the grassroots value is the personality and the effort.

"I've hunted several times with Chuck and I've never hunted with anybody that I thought was a better hunter than Chuck. And, you know what? Ninety-eight percent of the market would never do what he does. And because of how he approaches bowhunting, he knows what kind of product is going to work and not going to work. He is not soft on equipment. His stuff has been put to the ultimate test. Chuck is underrated. Really, based on what he's done, he's really way under-recognized."

BOTH SIDES OF THE FENCE

In Chapter Seven, we detailed some of the allegations and rumors that Chuck has endured as some angry observers attempt to rationalize how it is that he is so singularly successful. Some have claimed that he's broken game laws or trespassed to take record-book animals. Others wonder if he's abiding by the ethics of fair chase.

Up until 2001, the Pope and Young Club accepted certain trophy white-tailed deer bow-killed behind high fences. That year, they decided to no longer allow any animals taken within high fences, no matter how large the enclosure or how good the habitat within the enclosure. Before 2001, the club judged hunting properties on a case-by-case basis. Those deemed to have enough acreage and sufficient escape cover for animals naturally occurring and native to the region earned P&Y approval. Whitetails taken on P&Y-approved enclosures prior to 2001 remain in the record books today. In addition, the Safari Club International record book for bowhunters recognizes some high-fenced species.

"I've dabbled in high-fenced hunting," Chuck says. "I'd be the first one to tell you that an elk on a high-fenced ranch in Texas is not even remotely the same as a free-ranging Montana elk.

"I have a real simple philosophy about high fences. I think that if the animals are truly free-ranging in a large area, I don't have a problem. But for me to hunt in a place like that, I have to know that the animals are free-ranging and wild, not recently planted and dumb as a post. For that reason, I've taken several animals in Texas on high-fenced properties, but they are large properties designed to manage trophy size, not give archers an edge. I know there's a stigma attached to it. And there's a bit of a stigma in my mind. It's not something that I've done very often."

In 1992 Chuck queried the club about the Camp Verde Ranch in Kerr County, Texas. This was a large, famous whitetail property hunted by the likes of M. R. James, Ted Nugent, longbow shooter and singer Gary Morris, gun writer Grits Gresham and Gulf War icon General Norman Schwarzkopf. The club determined that it would allow Chuck to enter animals taken there into the record books. During the next three years Chuck tagged two white-tailed bucks annually at the ranch. Each of the three years, one of the bucks qualified for P&Y entry. The ranch and two large, neighboring properties supported other species including elk and a variety of exotic species. In addition to the whitetails, Chuck shot two elk, three blackbuck antelope and one aoudad during the three hunts from 1992 through 1994.

That's the extent of Chuck's bowhunting within high-fenced ranches. Yet, like the rumors regarding game laws or other contentions of impropriety, some people within the industry have exaggerated the truth.

One outfitter, speaking on condition of anonymity, said that he had hosted a large group of prominent outdoor writers on a hunt. Around the dinner table one evening, someone brought up Chuck's name, looking for opinions on his hunting ability and achievements. According to the outfitter, one of the writers quickly chimed in, claiming that some of Chuck's top P&Y record-book elk had been taken behind high fences. Yet, the only two elk that Chuck has ever shot inside fences were taken in 1992 and 1993 at the Camp Verde Ranch. Since the elk were non-native, Chuck knew that he couldn't enter them in the P&Y records. Safari Club International accepts many varieties of animals taken on preserves and is less stringent in the criteria used to determine acceptable preserves. Those two bulls are in the SCI records, along with the exotics that Chuck killed in the same area in 1994. They are clearly marked as non-native in a separate category.

For the record, as of this writing Chuck has taken 21 elk with a bow. Of those, 12 are listed in P&Y, including the current typical world record—all of them, he says, taken in a completely fair-chase setting.

"They (Camp Verde) were trying to get rid of the elk," Chuck says. "I'm not particularly proud of it, but I'm not ashamed of it either. One of those years I was in the middle of a divorce and didn't even go to Montana hunting, and I wanted to shoot something else. I knew that they weren't eligible for Pope and Young, but I would not call those elk easy. As far as my Pope and Young animals, everything's been free-ranging except the three Texas whitetails that the club accepted. Those deer were wild as hell, and the club was right to accept them."

DO AS I SAY?

As alluded to in the previous chapter, another thing about Chuck that has driven some industry insiders and fellow bowhunters crazy is their perception that he takes a "shoot first, ask questions later" approach to his bowhunting.

Since his childhood, Chuck has possessed keen accuracy whether with a BB gun, his Winchester .22 or a bow. He proved it at the local archery club in Chico and in competition at the collegiate level for Chico State. His well-practiced hands and painstaking attention to equipment detail instilled a strong sense of confidence in his shooting that he has carried with him afield.

"Chuck is a superb field archer," his old friend Richard Long says. Long has hunted with Chuck in Alaska and Montana several times, and once in Quebec for caribou. "He's one of the best field archers, with true hunting equipment—shooting broadheads at unmarked ranges—I've ever seen. Plus, he's an exceptionally skilled hunter. To top it all off, he's luckier than hell. Chuck is a very ethical hunter and a good sportsman."

But when Chuck would write about shooting a sheep or mule deer at 50 yards or more, bowhunters and the bowhunting industry gasped in horror. The thinking, of course, was that if Chuck said that he took a 50-yard shot, it meant that he advocated a 50-yard shot. Even though the gear had advanced dramatically during the '70s and '80s, bowhunting remains to most an ultra-close-range game. The average Eastern whitetail hunter, for example, shoots his deer at less than 20 yards. And since most of the nation's bowhunters reside East of the Mississippi, Chuck's accounts of 40-, 50- and 60-yard shots sounded especially foreign to most people. Where were the ethics? Shouldn't he suggest getting closer to game instead of openly writing about launching from half a football field away?

Chuck's defiance on this subject sparked debate throughout the industry that still smolders from time to time today. Many editors opted to remove any references to shot distances beyond 40 yards. Some still do. Others allowed Chuck to speak the truth, but then endured waves of angry letters from readers who argued that Chuck was doing the bowhunting tradition a disservice. It rang of arrogance, they said. Here's Chuck Adams grinning ear-to-ear over some huge animal and then openly bragging about shooting it from farther away than any sensible bowhunter has a right to. A lot of people, especially the "old guard" traditionalists were incensed.

"I've been criticized for talking about shots beyond 25 or 30 yards, and I'm saying, 'Man, when I was 16, it worked," Chuck says. "Fred Bear, some of his best animals he shot at distances over 30 yards."

So he continued to write the actual shot distances into his columns and feature articles. He continued in seminars to talk about the necessity of honing one's shooting ability at longer distances if a bowhunter aimed for consistent success when foot-hunting for most Western and Canadian big game species.

He even suggested viable shot angles that differed dramatically from the recommendations that you'd get in your average National Bowhunter Education Foundation class. The bedrock of formal bowhunter training, which is now required in many states before a hunter can purchase an archery license, is the discipline to wait for a standing-still, clear, broadside shot well within the archer's effective range. This presents the best odds for the incredibly lethal double-lung hit. The 8-inch paper plate is a common target used by many bowhunters because it represents the size of the heart-lung area from a broadside view.

Chuck's views on vital areas are more liberal. He's written that butt shots and frontal shots are deadly provided that arrow placement is precise. And he's advocated a wide variety of shot angles during his career. In fact, his book "The Complete Book of Bowhunting" published in 1978 includes illustrations of deer standing at every imaginable angle and shows an aiming point for each situation.

Many of the scenarios would be regarded as absolute "no-shot" situations in a bowhunter education class. But here's what Chuck advised in his book:

"A chest-on animal ... presents a fairly large vital target ... (A bowhunter) should hold dead-center where the neck joins the body. A hit here will catch one or both lungs and the liver if the arrow penetrates well."

And he offered this on the rear-end shot:

"Many bowhunters worry about the rear-end shot, but a deer or another big game animal with its butt toward you should be in one heap of trouble. A deer facing directly away cannot easily see a bowhunter move and presents both vital hams."

There are other references in the same chapter that might cause a bowhunter education instructor to cringe. However, it must be noted that Chuck introduces that section of the book by writing, "A bowhunter should always try to put his arrow in an animal's chest cavity." He goes on to discourage shots at the neck, shoulder and paunch. He adds that the quartering-away angle is, "the best shot of all."

"A lot of bowhunters over the years have criticized me because I've said that butt shots kill," Chuck says. "I don't blanketly rec-

238

ommend butt shots, but I've said that they take down animals most of the time. I've never personally lost a big game animal hit in the butt. Fred Bear used to say the same thing and actually recommended butt shots in some situations. So did Jack Howard, another well-known archer and bow maker in the 1970s. G. Howard Gillelan, *Outdoor Life*'s bowhunting editor, often advocated butt shots in his writing.

"I find it interesting that I took no immediate flak from bowhunters about the shot placement discussions and illustrations in my 1978 book. It was only from the mid-1980s to today that broadside became the only politically correct placement of an arrow. From then until now I have certainly heard complaints about my views on the subject.

"A whole different culture has emerged today in bowhunting—an ultra-conservative culture that says don't take anything but a broadside shot. I think the reason is current fear of what anti-hunters might say.

"What I'm more afraid of, though, is this. I talk to bowhunters who have actually said that they walked away from butt-hit animals and they didn't even look because they didn't think that they could find the animal because they didn't think it was a lethal shot. That's what I've always preached against. You go overboard on preaching a particular thing, and the general public buys it, and then you have other problems. I say don't shoot for the butt on purpose, but if you do hit one there, know that you're probably going to get the deer.

"I've modified my treatment of butt shots in articles and books the past few years not because I've been cowed by the critics, but because bowhunting has changed. Archery equipment is generally better—faster, more dependable, more accurate—but some setups no longer penetrate well enough to make the butt shot a success. Light arrows, nose-cone broadheads and mechanical heads do not always penetrate well. I believe that heavier arrows and welded-steel cutting-nose heads like the Bear Razorhead and Zwickey Black Diamond made old-time bowhunters more effective with butt shots. So I'm more cautious about touting butt shots to the general bowhunting public.

"There are times on animals that I know aren't going to jump the string, where I'll take a facing shot. In the case of a sheep, if you hit one in open country, even if he doesn't die right away, you're going to get him. I shot my former world record Sitka black-tailed deer straight-on dead in the chest because he stood up and gave me that little spot to shoot at. I'm going to take that shot and I don't really make any apologies for it.

"Fred Bear shot his world record Stone sheep chest-on. There's a famous article that appeared in *Outdoor Life* called "The Best Shot I'll Ever Make," back in, I think in the '50s. I read it as a kid and I remember it in detail. He shot that sheep at 60 yards in the center of the chest as it looked at him over a hill. He lobbed the arrow into the sheep with his old recurve bow and killed it deader than a wedge. That was the world record for many years. So I'm not the only one."

Again, Chuck offers qualifiers to every situation. While he might take a frontal shot at a sheep in wide open country, he likely wouldn't take the same shot on an elk—an animal that's more sturdily built and more tenacious. Ditto on a bear or moose.

"I believe the butt-shot and chest-on 'controversy' surrounding me is overblown. Sure, some people complain. For example, *Bowhunter* magazine ran a group of negative letters a few years ago after an interview article about me appeared in the publication. If you had picked up that particular issue, you might have thought that I was public enemy number one. But M. R. James, founder of the magazine, told me they received less than a dozen letters from angry readers. *Bowhunter* ran most of them, which did not make me happy, but when you consider that *Bowhunter* has hundreds of thousands of readers, a dozen or so people isn't that significant.

"Many people do not know that I have been an official Mentor for the National Bowhunter Education Foundation for several years. I worked directly with the late Bill Wadsworth, founder of the NBEF, to draft language about shot distance and other rules currently taught by bowhunter education instructors. There are certainly differences of opinion among those affiliated with NBEF, but I am, and always have been, a friend and strong supporter of bowhunter education programs."

Chuck's point is this: Each moment-of-truth situation presents a slightly different set of circumstances, all of which must be considered along with one's own ability at that split-instant before anchoring at full draw.

THE WORLD ACCORDING TO CHUCK

Ultimately, Chuck isn't the type to allow shot angle or distance debates to consume him. The way he sees it, there are larger issues that the hunting industry faces; issues that will more certainly determine our future. And based on the time he's spent working in the hunting industry and walking the mountains and forests of North America, his view of the future is mostly pessimistic. He's a hunter with serious environmental concerns.

"I think the decline of hunting in general is inevitable, eventually," Chuck says. "Habitat is disappearing. The human population is exploding. We're screwing up the world pretty badly, and animals are suffering. That is going to diminish hunting over the long haul, I think, more than any other factor.

"Coupled with that, hunting is not as socially acceptable anymore. The average person who lives in a house surrounded by concrete doesn't understand at all. And that's the person who's gonna create a snowball effect and limit hunters' activities even more."

What does Chuck think about that fact that so many people are now so far removed from our hunting ancestry?

"I actually feel sorry for them," Chuck says. "I feel sorry for them because I think a lot of folks who don't hunt don't realize how much more satisfied they would be if they were in touch with their true self. It's my belief that those people have lost touch because they're living in cities and surrounded by concrete. I think a lot of people are genetically frustrated the way a Labrador retriever would be if he were raised in downtown L.A. and never saw the water."

In 1978, shortly after venturing out on his own as a freelance outdoor writer, Chuck summed up his thoughts on the subject like this in his first book, "The Complete Book of Bowhunting."

"Before the filthy fingers of progress raped the land and castrated outdoorsmen by planting them in cities, hunting was a widespread and honorable lifestyle. Today, most men are out of touch with nature, living and dying in artificial worlds of concrete, steel and plastic. Most still satisfy their hunger for meat by hiring professional butchers to raise and slaughter dumb,

domestic slave animals like sheep and cattle. But most no longer hunt. Their only contact with 'wild' creatures consists of gazing at pitifully penned zoo animals on Sunday afternoons.

"The dedicated hunter is a much luckier fellow. He starts with the biological instinct to hunt and nothing more. He learns the basics of woodsmanship and shooting from his father, friends or magazines and books. He sharpens his skills through hours of enjoyable practice like a young bobcat chasing mice. If his instinct and determination are strong enough, he perfects his ability to hunt. In the process of learning his art, he develops an intimate knowledge of wildlife and a realistic view of his own limitations and abilities. His raw urge to hunt and kill turns to deep and abiding respect for wild things in general, respect which comes from being an active part of nature—not an outsider looking in.

"I enjoy all kinds of hunting, but bowhunting is my first love. I eat, drink and sleep this wonderful sport. It has taught me more about the woods, more about wild animals, and more about myself than everything else combined."

Given his experience as a hunter back in the 1960s and '70s, and his gloomy view of what the future holds, Chuck is happy to have lived during a generation that he considers the best possible time to be a hunter.

"We have airplanes and vehicles to get us where we want to go," Chuck says. "Two hundred years ago I would not have been able to hunt all the species I've hunted in my lifetime. One hundred years from now it might not be possible. It certainly is now. Shooting equipment is the best that it's ever been. Optics are better, accessories are better, and I enjoy the heck out of all that stuff.

"Animal populations are growing in a lot of places. It's just a great time to be a hunter, and a bowhunter, in particular. In metropolitan areas, a lot of places the only reasonable hunting tool to hunt with is a bow, like for white-tailed deer. That's bound to change at some point also as that habitat disappears. I really wouldn't have wanted to live during any other period as a hunter. Sure, there were good old days. I'm sure it would have been nice to have been the only elk hunter in the whole Bighorn Mountains of Wyoming. But there are a lot more animals in some categories now than there ever were, and the opportunities are certainly there to get to the animals."

So could some young, cock-sure hunter set out today to model his career after Chuck? Given the God-given physical skills and persistence, could he hope to achieve the Super Slam and rival Chuck's incomparable number of record-book animals?

"If this were the 1960s I would say, 'Sure,'" Chuck says. "Records are made to be broken, and there's always somebody who is going to come along and be more motivated with the hand-eye coordination and other God-given talents who might surpass what I've done. I think it would be great if someone did. If that person would have as much fun as I've had, I'd be happy for him.

"But I worry that if I had been born 20 years later that I couldn't do what I've done already because I think that hunting is likely to decline because of habitat loss. There won't be as many opportunities to go out and shoot 111 Pope and Young animals. I hope I'm wrong, but it seems like that's the way things are trending. The yuppie generation is probably going to be the biggest group of hunters ever. I hope I'm wrong."

CHAPTER TWELVE:
THE BOWHUNTING BUSINESS

PART II: WHAT THE INDUSTRY INSIDERS SAY

"Chuck does what every welder, every farmer in America does. He goes out and he works during the day for the maximum dollar he can get. It's what you do, it's what I do, it's what America does. And to level criticism at anyone for doing that proves you are a numb-nut."—Ted Nugent

In the nearly 30 years that Chuck Adams has earned a living in the hunting industry, he has raised eyebrows and rocked the boat. He has navigated uncertain political waters by combining hunting, writing, seminars and product promotion. That balancing act requires a delicate touch in a tightly knit business where one's loyalty, objectivity and ethics are quickly questioned at any minor misstep. Make a mistake, and word travels fast.

Here's how a cross-section of hunting industry insiders privy to all of the rumors and innuendo see Chuck and his career.

Craig Dougherty, vice president, North American Archery Group (Bear, Golden Eagle, Satellite, et al):

Question: Where does Chuck stack up in terms of what he's meant to bowhunting and the bowhunting industry?
Answer: "I think Chuck, with some of his hunting accomplishments and his writing accomplishments, has been able to position himself as the most recognized bowhunter in America. And I think he pretty clearly holds that title. I'm not going to compare him to a Fred Bear. They're totally different people at different times. There will never be another Fred Bear in terms of pioneering work. But what Chuck has created is a whole level of recognition. Through his bowhunting exploits and the amount of print that has been dedicated to his bowhunting, he has also been able to share that with literally millions of bowhunters. And I think that counts for a lot. That's a good thing."

Bowhunting Hall of Fame member, Jim Dougherty, right, is one of the industry insiders who has had the opportunity to share hunting camps with Chuck.

Question: What about the way that Chuck has gone about all this? His approach rubs some people the wrong way. Is he, ultimately, a help or hindrance to the health of bowhunting?

Answer: "From where I sit, my biggest agenda for the bowhunting community is the survival of our sport and the development of our sport, and seeing that our kids participate in our sport. In order for us to survive we have to have numbers of people. We have to have people exposed to bowhunting. If Chuck has shared his hunting experiences through the printed media with millions of bowhunters, what's wrong

245

with that? If he's turned guys on to elk hunting, if he's given them strategies, if he's suggested how he tunes a bow to make them a better bowhunter, is there something wrong with that program?

"There are certain groups of bowhunters in this country who have a different view of mainstream archery. The guys who are not mainstream—a small segment—react negatively to high-profile bowhunters. If Fred Bear were alive today and hunting, you'd hear the same thing about Fred Bear. Some people don't want to see archery promoted."

Question: You've known Chuck for about 15 years as a friend, and the company that you work for has had a business relationship with Chuck for approximately five years. How would you characterize him as a person and as a hunter?

Answer: "As a person I would say Chuck is a very private man. Chuck has also been a very good friend and honest individual and a very thoughtful man. Chuck is a deep thinker. He thinks philosophically and strategically about things.

"On the hunting side, I see him as what I would call a technical hunter. He's a technician. He understands equipment better than most manufacturers who make the stuff. He understands how it all works, how it all fits together, how you make it work for you. That's one of the reasons he's so capable. One of the reasons that certain people get frustrated with Chuck is because he can shoot things at 42 yards, and a lot of people can't. And Chuck always qualifies it by explaining that he can do this; he can make that shot at that range and he seems to prove it. The truth is what should carry the day."

Question: In your final analysis, at some point down the road, how will the hunting world look back on what Chuck has done?

Answer: "I think Chuck deserves a very high place in the sport. I've never seen him portray himself in any promotion that was anything but ethical, anything but honest. And like Yogi Bera says, 'If you've done it, you ain't bragging.' The guys that we should raise our eyebrows about are the ones who are sneaking into pens, doing things like that to promote themselves. If Chuck spends two weeks on a mountain and kills a Pope and Young record animal, he has every right, especially since he makes his living doing it, to go out there and share that information.

"He's taught, through his writing, millions of people how to make their gear work better. I really, really believe that. And I hear guys like Dave Samuel say to groups of people that Chuck Adams has done more for bowhunter education than half of the bowhunter education instructors in the country."

M. R. James, founder *Bowhunter* magazine; first vice president, Pope and Young Club (1990 to 2000).

Question: **How would you quantify the significance of Chuck being the first bowhunter in history to take the North American 27, the Super Slam?**
Answer: "In *Bowhunter*'s 30th anniversary issue, one of the things I did was look back over the past 30 years and I tried to present the top 10 most important, memorable milestones. And at Number 5 I had Chuck completing bowhunting's first Super Slam in 1990. And again, this is just personal opinion, but Chuck certainly is significant. There's no question that when you write bowhunting history as he's done—the number of Pope and Young heads—it's no insignificant accomplishment, and Chuck has a rightful place in modern bowhunting history.

"To think that a talented writer, a kid from California who is so passionate about the out-of-doors and passionate about bowhunting in particular, to embark on a journey like that ... it's a remarkable feat for anyone to accomplish. There's only one first, and for him to do this is certainly one of the top achievements in the history of bowhunting."

Question: **As a magazine publisher and editor for a long time, you had a prime vantage to gauge public and industry perspective of Chuck Adams. What have you seen?**
Answer: "Chuck and I have talked about this. Chuck is an extremely proud person. And he is stung and hurt deeply by

some of the criticisms he's received. A number of years ago, we did a profile on Chuck for *Bowhunter*. And I published a series of comments after the fact. And in the letters that we received Chuck was just ripped unmercifully. And Chuck called me after they had appeared in print, and he said, 'I understand the fact that there are people out there who don't like me and don't understand me,' he said. 'But you didn't print one, single positive response.' And I said, 'Chuck, we didn't get any.'

"And one time at a Pope and Young Club convention, Chuck and I sat down and talked about how he is perceived by a lot of people. There are the traditionalists who just despise him. He is the epitome of the gadgeteer, and not just a gadgeteer, but he's regarded in many circles as a pimp because (supposedly) for a price he will tout whatever modern gadget or gimmick that comes down the line. This is their opinion; that he is just someone who will sell his soul. That's the perception in the radical camp.

"On the other hand, some modern bowhunters dislike him because of his success. And Chuck and I talked about that and I said, 'There are a couple of things wrong with what you do. One is that you're an extremely successful hunter and the only picture that people have when the name Chuck Adams comes to mind is they see your photograph in a magazine grinning over some animal that they'd have liked to kill. There's a lot of jealousy. There's a lot of misunderstanding as to who you are.' I've had people tell me, 'This guy can't be that good, there's just no way.'

"We traveled together (for 30 days on the NRA Tour in the early '90s), and I got to know Chuck. We had a lot of chances to talk. We shared a lot of thoughts. I said, 'Chuck, one of your biggest problems is people don't know you. They see your picture, but they don't know you. They read your words, but they don't know you. Most people will never share a hunting camp with you. They don't know what a personable guy you are. They don't know that that smile is not just some toothpaste advertisement, but that it's genuine and that you are a nice guy.'"

Question: **Isn't the level of misunderstanding a bit tragic?**

Answer: "Sure it's tragic because, as I said, here's an extremely gifted bowhunter. He's a good shot, he's a good hunter and he's committed. I've had people tell me, 'If I had Easton and I had Hoyt and I had these companies paying my way I could do exactly what Chuck's done.' And I tell them, 'No you couldn't. Yeah, you could kill some animals, but you could not tell the story, you could not test the products, you could not do the public presentation of information the way Chuck Adams does because he's got this unique gift of being able to communicate.' He's doubly blessed with his hunting ability and his ability to share those experiences with others. So, yeah, it's tragic that the perception undermines what he has done. He has his legions of fans, but I would speculate that he's got a number of people who hate his guts. And that is extremely sad when you consider what he's accomplished."

Question: **You and Chuck have not always seen eye to eye. Has anything in particular caused conflict between the two of you?**

Answer: "Chuck's human. He misses shots. He does all the things that every bowhunter does. And Chuck has a tremendous amount of pride and rightfully so. Criticism hurts his feelings at times, which I can understand.

"One of the things that Chuck and I have had personal and professional differences about is that when Chuck Adams writes about taking a 60-plus-yard shot, I tell Chuck, 'You can do this and you can succeed more often than not.' I'm not as good of a shot with a bow and arrow as Chuck is and I'm not going to begrudge him of the fact that he has a rangefinder and he spots a sheep at 60 yards and ranges it and kills it.

"But ... when people read that, these are people who generally don't have Chuck's dedication, practice regimen or ability. Yet, 'Chuck Adams takes 60-yard shots, why shouldn't I?' And this is just one difference that we've had. The majority of the people who read it are never going to be able to shoot like Chuck.

249

"That's a little irresponsible on our part (to publish it), unless it's qualified in some way."

Question: So is Chuck good for bowhunting, or does the negative perception outweigh the good?

Answer: "He's good for bowhunting. There's no question about it. When you look at what he's accomplished; when you look at his communicative abilities; when you look at the number of people he's touched in a positive sense; he's definitely good for bowhunting.

"Chuck understands that there are people who don't know him who still are going to hate his guts for grinning that grin over this big critter. But he has earned this. I know what he went through as a writer to have accomplished what he's done. And I for one am not going to begrudge him. I know for years, he did without. I know just how tough a row he had to hoe there as a freelance writer trying to make it. Well, he made it. So, I don't begrudge him for the endorsements. I don't begrudge him for the fees that he charges for personal appearances. I don't begrudge him for making money off of what he's accomplished over a lifetime in the field because I think he's earned it."

Jim Dougherty, member Bowhunting Hall of Fame

Question: You've shared hunting camps with Chuck. How is he just as a guy to be around hunting camp with?

Answer: "He's a great campmate. He's fun. He's maybe a little bit more focused than I like, but then I might have been that focused when I was his age. He's pretty much into it, but as far as a guy who's a good hunting companion and a guy who's good to be with and everything, he's fine, he's great."

Question: Chuck focuses on killing trophy animals and promotes that end result through his writing and in advertisements. Does that rub you wrong?

Answer: "Let's face it. He's an incredible marketing guy. He's done a hell of a job. He's turned it into a hell of a career, and some people resent that. But I don't know why it would be bad for bowhunting. What the guy's done, well, a lot of big stuff that he's shot consistently proves that bowhunting is effective, and I think that's good for bowhunting.

"His notoriety, if you will, I think is good for bowhunting. He's turned what he loves to do the most into a career. I can totally understand it. I grew up in this industry and I've been bowhunting all my life and that's what I do. I can certainly understand it."

Question: **What about the common claim from bowhunters who say that they could duplicate Chuck's achievements, given the same opportunity?**

Answer: There are probably some guys who can say that to which it's true. But they're probably 10 percent of the bowhunting public. Chuck is an excellent bowhunter. He's very tenacious. He's smart. He's an incredible stalker. He's a deadly shot. He's got the patience of a mountain lion, so he can get the things done. He's the whole damn package. If you've got the time and wherewithal to get to all these places, then, yeah, some people are going to have a pretty good chance, but others are not going to get the job done either way.

You've seen some of these guys I'm talking about. You know who they are. They're all, 'Look at me, look at me, and how come I'm not in your ads?' that kind of thing. They bounce around from bow company to bow company. The world's full of them and always will be. But they don't have a solid foundation like he's got. He's done well and he deserves what he's obtained, reputation-wise, financially, the whole nine yards."

Ted Nugent: hunter, rocker:

Question: **What's your take on Chuck Adams?**

Answer: "I have great admiration for killing machines. I think you've just got to salute and appreciate the level of predator awareness and application of someone like Chuck Adams. He is certainly, I believe, one of the all-time most knowledgeable human predators in my lifetime. I truly believe he ranks right up there with the very best.

"I can't fail to comment how I applaud and have learned

from Chuck's progress over the years. I think his writing reflects the maturity as a man and the maturity certainly as a hunter. His writings are still campfire basic, but extremely progressive in the knowledge that he brings forth from his vast experiences. He plays an important, important role in our industry."

Question: It appears to many people quoted in this book that Chuck has worked hard for what he has and that he's played by the rules. So what's up with all the critics?

Answer: "I'll tell you what's up with that. Now, remember, you're talking to a 53-year-old guy who's been clean and sober for 53 years. My 53 years clean and sober, and a certain level of awareness; I've been very successful in anything I've chosen to do. I understand the human experience.

"I just spent a week with a dying child who is something like the 36th or 37th dying child who has requested his or her last campfire with me. The reason I'm mentioning that is ... I have an *amazing* amount of critics. But if a dying child and a dying child's family and a dying child's pastor authorize a last wish with Ted Nugent, I gotta tell you, I gotta be a pretty good guy. That's the ultimate screening process a reputation could ever go through.

"That being said, as I share the critic orgy of Chuck Adams; it isn't Chuck Adams. There is good, bad and ugly in the human species. That's not an opinion. That's an observation. We all have to be aware of this truism. You and I and Chuck and a vast majority of hunters have shared campfires with the very best of the good. The most profound, compassionate, giving, loving, thoughtful, good, decent, funny, positive people available in the human experience—the best of the best—can be found around hunting camps, without question.

"That being said, sadly, Chuck Adams' critics, like Ted Nugent's critics, in every instance I've reviewed, are the *worst* of the bad and the ugly. The resonating term that best identifies Chuck Adams' critics is PETTY in all capital letters. (The critics) are unfounded; they are self-righteous to a vulgar degree; the very content of their criticism is intellectually vacuous and historically defied.

"They criticize his choice of equipment, his style of hunting, the claim that he is commercializing his sport? I have to digress a moment here. Who in God's green earth would have criticized Dale Earnhardt for accepting a paycheck for racing a car? They (the critics) are pompous. I have watched them, and horrifically they have somehow lied and manipulated their way into leadership positions (in this industry). They know who they are. They are the most unsophisticated dolts who I have ever witnessed. And in their petty lives they scramble to make something of themselves in a feeble mindless attempt to belittle those who are successful. It's insanity.

"I'm constantly saying, 'Wait a minute. Don't you dare criticize Chuck Adams. You mean to say you wouldn't take a free hunt? You mean you wouldn't take free equipment? You mean you wouldn't take a paycheck for celebrating your last dynamic soul-stirring hunting experience on paper? You're going to turn down the check? (Expletive) you. Give me a break.' Chuck does what every welder, every farmer in America does. He goes out and he works during the day for the maximum dollar he can get. It's what you do, it's what I do, it's what America does. And to level criticism at anyone for doing that proves you are a numb-nut."

Question: Still, is he out there doing as much for bowhunting and our hunting future as you'd like to see him doing?
Answer: "With his position comes an immense responsibility in a cultural war of penetration. And that's my only current constructive criticism of Chuck Adams. He has got to reach out. He just shot the biggest (bow-killed) elk in the history of record-keeping. What does that mean? It's the healthiest elk ever taken which means it's the healthiest elk herd ever! But that's a secret (to the mainstream, popular media). How dare we keep it a secret that (because of us) wildlife is thriving! We're so afraid that we'll be called a braggart if we say we shot a monster that we actually retract our claws. I say sharpen them (expletive) and go to some clinic to get the claws bigger and badder and more dangerous! That's what we ought to be doing. This is a cultural war. With Chuck Adams' expertise, I'm asking him, Chuck, go to the front lines."

CHAPTER THIRTEEN:
IS BOWHUNTING STILL FUN?

"Quite frankly, I could hunt less, I believe, at this stage of my life, take fewer animals, and very easily maintain my career. And yet, I still feel like I don't bowhunt enough. I would love to bowhunt more than I do."

To anyone reading this book it must sound like an absurd question: Is bowhunting still fun? Consider, however, having taken literally hundreds of big game animals with a bow. Consider bowhunting for something approaching 100 days each year over the course of nearly three decades. Consider your whole life consumed by bowhunting. Would opening day anticipation evaporate? Might you rather be fishing, bird hunting, taking in a football game, spending time with your family or simply relaxing? Might each day spent bowhunting seem less precious than it should?

Some people do not mix business and pleasure well. The infamous case of Donald E. Lewis is one example. Lewis, of Huntsville, Alabama, made something of a name for himself and a modest living in the hunting industry because of the many trophy animals he claimed to have legally killed during the 1980s. In fact, his assertions earned him paid-for pro staff positions with at least three hunting equipment manufacturers at the time.

But in July 1993, he pleaded guilty to killing three elk in Yellowstone National Park. As part of a plea agreement, Lewis was fined only $15,000—$5,000 for each of the three elk—despite his admission that he and friends had made annual hunting trips to Yellowstone from 1983 to 1991 and had broken game laws in several states. Records show that Lewis and his companions killed approximately 14 elk in Yellowstone Park and that in 1991 they videotaped themselves shooting at 13 elk. Although Lewis had boasted of his bowhunting skills, investigators eventually discovered that he and his companions had shot several of the park elk with rifles.

"People look at major law-breakers like Don Lewis and others, and they bring those people up to me and say, 'You know some of those people like Lewis after he was indicted for poaching in Yellowstone National Park, said they were trying to be the next Chuck Adams,'" Chuck says.

"In Lewis' case," Chuck continues, "in an interview he said that the pressure to perform in this industry is huge. I've never felt that. I think that's a bunch of baloney. I think you either put it on yourself or not. And this is the honest-to-God truth: If the enjoyment of what I do decreased, I'd try to make a change because that's the only reason I work so hard—so I can truly enjoy hunting. People often ask me, 'Does the pressure of having to get animals dampen your enjoyment of bowhunting?' And I can honestly say that it never has, except in that one case (the lion hunt to complete the Super Slam) where I was feeling extra pressure.

"Part of it is that I'm a multi-species hunter. The hunters I talk to, the ones who feel pressure are the ones who are specialized with one animal. They might go two or three years to get one big whitetail with a bow. Those guys and gals seem to feel pressure. With me, I go on several hunts every year for different species and I figure sooner or later something's going to work out. And that's a pressure valve, too, I think."

It's an extreme example, of course, but it's common for hunting to lose some of its sparkle when it becomes one's profession. "I have to go on a hunt next week," instead of "I get to go ..." is a lament that can be heard from hunting writers late each hunting season. Being away so much can be a drag on even the most ardent hunter's quality of life. To Chuck's credit, though, hunting has not come to that. Each September brings the promise of elk bugling in the Montana mountains. And when the whole adventure finally winds down in January, it is not a sense of relief, but one of disappointment and longing for next season.

"I think I actually enjoy hunting more today because I feel I'm more in control," Chuck says. "Not a lot, but there's an amount of satisfaction derived from doing something right on purpose. I get just as excited as I ever did. If that ever stopped, I should probably go play golf or something else, but at this point I'm sure it never will. The thrill is still there.

255

"Quite frankly, I could hunt less I believe at this stage of my life," Chuck continues, "take fewer animals, and very easily maintain my career. And yet, I still feel like I don't bowhunt enough. I would love to bowhunt more than I do. And that's because I love it. But like everybody else, I need to make money, I have to work ... so I can't just go bowhunt year-round."

I'D RATHER BE HUNTING

Still, Chuck manages more bowhunting days each calendar year than many bowhunters enjoy in five years. On average, he's afield with bow in hand approximately 90 days annually. Like any bowhunter, though, Chuck must make hay primarily from September through November. The rest of his year is eaten up by "the job."

In January, depending on when the bowhunting industry's big trade show occurs, Chuck sometimes manages to sneak to Texas for whitetails or to Mexico or the desert Southwest for Coues' deer.

By February, the sportsmen's show season gains steam, and Chuck racks up thousands of frequent flier miles attending shows to give bowhunting seminars and sign autographs. The show circuit typically continues, with a show nearly every weekend, right into April.

"I love to hunt spring turkeys, but I haven't for probably seven or eight years because I'm simply too busy at that time of the year," Chuck says. "I'd love to hunt red stag in New Zealand or someplace during the rutting season in March and April, but I'm too tied up doing public appearances. So I live out of a suitcase during those months basically. I'm barely home in time to do my laundry and hit the road again."

"This year I'm going spring black bear hunting in New Brunswick in late May. The year before I was fortunate to be able to buffalo hunt in Arizona in spring, and I'm going to have to figure out some spring outing somewhere so I can maintain my sanity. Since the AMO (Archery Manufacturer's and Merchant's Organization) Show has been starting too early in January, I haven't been able to go to Arizona or Mexico for Coues' deer. Between November and August is a long time for me not to hunt, so I would bet that my black bear hunting, which I haven't done too much of lately, is going to come back."

Chuck says that he tries to limit his public appearances to 40 or so days per year, but that it sometimes stretches longer and is almost all jammed into late winter and early spring. Of course, he is paid well to appear at outdoors shows where he presents bowhunting seminars and signs autographs. And he realizes that beyond the paycheck from the show organizers it's also important to the companies like Easton, Hoyt and the others whom he represents.

In one year, Chuck estimates that he signs more than 30,000 autographs at sports shows. As for the seminars, he says that standing up in front of a crowd comes fairly naturally to a former teacher like himself.

"When you're immersed in this subject matter the way I am—when you eat, sleep and drink it and breathe it—I think you naturally know the subject matter backward and forward," Chuck says. "I write literally hundreds of articles on bowhunting and archery, and Lord help me if I don't know the subject backward and forward. If I don't, I shouldn't be doing seminars."

At the Anderson Archery Clinic in Grand Ledge, Michigan in June of 1990, Chuck gave his first seminars and was astonished when lines of 50 to 100 fans waited in the hot sun for a handshake and an autograph. He signed more than 5,000 photos during that three-day event. "I had a shaky hand when I finished that one," Chuck says. "I wondered what Mike Anderson had gotten me into."

Anderson, promoter of that popular event, takes credit for talking Chuck into public appearances.

"We had all the big names at the Anderson Clinic over the years," Anderson says. "That includes Fred Bear and Ted Nugent. Chuck is the most popular we've ever had, with longer lines for autographs and more people calling about him before the show. He greatly boosted attendance."

Chris Fassnacht is president of Expositions Inc. which runs the Pittsburgh and Cleveland sportsmen's shows. Chuck conducts seminars at both and has for seven years in Cleveland. According to Fassnacht, there are some basic reasons why.

"He has a very low-key style that attendees like," Fassnacht says. "He's very approachable. He encourages a lot of questions which is great. He doesn't speak down to people because a lot of time people ask what some might consider a stupid question and he takes that in stride. And his photography is just incredible. The best thing that I like is that the world of seminar speakers is so commercialized that it seems like you can't look at any part of a presentation without seeing company logos everywhere. Chuck doesn't do that.

"We have not seen a decline in the attendance to Chuck's seminars which would be typical for any seminar speaker after you use someone for seven years like we have with Chuck," Fassnacht continues. "When people ask via e-mail and letters, 'Is Chuck Adams coming back?' We're happy to say, 'Yes.'"

When the seminar season winds down by the beginning of May, it's time to crank out articles to meet the many converging deadlines for the various hunting magazines for which Chuck writes. He still turns out an amazing 12 to 15 articles monthly—almost one every other day.

"It takes a toll," Chuck says. "I'm sitting here talking to you in late April and I am absolutely whipped from traveling. I'm writing articles all the time. I'm writing articles on airplanes, between seminars, even in hunting camps. But I continue to write in May, June and July at an accelerated pace to try to get ahead before hunting season. That's a brain drain.

"I do it because I can jam most of my work into eight or nine months a year and then take off significant amounts of time to go hunting. But I certainly don't work less per year than other people. It's just apportioned differently throughout the year. And I don't think it's for everybody. As I've said, it wasn't a factor in my marriage, but it is very hard on relationships. I'm gone so much that it limits the number of women who would put up with me, that's for sure, and I understand that and appreciate that. It requires a high amount of enthusiasm to make it all work."

SEASON SNAPSHOT

In between writing sessions during summer, Chuck slips out to shoot his bow or to make a telephone call to a big game biologist, outfitter or bush plane pilot. It's time to make certain that everything is planned as precisely as possible for the coming fall.

Chuck and friend, Frank Addington, at the 1997 AMO Show. The bowhunting industry's big trade event in January kicks off what for Chuck is a whirlwind four-month show circuit during which he signs thousands of autographs and presents dozens of seminars.

"I start anticipating a lot earlier because I'm planning as best as I can to go to the best areas and, if it's an outfitted hunt, to find the very best outfitter and guide," Chuck says. "The anticipation for me is half the enjoyment. The planning and the looking forward; the same as it was when I was a kid in California and I had one deer tag a year and I anticipated all year to go and hunt that one deer. That's a big part of it for me and what I missed when I started this job.

"The first 10 or 15 years I was scrambling so hard to write articles that I was pulling all-nighters before I left on a hunting trip. That didn't leave me enough time to anticipate properly and that took something away from the experience. Now I can relax a little bit more during the three or so months before hunting season and really anticipate and savor it."

In July Chuck says that the serious bow-shooting kicks in as he dials his shooting setup to razor-sharp precision. Muscles are tuned, products tested and the gear that makes the cut prepped for travel. "Then it's hunting season, and I disappear," Chuck says.

For the entire decade of the 1990s, Chuck launched his bowhunting season with a week or two in July at Phil Phillips' Colorado pronghorn camp. But with Phil's operation dramatically curtailed, Chuck now marks August as the official season opener, likely somewhere in the remote wilds of Alaska.

"For the last 25 years I have always hunted in August," Chuck says. "Alaska was a big event most years. I was either up there hunting caribou on my own in a drop-camp situation, or Sitka black-tailed deer on Kodiak Island, or both on back-to-back trips in Alaska. In 1999, I spent almost all of August chasing that big antelope at Phil's. I expect this year that I'll go back to Alaska. The other thing I've done in the end of August quite often is hunt Quebec-Labrador caribou or in the Northwest Territories hunting Central Canada barren ground caribou."

September is no surprise. You'll find Chuck somewhere in the Montana mountains listening for a bugling bull elk as he has for decades. Sure, he might hunt another species or two in September, but elk take center stage.

"I'm happy to say that I've hunted elk every September except that one year that the divorce was imminent and I just wasn't in any mood," Chuck says. "Elk are way up there, and as long as I can get a tag, I'll be hunting elk during the rut in September. Some years I've hunted moose in September. I hunt early-season mule deer in September sometimes. I've hunted a second pronghorn antelope some years.

"September's gone. I'm never around in September. I laugh when someone asks me if I can do a public appearance in September because it just ain't possible."

October is a mixed bag of bowhunting, with whitetails a concentration in November and December. Between the hunts there are deep piles of accumulating mail and strings of voice mail messages that require attention to keep ahead of the game. Usually there's only a day or two to dig out and get things organized before heading back out the door. Then the Holidays, the AMO Show and the seminar circuit all over again. Would you want to walk a year in Chuck's boots? Has it been worth the sacrifice to him?

"I've thought about that a lot," Chuck says. "You never know what could have been, but I don't believe that there's any point in speculating much about that anyway. There's almost nothing in my life that I would change. I'm living a boyhood dream right now. It's a great job.

"I've sacrificed having children. I've sacrificed being able to leave the job at the office on the weekends. I've sacrificed alone time during the late winter and early spring and the peace of being able to go back to a home and not worry about climbing on another airplane for a few days.

"But this was the only way that I could figure out where I could take off and go elk hunting and caribou hunting during the fall without worrying about a set number of days of vacation time. I can't think of any other scenario that would let me do what I love to do most pedal-to-the-metal."

KEEPING IT FUN

For Chuck, a few steadfast rules ensure that each bowhunting season and each bowhunt generate the natural high that he craves.

To start, bowhunting and work are two distinctly different things. Chuck won't even carry his still camera along in his backpack while he's hunting. If he kills an animal, he returns to camp for the camera gear, and then the photo work begins.

Similarly, it is extremely rare for him to accept a hunting invitation from an equipment manufacturer. These "sponsored hunts" abound in the industry and are seen by many outdoor writers as the most economical means of gathering article fodder. For the manufacturer, it's a way to get his product promoted. For the outfitter hosting the hunt, it's a chance to get ink for his business—a win-win-win.

The downside is that the "hunting" part of these "hunts" is generally conducted in a leisurely manner and rarely in top trophy-producing areas. Thus, Chuck doesn't consider these trips hunts at all; more like business travel to be accepted only if absolutely necessary. And he won't spend a week on a business trip when he could be hunting daylight until dark during the prime, fleeting days of the hunting season. Chuck will occasionally hunt with a handful of select friends from within the hunting industry, but almost always on a hunt that he researches and schedules on behalf of the group.

In short, Chuck hunts where he wants, when he wants and with whom he wants. This approach rubs some the wrong way, but it's common knowledge in the business that Chuck won't compromise what he considers "his" hunting time. So he's rarely bothered about it anymore.

Along the same lines, Chuck has shied noticeably from the video cameras during hunting season. He's accepted a handful of offers to go on treestand whitetail hunts and allow a cameraman to be perched alongside him. But he's never done it while foot-hunting for any big game species. To date, no one has ever taped Chuck bow-killing a big game animal. That makes him something of an endangered species today when most hunting "celebrities" gain their notoriety primarily from hunting shows or videos. And despite the potential for Chuck to make a good deal of money in the hunting video business, he's stubbornly refused to venture down that road.

"I've tried to separate the two—bowhunting and work—entirely and I don't remember a time when I didn't try to do that," Chuck says. "If I ever let the two come together, I think I would enjoy bowhunting less. And that's one reason I have religiously refused to bowhunt on camera. Whenever you put a camera crew behind you, hunting becomes work. I'd be hunting for the right camera angle instead of a big animal. Without exception, the biggest animals that I've taken would not have been taken had there been another person there with a camera."

Chuck says that he's never heard his critics use the fact that he doesn't hunt on camera as evidence that he's not taking his trophies legitimately.

"Virtually all of the animals I've taken have been witnessed in one way or another," Chuck says. "Obviously if I'm hunting with an outfitter, I've got a witness right there. And I prefer to hunt with good friends, so there's almost always someone in camp or hunting with me."

PERSISTENCE, START TO FINISH

In Chapter Eight many of the men who've hunted side-by-side with Chuck echoed a simple and straightforward assessment of his hunting prowess: dogged determination, a persistence almost to the point where it would seem that he's hunting to eat, to survive. Of course, he's not literally, but he is figuratively. Take bowhunting from Chuck and you rob his soul.

And while there is extreme exhilaration in even the most lung-burning pursuit, the dirty work after the shot can be downright agonizing. Some blood trails are longer than others. That's part of hunting no matter what your choice of hunting tool. Yet some who call themselves bowhunters and revel in the record books would rather not deal with the inconvenience incurred when they make a marginal hit, especially if that animal wasn't particularly large anyway. It takes time that could be spent chasing a different animal. And it requires an "expert" hunter to face the harsh reality of failure. Some egos don't accept such humility and, thus, ignore the unwritten rules of ethics and duty that go along with being a hunter.

One might think that a guy like Chuck would rather not roll up his sleeves and get his hands dirty after the fact. Doesn't have time for it. Gotta tag P&Y animal No. 112, can't be burning daylight blood-trailing an animal that will probably get away and survive anyway. But Chuck says that his hunting persistence doesn't end when the bowstring slides from his fingers.

"I can honestly tell you that I never give up," Chuck says. "I know that even the most downer hunt can turn around so quickly that it would amaze even me sometimes. So I never give up. I'm always out there trying and hunting from daylight 'til dark. One of the good examples of this is recovering animals because you don't always get good hits and you always owe it to the animal."

One hunt that Chuck described was a Coues' deer hunt in Sonora, Mexico, in January 2000. Late afternoon the hunt's final day, he spotted a huge 8-point buck more than a mile away on a plateau. Hours later he'd stalked to within 30 yards of the bedded deer. With the deer slightly quartering toward Chuck and no way for Chuck to shift and set up a perfect angle, he drew his bow behind cover, eased up, aimed and released. At the sound of the release, the deer lunged from its bed and the arrow hit farther back than intended, behind the ribs and angling toward the hind.

A good situation suddenly turned bad. Little daylight remained, and Chuck's outfitter, his only ride out of Old Mexico, had to leave the country the next day. And Chuck had commitments at the archery industry's trade show a couple of days later. Hoping against hope, and knowing he had no alternative, he jumped on the blood trail immediately.

"The deer was leaving virtually no blood on the ground," Chuck says. "And I looked for that animal the rest of the day. It was a high hill, and he ran downhill. There were a whole bunch of different places he could have gone. At dark I still hadn't found him, and I was heart-sick. I had to leave the next day. I didn't have a choice. So I left with my outfitter, went to the AMO Show and as soon as that was over I made plans to go back to Mexico on my own."

Chuck and his dad flew south, rented a vehicle, crossed the border and blood-trailed the deer two weeks later. Of course, they knew that even if they were lucky enough to find the buck, only a skeleton would remain after two weeks of scavengers feasting on it. But Chuck still felt an obligation to try to find what was left of the buck, to see the hunt to its conclusion, and to take home with him, at least, the skull and antlers so that the animal could earn its rightful place in the Pope and Young records.

"Fortunately it hadn't rained, and we probably found 10 or 12 small match-head sized drops of very black blood at that point, and we found that buck," Chuck says. "The coyotes had eaten the meat instead of me eating the meat. But I did find that deer and I have the antlers, and he's one of the top award winners at the Pope and Young convention. And I if I do say so myself, I call that persistence, both in time and money and effort. And it's interesting that Pop and I both found the opposite end of that blood trail and we followed the whole blood trail, and I got to that deer about 150 yards ahead of Pop. And that deer had gone about 600 yards down a direction that was not one of the more likely routes I thought he'd take."

It's a trail that Chuck had been down before, the same as any veteran big game hunter. Years earlier, it happened in Texas under eerily similar circumstances. Again it was January and the last day of a hunt with the busy AMO Show waiting. Again a jumpy deer lunged at the sound of the string, resulting in a long track. This time the arrow angled forward through the front of one ham and out through the liver. The deer ran off and left no blood on the ground for Chuck to follow. He searched the rest of the day to no avail.

"I had to leave the next morning for the AMO Show because I

Although he admits that he's not a whitetail fanatic like some, Chuck has taken 43 whitetails with a bow, including seven Pope and Young bucks.

had commitments that I couldn't get out of," Chuck says. "And I asked three friends of mine on that big ranch to look for that deer on my behalf. Two of them were bowhunters. They looked for five days and didn't find the deer. I went back after the AMO Show and found that deer in an hour and a half, following his tracks from the week before. And I was really proud of that. That particular deer went 690 yards. I always figure even a paunch-hit animal, if you don't push it, is going to be inside a half a mile from you. If you have to, you grid-search the whole area, no matter how many hours of the day it takes, and you will find that animal.

"The only reason I went back to Texas was to find that deer, not to hunt anymore. So I also call that persistence. And I don't think every bowhunter would go that far to find an animal. And that was a nice 10-point Pope and Young whitetail, but if it would have been a little 8-point whitetail, I still would have gone back. Again, the coyotes ate the deer, but I got the antlers. And I'm proud of the antlers and I wish I had the meat, but life's not perfect, and the animal's dead either way.

"I've never felt lackadaisical about individual animals or hunting. I just love it too much and I've always valued every animal. Yes, I try to shoot especially big animals. But I would never say that one animal is more valuable than another. When I spend a great number of days going after a particular animal, I think, as the days go by, that animal becomes more and more valuable in my mind. So if anything, the longer I hunt an animal the more valuable it becomes. But I always go back just because that's my responsibility and I know what a good feeling it is to button up a hunt with a successful ending to it."

BASIC TRAINING

Chuck believes that his father was instrumental in instilling this hunter's ethic at an early age. Hand-in-hand with the emphasis on hard work and discipline went the responsibility for seeing a hunt through to its completion. And that meant searching for wounded animals until every last ounce of hope had been exhausted. It also meant the utmost effort in field care to ensure that every possible ounce of venison be salvaged before spoiling.

"I'm fortunate that I grew up in northern California and had my dad as a teacher because when we started black-tailed deer

With deer hunter success rates below 10 percent in California back when Chuck was in his teens, he learned to hunt hard and to work hard to preserve the precious venison.

hunting, we were hunting in a state with the lowest success rate for gun hunters on deer in the nation," Chuck says. "It was down around 6 or 7 percent. The way we got deer was to hike into the most God-awful roadless places that we could find, and go in on a day-hunt basis. Two places had names that speak for themselves. One was called the Devil's Den, and the other was called the Devil's Parade Ground.

"We would hike and hunt down in the middle of these very steep roadless areas, usually hunting downhill, ... so it was tough to get back out. We never saw anybody and we would shoot deer with our rifles, and the average amount of time that it took for two of us to pack out one of those little 120- or 130-pound black-tailed deer was six hours. I remember many times that it took eight or nine hours when we carried half a deer apiece, and we were scrambling uphill and sweating in warm early season weather.

"And I always thought that hard work and that never-say-die attitude stood me in great stead for the rest of my life because I grew up scratching and clawing for the little forked-horn and 3-point bucks we took with rifles. By comparison, everything else was not any more difficult. And I, as a result, was never scared to go work hard and break my butt to get the meat back out."

HUNTING WITH DAD

Those traditional deer hunts that Chuck and Charles enjoyed back when Chuck was still a kid did more than ingrain in Chuck a strong sense of ethics. They forged an unbreakable bond between father and son—a bond that would make them life-long hunting partners.

Charles was there on Chuck's first blacktail kills in the California hills. In fact, he built for Chuck the .270 Winchester that the boy shot his first deer with. And Charles watched and smiled on the way home with that buck as Chuck would prop the deer's head up repeatedly to make sure that one of the little antlers didn't get chipped. In the years since, Charles has been by Chuck's side in Alaska, Colorado and other hunting camps stretching across the continent. While Chuck has gained strong friendships with other hunting partners, the one guy who's always been there has been "Pop." And with him, Chuck is able to rekindle the best of what hunting has meant to him.

"Hunting with my dad is a lot of fun," Chuck says. "Our relationship is real important to me. I write about it pretty regularly, too. We hunted more together before I got into this business and less in the middle of my career and we're hunting together more now again. I make a concerted effort to do that just because I missed out when I was so busy. I just missed hunting with him."

By the time that Chuck passed hunter education at age 7, hunting had taken on new meaning for Charles in his adult life. Raised during the Great Depression, Charles taught himself how to hunt by age 10—not for fun, but for food. Still, he was able to find joy and life lessons in something that at the time was mostly utilitarian—nourishment for his family.

"My dad (Grandpa Paul) bought me a Remington .22 single-shot when I was 10 years old," Charles says. "And I remember him stabbing his finger at me and saying, 'Your assignment is to get meat for the family.' So that's the way I started hunting.

"That's always been part of the code. Of course, we grew up in a Christian context. And what I tell people now when I get guff about hunting, I say, 'Look, I'm not even going to argue the point with you. I'm committed to the idea of every creature of God is good for food and nothing to be refused if it be received with thanksgiving.' That's a New Testament quotation, and that's it."

Today, though Chuck and Charles don't need to hunt for food, they maintain an understanding as hunting partners built on that "code" of ethics. Yet one could imagine where Charles would have worried about how those "middle" years, when the two were apart, would have impacted Chuck's perspective. At the time, after all, Chuck's hunting became a means toward a different end, one measured at least in part in dollars and antler inches. There was a Grand Slam, the Super Slam and a world record animal. And in those middle years Chuck had become a bowhunting icon. What kind of hunting partner would Charles get at the end of all that?

"The same love of the out-of-doors, the same love of game, the same intensity, ... it's still there," Charles says about Chuck. "That was something that was drilled into him right from the beginning. He wounded that buck in Mexico in 2000 and he just simply insisted that we look for that deer even though it was difficult because of the timing and so forth. But it's always been that way. It's been a passion."

As Chuck pointed out way back in Chapter One, he and Pop have been an odd couple of sorts ever since Chuck decided to handicap himself with a bow. Yet they've accepted one another for their different tastes in hunting, and they've managed to find ways to share hunting camps, even if they might strike out from camp in different directions to hunt. Still, Charles, now 74, has walked alongside his son often enough in these later years to recognize and witness for himself the hunter that Chuck has become.

"It never really was something that I said, 'Oh well, I'm a rifleman. He's going to come back home after a while,'" Charles says. "He's a bright kid and he was just so dedicated with things he did that I figured he would do all right at bowhunting. You're talking to a proud father here, but he's good. It never occurred to me but that he might be good.

"I have a range set up here in my backyard in California. When he's here visiting, even just for a week, he brings his bow and he shoots. I mean, I don't need a range, but we have it staked out and I keep a couple bales of straw, and he practices."

"Pop always thought that I should do what I wanted," Chuck says. "Yeah, he teased me about bowhunting all the time. To this day he does. And his philosophy is, 'If you can't join 'em, beat 'em.' We hunt a lot to this day, and I've learned to manage the built-in conflict between gun and bow. We like to hunt Alaska for Sitka black-tailed deer. And we went seven years in a row. I'd draw a circle around camp and I'd walk outside the circle and then start hunting with a bow because the two mix like oil and water. We've learned to stay away from each other in the field. I don't want gunfire in my ears, and he doesn't want me scaring things away.

"He admires the skills involved in bowhunting, and I know he's proud of what I've done, like fathers tend to be of their sons," Chuck continues, "but we have admiration for each other because there's a lot of skill in rifle hunting done right. Dad's one of the best rifle shots I've ever seen. I've seen him a number of times shoot running deer at several hundred yards, and it wasn't by accident. He's into his thing, I'm into mine, and we respect each other a lot."

It's been a long time since Chuck and Charles set foot together in the Deer Creek country or any of their other old blacktail stomping grounds. Times have changed the hunting landscape around Chico. The human population has increased dramatical-

Pop was there in April 2000, when Chuck arrowed his world record bison in Arizona and this second, smaller bull. He says that buffalo hunts with Chuck spark some of his fondest memories of time spent afield with his son.

ly and so has the hunting pressure on the available public land. Private land with good deer and wild pig populations is leased by wealthy hunters or hunting clubs.

These days, Chuck and Charles are more likely to be camped together on a forgotten lake somewhere on Kodiak Island. Still, despite all the exotic hunting locations and all of the record-book animals that the hunters have shared, the fondest of Charles' memories come from simple pleasures and simpler times.

"Before Chuck started hunting with a bow, we went up into the Sierra Mountains and killed two really nice bucks within two hours on the first morning," Charles says. "We were so pleased. We got back home by the middle of the afternoon. The neighbor just couldn't believe that we were back that soon, much less that we had killed two bucks.

"Then, when Chuck got his world record buffalo in 2000, we spent the whole night together butchering that. I don't know, there was just something about that—kind of a bonding. The buffalo was wedged down in some pinions and we just couldn't move it. So we had to skin it and butcher it piecemeal. We had the meat in the truck and ready to go to the cooler at 2 p.m. the next afternoon. That, I think, is one of the great memories that I have about working with Chuck. We had a great sense of accomplishment once that was done. We thought, 'Well, we did it.'"

Chuck knows that Pop isn't going to be able to help him butcher 1,800-pound buffalo for many more years. He knows that the remote, do-it-yourself hunts on Kodiak can't last forever. But, as is his tendency, Chuck opts to live life in the present and to plan for a future of maximum hunting pleasure.

"I've thought about that a lot," Chuck says. "It won't be the same; there's no one like your Pop. But Pop and I are talking about going back to Kodiak again next year if there's another mild winter. He'll be 75 at that point, and I have little doubt that he'll go do it."

DRIVING FORCES

Even though Chuck has achieved more in terms of record-book archery animals than any other bowhunter in history, he remains driven toward additional bowhunting goals. And striving toward new challenges is what provides the zest for the pursuit.

For seven straight years, Chuck and Charles hunted Kodiak Island, Alaska together. Here they display the results from a fantastic hunt in 1997.

Chuck admits that there are North American big game species that he has no interest in hunting again. He's taken them all. Some still spark the fire in his gut, others don't.

He doubts that he'll ever hunt muskox again, for example. And because of the great expense and the great specimens that he already has, another polar bear or Alaska brown bear are doubtful. Rather, now that he's experienced everything that the continent can throw at a bowhunter, he chooses to focus the magnifying glass more narrowly on the big game species that stoke his fire.

"My main goal is just to go back and hunt animals that I enjoyed hunting the first time around and try to get bigger specimens, only because that increases the challenge," Chuck says. "I could hunt elk once or twice every year for the rest of my life and be very happy about it. Any type of big deer is great. I'm going to try to hunt big white-tailed deer, mule deer and black-tailed deer for as long as I'm able to do that. As far as grandiose schemes, I don't know what else I would do. I'm asked that quite a bit, but it's not something I've thought about.

"I went and got the Super Slam to see what it was like to hunt all the North American animals and have that variety. I've done that, and that has given me a window, a very clear view of what's

273

out there. That allows me to go back and do what I enjoyed the first time around. So I think I am moving ahead all the time. I found out where I had the most fun. I don't have any desire to do a world slam or anything like that. I like hunting North America the best."

Especially Alaska. Chuck says he loves "The Last Frontier" most because of the variety of big game species that can be hunted in this wild, remote state. Famed Kodiak Island, in particular, marks a favorite place in Chuck's bowhunting memories and dreams.

"When you can go someplace and sit in one spot and see more than 100 branch-antlered bucks in one day, and pick and choose which ones you want to go after, I don't know how it gets better than that," Chuck says. "They don't have the biggest antlers in the world, but who cares? Everything's relative. I know what a big Sitka deer looks like, and that's what's important to me."

In the Lower 48, it's no surprise that Montana steals the show for Chuck. His home for nine years, the state that gave him his first elk in the mid-1970s and a P&Y world record typical bull in 2000, "Big Sky Country" is a close second to Alaska.

WHAT'S NEXT?

Though it might sound as if Chuck is backing away from his record-book pursuits, he maintains a keen focus on the top of the charts. With five world records in his history, including three current Pope and Young world records under his belt, taking the best of the best is definitely Chuck's type of thrill-seeking.

But he acknowledges that many of the P&Y world record animals are simply out of reach for all practical purposes. Topping his current world record elk would be a freak accident along the lines of being struck by lightning twice. Intentionally targeting and arrowing a new world record typical whitetail is virtually impossible. And Chuck's never been one to rely on blind luck. He'll keep hunting elk and deer, but he'll do so with the realization that it's not a world record he's after. Other big game species, though, might present an off-chance for world record number six.

"The world record scores are getting so high that there are not too many Pope and Young world records that are deliberately reachable anymore," Chuck says. "When I got my Sitka blacktail—the previous world record in 1986—that record was deliberately attainable. I felt at that time, and I was right, that if a person went to a remote area and hunted hard he could lay eyes on a world record. And if that person had the skill and the luck, he could shoot that deer. Today the world records have such high scores that in most cases, like my world record elk, you're talking pure luck if you ever lay eyes on an animal like that. But there are a few categories."

After a brief hesitation, Chuck revealed a few of the categories where he thinks he has at least a slim chance to stand atop bowhunting history.

Woodland caribou, the variety found on the island of Newfoundland in eastern Canada, is one species with a beatable score. He points out that gun hunters today, almost annually, are killing stags that would shatter the standing P&Y record. "That tells me those animals are there, and a person who went to the exactly right area might after several years of hunting lay eyes on a new world record. Then it's up to him to go kill that stag." Is Chuck strategizing to do it?

"I have plans," he says. "I do actively seek really big animals and check the record books periodically to see which categories have world records low enough that I think I could beat. I think there's a bigger mountain caribou out there. I think I actually have a chance to beat my own world record in that category. I think there's a bigger buffalo out there somewhere than what I shot last year, and I bet that I'll hunt buffalo again trying to beat that.

"There are a handful of attainable records out there, but as the years go by it's getting increasingly difficult. You look at the first record books from Pope and Young, and they're fairly thin books. You look at the latest one, and that is one big, heavy book. The more bowhunters there are, the higher the world records are going to go and the tougher it's going to be to beat 'em. But that's not my goal. If I never shoot another world record in my life, if I can just hunt and take nice animals, I'll be happy."

How happy? By all accounts, Chuck's bowhunting flame burns as bright as ever. Sure, he might not jump up and down with overwhelming euphoria anymore like he did when he was a kid; but the revelry and the appreciation for the art of bowhunting continue to drive him full-speed and head-long down this narrow, ancient path. And, yes, for Chuck, many of life's other pleasures have fallen casualty, left in bowhunting's gentle wake.

Some people rightly wonder then how long he can push himself season after season, hunt after hunt. Why does he? What's left to prove? Why not slow down and bask in the warm glow of success that he's earned after pressing himself so hard for so long?

The answer is the same as it was when he was a teenager falling in love with archery. The goal wasn't then and still isn't fame or fortune from bowhunting. Though he remains keenly competitive and keeps on counting those record-book certificates, the competition isn't with anyone else. If it were, it would have long since been over. Instead, the fire burns entirely within. And at the center of the flame are moments—a deft foot-fall indiscernible to wild ears; a predator eye probing broken country for antler; a dead-steady hand balancing a bow grip, the other hand's fingers tuned to hair-trigger precision. Satisfaction in the elements of bowhunting can come in small packages. And as long as those moments await, Chuck will chase them.

"I'll quit bowhunting when they bury me with my bow and typewriter," Chuck says. "I can't even imagine that. I guess I'll quit bowhunting when I'm no longer physically and mentally capable of getting out there. If I'm physically handicapped and can find a wheelchair with a motor, I'll still be out there. I suspect that my adrenaline level would still be high even if the success level were not. My guess would be that I would do the best I could and still enjoy the heck out of it. Even if I were camp-bound most of the time or had to just shuffle out of camp a little ways and sit on a stand. I just can't imagine not hunting."

CHAPTER FOURTEEN:
THE ONES THAT GOT AWAY

"The animals that get away are worthy adversaries. And if anything, I remember them more clearly than the ones I got because I didn't get them. They're tool sharpeners. I'm a better bowhunter because of those animals, not the ones I got. Every time I think about one of those big deer, I think about the mistakes I made and how I vow I'll never make them again."

A s memorable and momentous as so many of Chuck's bowhunting big game trophies are, so too, for Chuck at least, are some of the bucks and bulls that have escaped. Much has been written about the trophies taken, but precious little has been published about the ones that got away—because that doesn't sell as many magazines.

In more than three decades of bowhunting, Chuck has crossed paths with more than his fair share of world-class animals. Here are the accounts of the ones still standing after a dose of Chuck's best.

THE SPACE MONSTER
By October 1998, white-tailed deer hunting insiders near and far had heard of the "Space Monster." Living near Dinosaur National Park in Alberta, Canada, this buck had been shedding jaw-dropping antlers for the locals to find on a neighboring ranch. Each summer and into early fall, the buck could be spotted grazing the alfalfa away from the security of the park. But as soon as gun season opened, he'd vanish. His unearthly antlers and mannerisms earned him the Space Monster moniker.

On and off during the mid-'90s, Chuck's friend, Gerald Molnar, invited him to come to Alberta to hunt mule deer. In 1998, Chuck finally agreed and was rewarded with his best mulie buck ever—a hunt recounted in Chapter Five as one of Chuck's all-time best. With the mule deer tag filled, time to kill and a separate whitetail tag, Chuck wanted his shot at the Space Monster.

For three straight days at the end of his 1996 Kodiak Island blacktail hunt, Chuck spotted a buck that still haunts his memory.

The old buck was on his last legs in 1998 and so hungry that he hit the fields during bow season like he never had before. The ranch owner and other locals spotted the Space Monster sporadically during bow season, and Chuck got to see the deer alive, twice.

The first glimpse came during surveillance a mile from a fence corner where the rancher had told Chuck that he'd seen the buck cross. Well after daylight, Chuck manned a spotting scope on a distant rise. Sure enough, the old buck did just as the rancher had said. Out of the alfalfa, over the fence, across 150 yards of wide-open, flat prairie and into the depths of Dinosaur National Park.

"The rancher had told me, 'I haven't seen this buck enough to pattern him, but I've seen him cross there a couple times before. And he always jumps the fence right at this corner.' I went over there and glassed it and saw it for myself and I thought, 'Ah-ha!' I'll never forget that deer," Chuck says.

Midday he set his trap. Calling on a decade of pit-blind pronghorn hunting experiences gathered while hunting the Colorado high desert with Phil Phillips, Chuck deduced that a pit provided the only chance. He fervently dug the pit waist-deep along the fencerow. Seated inside, only his head, shoulders and the top half of his bow protruded above ground level.

Rather than build a roof over the top, and to keep it as natural as possible, Chuck gathered armloads of tumbleweeds and constructed a thick wall around him to camouflage his form. He left a small gap where he could shoot the unsuspecting Space Monster broadside, just as the buck prepared to jump the fence.

"And the very first morning I waited, here he came, after sunup, out of the fields," Chuck says. "I could see him coming for like half a mile. He had at least 12 or 14 points total. I didn't take time to count points. His rack was narrow, I bet it wasn't more than 15 inches wide, but he was a goal-poster. His rack went up forever, and he had extreme mass and long, long eyeguards.

"As that buck came across, he was all stove up. He was obviously arthritic. He wasn't limping per se, but just acted stiff. And he had his head down and he was very skinny and kind of reddish and sickly colored. And he had this awesome rack on his head—not as big as his sheds from his heyday, but still awesome. He came across and disappeared behind my little barrier. I figured he was going to jump the fence at about 40 yards away. I came to full draw, and he stopped just before he was going to jump the fence. I shot, and he jumped the string. All of the arthritis and old age disappeared for a few seconds, and he was 10 feet from where the arrow hit. He squirted down into Dinosaur National Park, and I never saw him again.

"It was a dead-calm day with a little bit of frost on the ground. I was shooting a quiet bow, but that son-of-a-gun heard me and goosed out of there. It was a difficult situation because it was wide open. And I don't know if he suspected something. I mean, those tumbleweeds were new along that fence, and he might have been spooky because he grew up there; suddenly, there was a huge wad of tumbleweeds where there weren't any before. I don't know. He did not see me. I had a solid wall and I was down in a hole, which allowed me to draw my bow unseen. But he didn't stand for it. And I figured he was just right at 40 yards where he stopped there, but it wouldn't have mattered."

Rifle hunters killed the Space Monster later in 1998. Aged at more than 10 years and in declining health, the buck still sported a rack that netted in the 180s non-typical. The shed antlers found during the buck's prime consistently grossed in the mid-200s with ungodly eyeguards approaching 19 inches. "You know," Chuck says, "if I would have gotten that buck, I might have said that 1998 (not 2000) was my best year ever. But I do feel fortunate that I laid eyes on that deer because he was a legendary whitetail."

MORE MISADVENTURES

Even in 2000, when it seemed that nothing could go wrong for Chuck, a Montana mule deer proved otherwise. This wasn't just any mule deer; the buck dwarfed all other Montana mule deer that Chuck had ever tailed and, he says, might have even rivaled his 1998 Alberta buck. Maybe the fact that this buck got away is one of the reasons that Chuck puts mule deer among his top four most difficult North American big game species.

"That deer just made a fool out of me, too," Chuck says. "I hunted him for probably two full weeks. I was in there every day where he was living and I found him most days. He was always in a different spot and always with a bunch of bucks. He was so sharp.

"The one opportunity I had at him, I saw him standing on a ridge, and he walked down and stood above his bed, straddling it for almost two hours before he lay down. And while he stood there he never moved, except for his head and his neck. That deer was so watchful. I tried to stalk him that time and I got within bow range over the curve of the hill. The wind was marginal; it was my only approach, and he smelled me before I got a shot. He got away clean."

So did a mountain caribou that still haunts Chuck's dreams. For 10 years, from 1985 to 1995, Chuck set his sights on breaking the Pope and Young world record for that species. He knew that gun hunters were taking bulls annually that were larger than the standing P&Y record and surmised that, given enough time in the right territory, he could, too. In the early '90s, a huge bull appeared—one that Chuck quickly judged to be much larger than the world record.

"That bull was very different from the world record caribou that I finally got in 1995," Chuck says. "The caribou that I got was massive and heavily palmated at the tops—more of a classic mountain caribou. The one that got away was very long-beamed and had tremendously long top points; he looked more like an Alaskan barren ground caribou. But he was very clearly way over 400 inches, and I almost got him in the middle of the day."

The bull and some of his bachelor buddies bedded in tall brush in a place where Chuck could slither to within 50 yards. Hunkered there inside solid bow range, he waited for the chance sure to come as soon as the bulls stood. But it never happened.

"When they stood up to go, they just started walking," Chuck says. "And I chased. You can't chase a caribou, and I knew that, but I tried. I chased that caribou for about five miles around a lake with my guide trying to keep up with me and I almost got that bull twice during that chase, when they'd stop briefly to feed. But I never got closer than 100 yards after that. I'll always remember that caribou. I think he was a higher-scoring caribou than the 413⅞ caribou that I got in 1995."

A huge mountain caribou, whitetail or mule deer getting away hurts, even if you get to hunt a lot and know that you'll eventually encounter other chances at other fine animals. Individual animals sometimes take on great importance to hunters, especially a trophy hunter like Chuck. And if it's a species that a hunter has a lot of history with, the significance is compounded.

For a kid who cut his teeth on northern California Columbia blacktails and thrilled to filling a tag with a fork-horn, imagine the agony of finally finding a giant blacktail one moment and watching it evaporate in the next.

"I was backpack hunting in the Trinity Alps Wilderness Area in northern California back in the early '80s," Chuck says. "Some friends of mine and I went in and set up a camp, and I saw the most tremendous Columbia black-tailed deer that I've ever seen in my life. I figured he would have netted 150 inches or better. He had like 15 other deer around him. I didn't get within 200 yards of that deer. It was in the evening, and I finally had to push it right

281

before dark and I spooked the whole bunch out. He was the biggest blacktail I've ever seen. I have several Columbia blacktails in the Pope and Young record book, but all in the lower half. This deer would have been near the top. He was in a class by himself.

"I think about that hunt pleasantly and I didn't get that buck. Bowhunting is always fun for me. Some of the most memorable hunts I've had, I haven't gotten an animal. The animals that get away are worthy adversaries. If anything, I remember them more clearly than the ones I got because I didn't get them. They're tool sharpeners. I'm a better bowhunter because of those animals, not the ones I got. Because every time I think about one of those big deer, I think about the mistakes I made and how I vow I'll never make them again."

TIME'S UP

Mature, hunter-wise big game animals don't tolerate mistakes. A mistake, in fact, often marks the end of a hunt. Every hunt, after all, must end at some point. Even if you're Chuck Adams with the luxury of a flexible schedule, seasons end and other business sometimes can't be re-scheduled. So what happens when you're on the brink of check-mate, but just can't put all the pieces together? How do you decide to throw in the towel and move on?

"It depends on the situation," Chuck says. "Sometimes I have another hunt coming up and I just have to bag it and go to the next trip. Usually I have work I just have to get done, or I have another hunt with other people who I don't want to disappoint. Occasionally the animal will disappear, and I know I've bumped him and it's over. If I can stay without jeopardizing my career or another hunting trip, I'll stay."

In 1996 Chuck prowled Kodiak's mountains for Sitka blacktails and on the third-to-last day of the hunt spotted the best buck he's ever seen. A Quebec caribou hunt with his colleagues from Easton awaited immediately following Kodiak. No choice. Chuck would have to intercept the buck in three days, or the buck would win.

Each of the three days, Chuck found the massive, 24-inch-wide, 5x5 buck in the same basin surrounded by six of his bachelor buddies: too many eyes and ears. Over the three days, 120

Chuck went on from Kodiak Island, Alaska to Quebec where he met up with friends Randy Schoeck, left, and Pete Weaver, center, But even an awesome caribou migration couldn't erase the giant Sitka buck from his mind.

yards is as close as Chuck could get. Game over.

"I had to walk away from that deer," Chuck says. "And I think he would have broken the world record. He was like a 120 Sitka, net. That broke my heart, to have to get on a bush plane and leave. But I had no choice. If I had another hunt, solo hunt or a hunt with casual friends or a guided hunt that I could have just cancelled, I would have stayed and hunted that deer. But in that case, I didn't have a choice. I think the chances were pretty good that I would have had an opportunity to take him if I would have had a week to 10 days, but I just didn't have it.

"I told the Easton guys about him. I told them, 'You guys need to know how much you mean to me.' I mean I went to the best Quebec-Labrador caribou hunt I'd ever been on in my life. We saw several thousand bulls on that trip. We hit the migration just right. But I still was wishing that I was back in Sitka country."

In 1997, Chuck trekked to the same Kodiak basin and searched for the buck to no avail.

Searching, hunting, focusing. This is what you get with Chuck Adams: a man with a singular life quest—perfection in bowhunting. Maybe for all his sacrifice and focus, he's approached that perfection more closely than any other human hunter in history. Still, many want more from him. We want him to be more like us. We want him to be the neighbor who brings us beers, slaps us on the back and talks about the football game. We want him to miss shots, drop his arrow off the rest and tell us all about it. When we don't get that satisfaction, Chuck Adams is difficult for some of us to accept simply for what he is and what he is not.

"When I go hunting it's like I step into my true element, and there's just a constant feeling of well-being when I'm out there," Chuck says. "It's just like all the invisible wires extending from my body are suddenly plugged in to everything around me. And I feel totally a part of it, and that's a tremendous feeling. That is one of the reasons why I enjoy hunts where I don't get anything the same as I enjoy hunts where I do get the animal. The adrenaline high is there, the sense of success and heightened satisfaction, because the challenge has been met. Just being out there makes me part of what I think I'm designed to be part of. I'm not designed to be part of an office with sheet-rock walls and maybe a window. I'm designed to be out there."

CHAPTER FIFTEEN:
BEYOND BOWHUNTING

"You never know what could have been, but I don't believe that there's any point in speculating much about that anyway. There's almost nothing in my life that I would change. I'm living a boyhood dream right now. I have sacrificed things. ... But this was the only way that I could figure out that I could take off and go elk hunting and caribou hunting during the fall without worrying about a set number of days of vacation time."

When the trade show closes, the hunt ends or the next article or photo shoot is complete, what is life like for Chuck Adams? There must be more to the man in the magazines and on the posters. What does he do in his spare time? Does he feel trapped by his bowhunting career? Has it consumed him to the point where he has "burned up the spot," but wishes for more from life?

"I certainly have other pursuits besides archery," Chuck says. "I love to cross-country ski, build furniture and other things from wood, and fish when I have the time. Although photography is part of the job, I also like to photograph scenery, landmarks and people. I watch TV occasionally to turn off my mind and relax, and I see all the top movies shortly after they hit videotape.

"I keep up on world events, though I'm not actively political, and I feel I can carry a conversation about a whole bunch of different subjects. I'm an avid chess and backgammon player. I'm not a culinary snob, but I do enjoy good restaurants.

"Most of all, though, I enjoy my down time with good friends," Chuck continues. "The majority of these folks are hunters, I'll admit, but we don't always talk archery. I suppose I'm mellowing out a bit as the years go by, and I certainly have more free time than when I was scrambling early in my career so that I could rub two dimes together.

"At the end of the day, I believe friends and family are the most important things in life. And when it comes to bowhunting, the trips I enjoy most are always with friends like Bob Breuder, Jeff Shimizu, Bill Hom, Richard Long, Craig Thomas, Roy and Angie Walk, Dave and Gail Griffith, Del Moore, and Doyle and Colleen Shipp. In that same category are industry friends like Erik Watts, Randy and Cathie Schoeck, Phil and Leslie Phillips, Randy Walk, Scott Shultz, Bill Jordan, Ev Tarrell, Craig Dougherty."

Mostly Chuck plays life fairly close to the vest. He gambles only during tricky stalks, never with hard-earned cash. His drug is fresh air, remote wilderness, a bow in his hand and a tag in his pocket. He has no taste for alcohol or tobacco, ordering iced tea or orange juice while others at the table enjoy wine or beer.

A DINOSAUR?

Though he's been self-employed for going on three decades, Chuck still conducts his business much the same way that he did when he started in the '70s. An editor or manufacturer can call and leave a message on Chuck's machine; and, provided that he is somewhere that has telephone service, he'll respond within a day. He has a cell phone, but wishes he didn't.

Chuck owns a computer but doesn't have e-mail, on purpose. He still composes articles on paper first and then keys the copy on his old IBM Selectric typewriter or laptop computer. As journalists go, Chuck is a throw-back. He'd be the laughing stock of an e-business convention. And, in some distinct ways, that is a reflection of Chuck the hunter, too.

He prefers to keep his equipment simple and reliable, rather than adding a lot of bells and whistles. His bow is not particularly fast. Neither is his typewriter. But both get the job done and don't let him down. He shoots aluminum arrows at a time when speedier carbon gets the majority of the press in hunting magazines. He trusts his fingers release more than a mechanical release aid. He's old-school. Some people choose to criticize him on that basis, saying that he's behind the times.

In reality, Chuck has tried racier bows. He's shot carbon shafts and monkeyed with mechanical release aids. He just happens to be in the minority of those bowhunters who prefer simplicity. And that approach also carries through into his professional life.

"I write everything in my own, impossible-for-anyone-else-to-read shorthand," Chuck says. "I can actually write faster than I can type, nearly 100 words per minute when I'm rolling, so I compose on college-ruled tablets. I have a laptop, but I still bang out a lot of stuff on my typewriter. It's not so much that I'm stuck in my ways. But I don't like to complicate my life. And a lot of the things that are supposedly life-simplifiers ... I don't think are.

"I think that I'm in pretty good company here because other successful, high-profile people avoid computers and hate cell phones just like I do," Chuck continues. "J.K. Rowling, of 'Harry Potter' fame, now has sold more books than any other author in history, and she writes everything longhand on legal pads in restaurants. I'm not so sure that following the thundering herd of humanity down well-worn paths of progress is always the best for every creative mind.

"I've religiously resisted having e-mail because I know highly visible people who have big problems answering the huge volumes of e-mail that they're deluged with. I hate the cell phone because it has complicated my life. I don't take the cell phone when I'm hunting because then it turns into work again.

"I don't know if you'd call me a dinosaur or not. I'm really quick at what I do the way I do it. It's just taking the time to change that's probably the biggest problem. I am so busy that I don't have time to stop and become truly adept with computer functions. And I know that if I decided to stop and do that, I'd totally stop and master the whole dang thing before I got back to business as normal. But it never seems like I have the time to do that. I don't like to dabble in stuff—I dive in headfirst and go all the way to the core."

Yet, despite the fact that Chuck resists communication technology in a concerted effort to find moments of peace, only when he's hunting in some far-off land can he escape the rigors of being Chuck Adams.

Chuck's the first to acknowledge that all of the attention and hustle goes with the turf. And he wouldn't trade this life for any other. But a wide gap exists between perception and reality: "He must be rich. All he has to do is hunt." Or as an old beer commercial used to say, "Wouldn't that be great?"

"When people come up and ask me at sport shows, 'How can

287

I do what you do?' part of my response is that I'm not sure most people would want to do what I'm doing," Chuck says. "I don't think most people would truly want to put up with the problems associated with being in business for yourself. You're with it day and night. You can't leave self-employment at the office. I don't know anybody who does that. They take it home with them in their head, if not in their briefcase. The successful ones do."

Maybe the 24-7 nature of Chuck's work is the best thing for him. He doesn't have time to sit around his Jackson, Wyoming, home and feel lonely. After all, at the end of the day, there's not always someone there to share the problems or the successes with. He's a 50-something bachelor living far from most of his family. He spends months each spring speaking mostly to strangers at sports shows, sharing his zest for bowhunting and trying to help them absorb more from the pursuit. Then he retreats to a motel room and orders up room service. He hunts with friends as much as possible, but there are also hunts where he's camped alone in a tent somewhere. Alone, but not lonely.

"I like being alone," Chuck says. "There's a big difference between being alone and being lonely. And I think the reason I'm not lonely, in part, is that I get my fill of people when I'm traveling and doing sport shows. I welcome the chance to be alone at other times of the year. If you go back to relationships, it seems like I've always had a special woman in my life. I have a terrific girlfriend now—a professional gal who has a busy life of her own. That pretty much takes care of being lonely, along with my immediate family and friends. My parents are really special to me, and I know that if I even start to feel a little lonely I can pick up the telephone."

MAN IN THE MIRROR

Maintaining a modicum of privacy when you have to be in the public eye for your career to succeed is a conundrum that Chuck fails to fully reconcile. He can't have his cake and a free bow, too. He enjoys the publicity, the notoriety and the celebrity ... to a point.

This is all an affirmation that he's "made it" and achieved his childhood dream—a dream that he almost didn't dare chase. All of that is good and gratifying and even humbling to the man who some claim has a world record ego. But there are those inescapable times after the show that he'd like to be someone who no one recognizes, just a bowhunter from a little town called Chico. Chuck knows better. He understands the reality. An English professor could have had all the privacy he ever wanted. "The world's most successful bowhunter" can't. Maybe the fact that Chuck's a Gemini explains why he enjoys the profile at the shows, but prefers incognito elsewhere. Has he ever thought about stepping away from the grind?

"More regularly than you might think, actually," Chuck says. "It's a burden sometimes. I love bowhunters. I love talking to bowhunters. But I also feel like I'm in a particle accelerator sometimes. I've had people wake me up at airports when I was really tired and had a couple-hour layover and was just trying to sleep. They recognize me and tap me on the shoulder and want to talk bowhunting. But in every case they were nice guys who just saw an opportunity to talk to me and thought they'd probably never see me again. I rarely run into anybody who is obnoxious or really intrusive. But one of the reasons I don't do seminars year-round is because I've had enough of it by the middle of the year. I'm ready not to be shaking lots of hands and talking bowhunting. It gets overwhelming sometimes.

"And I really like never to be recognized in the woods for two reasons. One, I like to just relax at camp with my friends in the middle of the day. And people come by and they might be well-intentioned, but you don't get to take a nap when you want to and whatnot. The other reason is that people follow you around. I fully expect people to try to find out aggressively where I shot that big elk in Montana in 2000 and I don't like to be watching over my shoulder. So, yeah, it's a burden. I don't really groove on being highly visible. I suppose it is nice to be recognized in moderation, but if I had to choose I'd probably choose to not be recognized. Yet, it comes with the territory. It's a responsibility that I'm willing to accept, but it's not necessarily fun all the time."

Of course, this might sound hypocritical to some. After all, Chuck has asked for this lot in life. He has fought tooth and nail for it. And if he didn't enjoy the attention, he probably wouldn't be where he is today. Whether it's autographing a hero-shot poster or putting his name or face on a product, or standing up in front of an audience and conducting a bowhunting seminar, Chuck brings an unmistakable air of confidence. Thrust most any bowhunter into a sportsman's show booth to autograph posters of himself and he'd feel queasy quickly. You can't pull that off unless you believe that you've earned it. If that's ego, Chuck definitely has one. But does he have an ego problem?

"First of all, I think ego is a positive thing if it is controlled," Chuck says. "I don't think anything in the world gets done without ego. I think every president of every successful corporation in America probably has a huge ego. But the key is that you channel the ego into trying to do positive things. I don't think mine's out of control. I view my current situation as a function of my job. I put my pants on the same way as anybody else. And I don't regard myself as being better than anybody else. I'm certainly happy and I feel confident in my abilities that go into my job. But I would like to think it's a quiet confidence."

MANIAC OR EGOMANIAC?

Chuck's self-review is echoed by his sister Becky True and her husband, Randy. Becky and Randy bring a qualified clinical approach to the table. Both of them are practicing psychiatrists, even though they might be somewhat biased in their assessment of kin.

"He's not an egotistical guy," Randy says. "He comes from humble roots. Honest, he doesn't have to control it, and I know him pretty well. I've bowhunted with Chuck some and I've seen how he acts in the spotlight. If anything, he has to kind of act like he's supposed to act because he's a celebrity. I've never seen him ever be anything but good old Chuck my brother-in-law who treats me great. He's certainly proud of his skill; he's not falsely modest. He's just a guy who, in a way, God has smiled upon."

"His career has not changed him in the slightest," Becky says. "He is one of the most patient people I know. Just the other day we had gotten bows and we were talking to him about tuning them, and he is talking about these things that are so basic to him. But the spark of enthusiasm and interest ... it's still there. He's still excited about what he does. He's still excited about people getting excited about the sport. He's still just real down to earth and enjoys it.

In the midst of the Grand Slam and beginning his quest toward Super Slam, Chuck still made time for family adventure like Montana elk camp with Joanne, left; sister, Becky, right; and brother-in-law, Randy True, center.

"He's always competing with himself," Becky continues. "So when we used to play as kids, when he would handicap himself, he'd do it not so that he could beat us, but so he could compete with himself. And he doesn't compete to squelch the other person and to feel good because he's won and they've lost. His goal is not to feel better about himself because you lost. He is non-affected. He's not stuck on himself. He's really hard on himself and asking himself, 'How could I do that better?'"

Ego and archery, according to Eugen Herrigel's book, "Zen in the Art of Archery," mix like oil and water. In fact, Herrigel notes repeatedly throughout the book how the archery master admonished his students whenever they attempted to put themselves ahead of the art.

"The right art," cried the Master, "is purposeless, aimless! The more obstinately you try to learn how to shoot the arrow for the sake of hitting the goal, the less you will succeed. ... Put the thought of hitting right out of your mind! You can be a Master even if every shot does not hit. ... You know already that you should not grieve over bad shots; learn now not to rejoice over the good ones."

Maybe Chuck has never read the book. Maybe Zen is bunk. Or

291

maybe Chuck really has mastered his place behind the bow and has found the necessary inner peace to accept bowhunting failure and success with an equal measure of humility.

He certainly remains grounded firmly enough to maintain strong business relationships and friendships within the archery industry—relationships that would likely erode rapidly if he exuded arrogance. Because as much as those companies are selling product, they're selling Chuck Adams. If a new customer is turned off by Chuck, the companies that Chuck represents and the magazines that he writes for are guilty by association.

To bowhunting greenhorns looking to the experts or the celebrities in this business, Chuck will likely be one of the first names that the individual will come to know. If Chuck's cool, bowhunting's cool. If Chuck's a jerk, maybe the kid buys a snowboard instead. And none of this is lost on Chuck. He's not afraid to carry the bowhunting torch in an industry-wide battle to recruit new people into archery. It's a competitive environment, and Chuck is savvy enough to know that he is either part of the solution or part of the problem.

"I think that doing this job is a high responsibility," Chuck says. "It's not something that I asked for or even anticipated, but I think it's a responsibility. I don't think if you put yourself in a high-profile position you have the right to let people down. I think role models and people to look up to are important anywhere, and there is a pretty strong philosophy that's counter to that in this country.

"I hear people say, 'You don't need role models.' I disagree with that. I think it's deep in the human psyche to want someone to look up to. I know that boys look up to their dad or uncle or another male role model. I think that's so deeply ingrained in us that the lack of it could be damaging. Young people want to look up to somebody and they're going to find somebody to look up to. And I often wonder if some of the violent kids in our society these days don't have the problem of never having had a role model.

"I will tell you that, and some folks would say that this is Chuck's ego talking, but one of the most common comments I get when I'm out in the public is that people tell me that they're really pleased that I am a down-to-earth guy."

Everybody has a bad day at the office, though, and Chuck is no different. It's one thing if he's "at work" on a bowhunt. But when he rolls out on the wrong side of bed and has to shake a lot of hands or perform an entertaining, informative seminar, the job isn't everything it's cracked up to be. And, inevitably, that's the day when someone catches him off-guard with criticism or wants to provoke an argument. Exercising diplomacy even in the most confrontational situations is a skill that Chuck has had to learn on the job. He long ago grasped the fact that everyone who comes to see him is more than just a fellow bowhunter who might want an autograph or a handshake. They're all customers. And Chuck's in the customer service business where "the customer is always right." Fortunately for Chuck, he says there's not a better group of people to work for than hunters.

"I don't think if you're in the public eye you can afford to ever get snappy or chew somebody out who's obviously off-base," Chuck says. "You have a responsibility to treat people right because they expect it from you. I wouldn't say that's a burden, though. I find it pretty easy to be nice to folks, partly because hunters are generally great people.

"If this job weren't fun, I'd be gone. I'd just quit it all together. That's not going to happen though. My bottom line is, I want to do what makes me happy, and that's what I'm going to do."

In December 1997, that approach to his career landed Chuck an honorary doctorate degree from Penn College, an affiliate of Penn State University. Chuck and his dad had gone bear hunting to Alberta together in 1997 and on that hunt met Bob Breuder, the president of Penn College. Breuder was an avid hunter, but says that he didn't know much about Chuck at the time.

By the end of the five-day hunt, Breuder came away impressed with the man behind all of the outdoor acclaim—so impressed that he pulled Chuck aside and made him an offer that he couldn't refuse.

"He said, 'I've been watching you the whole trip. You're not pushy, you're not telling people what to do, and I think you're a fine role model for archery. I think our college would like to give you an honorary degree based on your academic achievements and your distinguished career as an outdoors communicator,'" Chuck says, recalling the conversation. "And I was blown away.

He said, 'We've only given one other honorary doctorate degree in the history of the college.'

"So, the following December, Dad and I sat up on the stage at Penn College's commencement, and I was given an honorary doctorate degree for my writing. That was one of the highlights of my life. Better yet, Bob Breuder and I have become fast friends and great hunting pals since then."

Breuder today is president of William Rainey Harper College in Chicago and one of a few people who share an especially close friendship with Chuck.

"We would later go to the Northwest Territories to hunt caribou," Breuder says. "He and I shared the same boat and the same cabin and spent a lot of time together.

"On the first morning, Chuck simply left his bow behind. I said, 'Chuck, why are you doing that?' He said, 'Our first priority is to get you a really beautiful caribou, one that you can be proud of.' I protested, but he said, 'No. You're first. We'll worry about me later on.'

"I think that's a dimension of him that comes out no matter where you see him—the desire for this guy, as world-class as he is, to be more interested in others."

Breuder says that there are a number of reasons why he and Chuck have established such a close-knit bond. They share a lot in common coming from an academic background, but to Breuder, it once again comes down to Chuck's interest in putting others' interests ahead of his own.

"We were having dinner together at a sportsman's show," Brueder says. "And as I was talking to him he clasped his hands together in front of himself and I noticed his ring. I said, 'That is one beautiful ring. Can I see it?' It was a custom ring made with the ivory from his tule elk. It was absolutely a thing of beauty. I said, 'Before I die, I would like to have a ring like that. I have elk ivories, but don't know what to do with them.

"Less than a year later, Chuck and I were having lunch and it happened to be the day before my birthday," Breuder continues. "And I said, 'You know, I'm convinced that I'm going to get a ring like that one of these days.' And he took the ring off his finger and he said, 'This is my gift to you.' I almost fell off my chair and said, 'I can't take it.' He said, 'Bob, look at the inside of the ring.'

Chuck receives his honorary doctorate degree from former Penn College President Bob Breuder. Today, the two of them share bowhunts and a powerful friendship.

And it's on my finger now and it says inside, 'Chuck Adams to Dr. Bob, 2000.' He said, 'Bob, it's your ring,' and he starts chuckling and he pulls his own ring out of his pocket. Chuck had called my wife and said, 'Send me all of Bob's elk ivories and I will pick the ones that I think are the most spectacular and I will have a ring made for Bob.'

"You talk about who this guy is, ... he didn't have to do that. So I have the mate to his ring, and to me it is the single-most prized possession that I have. We have a friendship that is never-ending. If I said, 'Chuck, I need you here in Chicago tomorrow, I have no doubt that he'd be here, even if he had to give up a hunt.'"

Others have seen Chuck in action when it comes to helping out friends.

"Our youngest boy, Reo, was in a serious truck accident last year," Colleen Shipp says. "I called Chuck 30 minutes after he had driven 12 hours back to Wyoming from a mule deer hunt in Alberta. He dumped his gear, cancelled his commitments and drove most of the night to Montana. He spent the next three days

295

and nights with us at the hospital. It was a godsend.

"Montana's a hunting state, and several doctors and orderlies recognized Chuck. One asked, 'Why is Chuck Adams sitting here 24 hours a day with you?' I looked at him and said, 'Because Chuck is our friend.' And I think that pretty much says it all."

Reo is fine now, and Chuck spends as much time with Reo, Ryley, Colleen and hunting partner, Doyle, as possible. Much of it is fishing, rough-housing with the kids and just relaxing.

TURN-ONS, TURN-OFFS

Chuck readily acknowledges that bowhunting rules his life. "I'm doing what I like to do best," he says. But he also admits that there are times where he needs to get away. A Tom Clancy or John Grisham spell-binder far from reality sometimes works; and Chuck usually has one with him during his show season and during those hunts where he knows that he'll be spending long hours in a treestand or ground blind.

Fly-fishing is also an outlet and a stress-reliever and, more than anything, another challenge. Yet, it's a rare day when he'll set down his bow for a flyrod. He'll sometimes pack the angling gear on Alaskan hunts. But he'll only use it if his tags are already filled and he's waiting for an air taxi out or if the hunting is particularly bad. In fact, for years after moving to the Bitterroot Valley of Montana from California, Chuck lived a stone's throw from many blue ribbon trout waters. "Tomorrow," he'd tell himself when the flyfishing urge would tempt him. But tomorrow never came. Second-favorite doesn't count for much.

That's not to say that he can't find enjoyment in other things during the off-season or those fleeting moments when he has a little down-time. He might even flip on the TV and dial up a sporting event—preferably individual sports like golf or tennis, and ideally the final round or match for the title. Team sports rank a distant second, and, again, the games don't seem to mean much unless a World Series, Super Bowl or NBA championship is hanging in the balance. "I don't have time to be avid," Chuck says. "I'm basically not a spectator."

Yet he admires great athletes and great performances—especially those requiring precise hand-eye coordination delivered in clutch situations when all the pressure is on. A master in both regards made an impression on Chuck.

"I watched Jack Nicklaus throughout his career, especially on Sunday, the last day of every tournament," Chuck says. "I watch Tiger Woods today with the same rapt attention. I really admire people like that who seem to be self-contained and in control of their sport. I suppose when you think about it, we're talking projectile sports."

And even though all of his big game hunting is done with a bow, Chuck still gets a kick out of shotgunning when he can find the chance. His bow collection vastly outnumbers his firearms, but he's managed to collect close to 30 Winchester Pre-64, Model 12 shotguns over the years. Occasionally he'll find the time to grab one from the safe and flush pheasants with Pop. "That's the gun I grew up with," Chuck says. "I love to go out and shoot birds with them. That's really relaxing. It's more of a social thing."

His only big game rifle is a .375 H&H used as a camp gun for bear protection in places like Alaska. And though Chuck hasn't seriously rifle hunted for big game since he was a teenager, he doesn't categorize gun hunting as a "turn-off" in the same way that some bowhunters disdainfully view it.

"I'm not one of those people who sees a major dividing line between rifle and bowhunters," Chuck says. "I think it's a continuum, and it gets more difficult as you limit your weapon. My dad now has converted to blackpowder probably the last 10 years. He's shot a number of mule deer and elk in Colorado with blackpowder, and pronghorns at Phil Phillips' camp in Colorado. I think hunting's hunting, and it just depends on what tool you decide to shoot. It just gets more difficult as you head toward bowhunting."

Crossbows fall somewhere in between. While he doesn't view crossbows as a threat to game populations if legalized during regular archery seasons, Chuck clearly could do without the "string gun." Because it is shouldered and the arrow is not drawn by the hunter's muscles, he believes this shooting mechanism should be limited to disabled hunters during archery season. "But that's an arbitrary line, too," Chuck concedes.

Though one might not expect it from such a devout bowhunter, Chuck is a member of the National Rifle Association (NRA). When it comes to the 2nd Amendment, he's as conservative as they come.

"I think the NRA is doing a bang-up job," Chuck says. "I heard that the one regret that Bill Clinton voiced when he left office was that the NRA had bested him. He said that in so many words, and I think that's good. Any large organization is going to have its detractors. But by and large, I think that the NRA is doing a good job. You try to get in my house and I've got a riot shotgun loaded with buckshot beside the bed."

LEAVING A LEGACY

Some hunters, maybe even some reading this book, will forever regard Chuck as self-centered. His hero-shot smiles or even his stocking cap will always turn off some. Some will rail on Chuck for appearing in ads and "commercializing" bowhunting, whatever that means.

In many ways, though, Chuck has failed to capitalize completely on his achievements. The shortfall is not for lack of business acumen. He's sharp enough to recognize opportunities. Yet he has intentionally placed a low priority on profile and a high priority on his bowhunting satisfaction. Consider:

He has refused to allow his bowhunts to be taped, save for a few treestand hunts for whitetails with his good friend, Bill Jordan. At this stage of his career, he could effortlessly sell thousands of hunting videos if he chose. But he knows all that would turn the fun into work. How many instructional bowhunting or bow-shooting videos might he be able to sell if he wanted to market something like "Chuck Adams' Secrets To Success?"

For someone supposedly so driven by money and fame and his own self-importance, it's curious that he has disregarded opportunities to leverage his position as "the world's most successful bowhunter." Why? Chuck is comfortable, but not wealthy. He flies coach instead of first-class. He lives in a modest house with dreams of buying a few acres and building a bigger house out in the country. If these commercial ventures would help to secure his financial future and further elevate his stature, why hasn't he pounced?

At the 2001 AMO Show, when a writer approached Chuck to authorize this biography, the journalist fully suspected that Chuck had been asked before or that he'd already promised the project to some other writer. Instead, the inquiry drew a quizzical look from Chuck that finally turned to his signature smile. "No one's ever asked," he said. Clearly, he hadn't seriously considered an autobiography, either.

Other self-fulfilling avenues have also gone conspicuously unexplored. What about the 111 P&Y record-book animals, including two former and three current world records? Where are they and all of Chuck's bows and gear that he used during the epic journeys to the corners of the continent? What about the 60-some African trophies? Surely, there must be plans for a Chuck Adams museum. That is not the case.

"Most of my animals are in storage right now," Chuck says. "And that's part of the legacy from Joanne and me splitting up. We were going to build a house with high ceilings and lots of wall space to display our trophies. And I've never counted, but with probably more than 500 big game animals to my credit, there's no way I could display them all. So a lot of those hides and horns and antlers and skulls are in storage, and I'm commonly asked when I'll open a museum.

"It would probably be nice to put some of my critters somewhere where the general public could look at them—not because it would be an ego boost for me, but because there seems to be interest in that. I've talked to Cabela's about displaying animals in some of their big stores, and that's likely to happen. The Fred Bear Museum in Gainesville, Florida, has asked me to loan them a major display of animals, and that's a possibility as well.

"But I frankly have never been obsessed with trophy rooms and creating a shrine for Chuck Adams. I'm more interested in going out and enjoying the moment. I own every set of antlers and every set of horns and every skull of every animal that I've shot since I was 12 years old including all the gun kills early on of little black-tailed deer, and I love all of those. I go out to the garage and storage shed regularly and I handle them and I remember the hunts. I remember all of them in intimate detail. Ultimately, what I'd like to do is have a house with a modest trophy area."

What Chuck hasn't done speaks volumes about the man behind the bow, maybe in some ways more than his achievements do.

"I know right at the moment, he is concerned about finding a place to settle down," Pop says. "Part of the problem there is perfectionism. And I share some of that. I'm sitting in a house that I bought 42 years ago. But it was right. It's just right. And he hasn't found that.

"I think a big part of it is his concern that he may spend money on a place and then decide he doesn't like it or another place shows up that he'd wished he bought. And the trophies, he just can't quite bring himself to turn that stuff over to someone because he doesn't think it's going to be right."

In Chuck's mind's eye, all of those hundreds of trophies are perfectly preserved already, even if they are collecting dust in a warehouse. The museum ground-breaking can wait. There are bowhunts to be planned. It's quite possible, likely even, that Chuck will continue to dream most of his dreams, much as he did as a young boy, not about fame or fortune, but about hunting. After all, one bowhunt, he knows, will have to be his last.

Some have lamented in this book that only after Chuck is gone will he be appreciated for his singular achievements and, even more, for his enormous impact on bowhunting. For Chuck's part, though, there's no sense in worrying whether or how he'll be remembered.

"I was the classic example of falling off the turnip truck when I went to L.A. in my early 20s," Chuck says. "I grew up with what I consider to be good, solid values that are associated with country living and a kinship with the land and a love for hunting. I might have very well been one of those frustrated city dwellers with the instincts and the genetics, but not the wherewithal, to make good on those. So, again, that's just pure luck. You're dealt a hand of cards in life. Some people are dealt a stronger hand than others, and all you can do is play the hand you're dealt.

"It's never been my goal, to make my mark. My goal is to enjoy my life. If there was a legacy that I'd be really proud of it's that I have helped other people enjoy bowhunting and the out-of-doors more than they would have otherwise; and, hopefully, that I would have helped people enjoy bowhunting as much as I did. Because I love it completely."

Some day, one imagines Chuck Adams' spirit soaring to a campfire meeting beneath the stars somewhere unseen in the

"I hope that I would have helped people enjoy bowhunting as much as I did. Because I love it completely."

quiet summer hills high above Deer Creek. There, a barefoot, ancient Yahi hunter will welcome his friend home. The men will share vivid stories of black-tailed bucks that they stalked on this very soil many moons ago. They will share intricacies of bows and arrowheads that they crafted; tools that gave each of them great powers; tools with which they danced a timeless dance of survival. And when the final spark from that fire dances among the stars, they'll set out together, leaving their footprints unmistakably for anyone willing to take up the trail.